The Spanking Collection

A Charity Anthology

Edited by Abel & Haron

The Spanking Collection

A Charity Anthology

Edited by Abel & Haron

First published in Great Britain in 2011 by
Abelard Books
abelardbooks.co.uk

All profits from this book will be donated to cancer research charities

A catalogue record for this book is available from the British Library

ISBN 978-0-9558483-4-6

The Spanking Collection

Introduction

Eliane Chevalier

I used to feel alone. Strange, wrong. I used to believe that the thoughts and fantasies I had were twisted and dangerous: that they meant there was something fundamentally wrong with me. After all, who would want to be spanked?

I was alone for a long time.

Then I went online and discovered stories like the ones in this book, written by many of the authors who have contributed here. And I realised that all those things I'd been thinking about, while different from more traditional sexual fantasies, were thoughts shared by thousands of other people out there. And that felt good.

This book is the brainchild of Abel and Haron, authors of The Spanking Writers blog. They decided to bring together their favourite writers from around the world, inviting them each to contribute a story to an anthology.

If you have ever been online searching for erotic fiction about corporal punishment, you may be familiar with some of the authors here. If you haven't, you're about to discover the work of some of the best writers out there.

Either way, you have a host of delights to delve into. Canes, paddles, hands, slippers. Historical and contemporary settings. It's all here.

The anthology is not just the authors' way of expanding the body of published spanking fiction. There's also another aim: to raise money for charity. The profits from every copy of this book sold will go to cancer research charities, a cause which is close to the hearts of many of the contributors, myself included.

So if you are buying this anthology to re-acquaint yourself with old friends like Abel, Haron, Bonnie, Zille Defeu, Emma Jane, Pablo or the Lowewood writers, then welcome back.

On the other hand, if this is your first foray into spanking fiction, then a very special welcome to you. Dive in, enjoy, and - above all - remember that you're not alone!

Eliane Chevalier
newtospanking.blogspot.com

The Scholarship Girl

Abel Jenkins

The rule had been designed, in the first place, to *protect* the girls of St Columba's – to ensure that corporal punishment really was only meted out as the very last resort. Section 8.2 of the school handbook, to be precise: "Where a serious breach of school rules has taken place, the headmaster may administer up to eight strokes of the cane, provided prior approval for the caning has been granted by the governing body."

No summary whackings here: no girls called forward to touch their toes at the front of their classrooms; no masters patrolling dormitories late at night wielding their canes at the boarders. Rather, a period of quiet contemplation; a rational discussion of the facts of the case in front of the great and the good. Their consent forthcoming, a measured application of the rod would follow. Thoughtful, fair, calm. Considered.

But, of course, the governors only met three or four times a term – and even then it was relatively rare for such a 'serious breach' to be presented. The lucky girl – if lucky is an appropriate term in the circumstances – might therefore find her punishment debated and administered within a matter of days. But Ann Maitland was rather less fortunate.

That her offence that Saturday afternoon had been serious – and quite out of character – was beyond doubt. It was only thanks to Mr. Ingle's diplomacy that her case was being heard before the governors and not the local magistrates' bench. Even she couldn't explain why she'd done it: she'd never stolen before; abhorred thieves. She'd had the money in her purse. But the book had been there, in front of her; no-one had been looking. And it had all been so easy. Until, that is, Mr Dixon (he of Dixon's Booksellers) had barred her way to the door, and asked to look inside her bag.

Her subsequent encounter with the headmaster had been short and to the point. Her behaviour was quite unacceptable. It was a

3

good thing that Mr Dixon's daughter had attended St Columba's and so he was prepared to protect its reputation. "Provided," Ingle emphasised, "*provided* the matter is dealt with soundly."

"I didn't mean to do it," sounded pathetic in the circumstances. For she *had* done it; she'd been caught, and she trembled at the thought of the consequences.

"I will be recommending to the governors that you be caned, Miss Maitland, as I am sure you would expect me to do."

Caned. An abstract concept. Dreaded, talked about in hushed, awe-inspired tones. Something that happened to the very worst girls. Behind closed doors.

Only this time, she'd be the girl on the wrong side of the door.

He'd sent her away, "most disappointed that a girl of your calibre would find herself in this situation." Sent her away to creep into the dorm, to sob on her bed, until friends had found her and provided what little reassurance they could.

It'd been Mary who'd taken the practical step of looking at the school notice board, where the dates of the governors' meetings were listed; Mary who came back with the bad news, that the previous gathering had just taken place; and that there were three weeks until their next forum.

And three weeks is a long time, when you're waiting to be caned. Long enough for every other girl in the school to know, to point at Ann in the playground and the corridors. Long enough to imagine the worst.

Long enough, too, to forget, momentarily. To find herself deep in concentration in the library, absorbed in the game on the hockey field, giggling at a joke in the common room, waking with the rays of morning light sneaking through the curtains in the dorm, as if without a care in the world. And then, suddenly, for the bolt to strike and the memory of her predicament to take over her every thought.

Yet three weeks felt all too short, as the date encroached. "February 11th, 1pm – 2.30pm", the notice had said. Since she'd first arrived at St Columba's, she'd counted off the days on her calendar. Counted down, looking forward to the end of term and being home. This time the countdown was filled with a sense of impending doom, not joy. She wandered alone, rehearsing the governors' conversation: "A bright girl", "Not been in trouble before", "Knows she's done wrong", "A momentary lapse", "A little leniency in the circumstances?"

The morning of the eleventh passed in a daze. Double maths: concentrating on equations, when she could only think of one thing. Morning break – hiding from the others, lest they saw her tremble. (She'd be brave in front of them, of course. As best she could). A French vocab test – easy, brushed aside, a momentary distraction. English – the final lesson of the morning, during which the discussion of the set text scarcely held her attention. And then, as she gazed out of the window counting the seconds, the Rolls and the Daimlers and the Mercedes started to pull through the gates, and the neatly-tailored ladies and gentlemen clambered from their vehicles, greeted each another warmly, and headed for lunch.

They'd been there, at the top table in the dining room, in animated yet friendly discussion, as she'd toyed with her food. Could they see her, these gods who held her fate in their hands? Would they help her, if they knew she was a good girl; that they could give her a chance; that she'd never do it again?

And then they were standing, and leaving, and heading off to sit in judgment.

Geography, after lunch: old Mr Spencer, droning on as usual. Then time to change, for games. She'd be safe out there, on the hockey pitch. Free.

A jog around the pitch, three times, to warm up on the bitterly cold afternoon. Whilst *they* sat inside, in the warmth, debating.

Choosing teams. She'd been one of the first to be picked, as usual. As if the captains thought she'd be able to concentrate. (Would they discuss it first, or save it to the end of the meeting?)

One-nil. Two-nil. Three-nil. Easy.

And then Mrs Townbridge was asking them to wait for a moment, as she walked to the touchline to speak with the fast-approaching prefect. She turned, and blew her whistle: "Ann

Maitland, would you go and shower and get changed, and report to the headmaster's study. And quickly!"

Fingers trembling in the changing room, but not from the cold of the winter day. Shivering in the shower – despite the warmth of the water. Buttoning her shirt was a challenging task; she straightened her tie, brushed her hair, as if a neat appearance might save her from her fate.

Her fate. Not in three weeks. Not in three hours. Now.

She walked briskly across the playground, and skirted round the science block, opening the gate that led through to the headmaster's house. Oakland was set apart from the school buildings, surrounded by trees, its lawns neatly manicured by the school groundsmen. She scrunched across the gravel path, as another girl rushed cheerfully her way. Ann recognised Sam Wilson as the other girl who'd been due for a caning: the playground rumour mill had been quite gleeful at the prospect of *two* of their number facing sentence.

But she was smiling. "They decided to let me off," the older girl exclaimed, as if she'd won the Lottery. Which, in a schoolgirl way, she had. "Hope they did the same for you..."

So maybe, just maybe... Ann pushed at the open front door, and turned into the headmaster's secretary's office.

An abrupt, cold welcome: "You're late."

"I had to change. I was playing hockey."

The secretary looked back down at her paperwork, as if already moving on to more interesting things. "Well, Mr. Ingle is waiting. He wants you to go straight in."

Maybe, just maybe... She allowed herself to hope, as she walked down the corridor and knocked on his door.

Maybe, just maybe, as she heard his curt, "Enter", and walked into the office.

He was sitting behind the desk, reading a sheaf of papers. "Take a seat, Miss Maitland." Maybe, just maybe...

And then he was standing, and walking around the desk, and heading for a cupboard at the side of the room. Her eyes followed his every step; he reached into his pockets for a fob heavy with keys, unlocked the cupboard door. And her maybes were replaced with the chill knowledge of the certain outcome of their discussions, as he extracted a long, dark, crook-handled cane.

The headmaster walked back around the desk and took his seat once more, placing the rod on the table between them. She looked down, avoiding his gaze, avoiding the sight of the rattan.

"You'll be aware that we discussed your case this afternoon at the governors' meeting, Miss Maitland?"

A quiet, resigned, terrified, "Yes, sir."

"I told you last time we met that I viewed this as a matter of utmost severity, and I have to say that the governors fully shared my view. They particularly asked me to let you know of their displeasure that a scholarship girl should behave so disgracefully." He paused to let their message sink in, as if her own disappointment at herself didn't already suffice.

"I did remind them that it is usual to show a degree of leniency towards a girl who finds herself in trouble for the first time, but the governors were quite unanimous in their agreement that I should give you the maximum of eight strokes of the cane. Do you understand me, Miss Maitland?"

"Yes, sir" – understood the words, even if she couldn't quite comprehend that this was happening to her.

"I'm sure you'll also be aware, Miss Maitland, that it is customary, on the rare occasions that a scholarship girl like you finds herself in this situation, that the punishment be administered on the bare. So I'd be grateful if you could remove your knickers and place them on your chair, then take up position with your feet apart, touching your toes, facing the door through which you just entered my study."

Ann stood, as if on auto-pilot, and followed his choreography. Maybes had given away to "get-it-over-withs", much as she prayed that somehow it might never start. She glanced hopefully at the door as she walked towards it, yet knowing she couldn't hope for some winged messenger to knock bearing news of a miraculous pardon.

She bent forward, as he'd instructed, and only then did she sense him stand and walk towards her.

"Reach back and lift up your skirt."

Her fingers hesitated on the hem, and then she was bare.

"I hardly need to tell you that this is going to hurt, Miss Maitland. I only hope that you'll try and maintain a degree of dignity whilst taking your punishment." And then she felt the cold line of the wood, pressing across her buttocks.

The pause before the first stroke was the longest in her life. But when it landed, she lost any sense of time, of place. The blow itself scarcely hurt, but the momentary relief ("that could have been worse") was washed away by the floods of pain that seared a second or two later across the stripe he'd just inflicted. Not in her worst nightmares had she conceived that being punished like this could be so intense.

Deep breaths. Trying to regain composure. Deep breaths. He's stepping back. Stay calm... you know what it's like now... but the second biting stroke was even worse than the first.

So this was why the cane was so feared, so revered? Ingle walked away from her, turned, and waited. Waited. Then danced forward, cane lifted high, and striped her for the third time. She reached back, instinctively, unable to stop herself clutching at her backside, trying to no effect to soothe the anguish.

"I'd rather you stayed in position, Miss Maitland. With some dignity, please."

Her fingers reached forward again for her polished toecaps. Again, the wait; the dreadful anticipation, the fire burning ever more painfully, before the next stroke, and the next, and the next in rapid-fire succession.

And then he stepped back again, leaving her to absorb the consequences of the strokes he'd just inflicted.

This was unbearable, unbelievable. Tears dropped freely now onto the carpet. "I'm sorry, sir. Please, sir, I'm sorry," came from her lips, as he walked away again and turned.

The seventh stroke of the cane: itself excruciating. The seven strokes of the cane - merging, inevitably, into one blaze of agony, before the eighth cut home and the headmaster walked away for a final time.

"Stand up and sort out your uniform when you're ready, Miss Maitland, and come and sit back down over here."

Ready? She'd never be ready to face him. But ready to stand, and cover herself, and reach back, and try to calm the pain? She leapt up, turned, and tottered towards the chair to pick up her knickers. Putting them on, under his steady gaze, was excruciatingly painful. And then slowly, gingerly, she lowered herself down, with a wince and a gasp as she sat on the firm wood.

He passed her a box of tissues. "Do dry your eyes, Miss Maitland, and then we can bring this to a conclusion." He was scribbling on a form, which he turned and passed across the desk. "I need you to sign this: it confirms that you have been caned. A copy will go on your file, and another will be sent to your parents."

She looked at him, shocked. "Please, sir! They can't know...."

"I'm afraid you should have thought of that when you were in the bookshop, young lady. Now, the other matter to which we must attend is your apology to Mr Dixon. So perhaps you would go straight to the library and take a sheet of school notepaper? And you can write him a letter explaining how you have been punished this afternoon, and apologising for your conduct?"

Downcast: "Yes, sir."

"And then you can take the letter into his shop on Saturday. Be sure to hand it to him personally, and to wait until he has read it, and then that will draw a line under this whole sorry episode..."

****

This story © Abel Jenkins 2011

About the author:

Abel Jenkins is one of the best-known British authors of spanking erotica, featured on his website - "Abel's Spanking Stories" – since 1999. His writing has won various awards, appearing on "Laura's Spanking Corner" and in print in "Kane" and other publications.

With his wife Haron, Abel is the co-author of "The Spanking Writers", the popular blog updated daily since 2006. They also present SpankingCast, the spanking podcast (downloadable from iTunes). Together, Abel's websites have attracted some eight million visitors.

A selection of Abel's stories, "The Punishment List", was published in 2010. He and Haron have edited this volume, "The Spanking Collection".

Abel has been an active spanking roleplayer for many years, enjoying scenes with friends in the UK and around the world.

Abel welcomes feedback and friendly emails (abel1234@hotmail.com); for more of his writing, please go to spankingwriters.com.

Slipping Up

Emma Jane

Kicking the door shut behind her, she dropped her bag with relief; Friday night at last. It had been a long week. Happily she noticed he was home too, his keys and jacket in their proper places. It made her smile, the contrast to her hastily strewn items.

She went in search of him, suddenly giddy to have a whole weekend ahead, just them, no interruptions. He was in the kitchen, peering at the wine rack, studiously choosing the wine for the evening. A rich smell wafted from the oven and she smiled in appreciation.

Placing his chosen bottle on the counter, he turned to greet her, smiling. Their hug was long and lazy, neither eager to disentangle. When they eventually broke apart, she found two glasses and proffered them hopefully.

He shook his head. "Not just yet, missy, that's for later with dinner. In the meantime we have some things to discuss, don't we?" His tone was light, but his look was serious.

A flash of irritation swept over her. What a way to ruin a lovely evening, their first alone in far too long. Swallowing the sharp retort that bubbled up, she smiled sweetly at him, making the glasses dance. "Let's leave it for now, huh? You me and a bottle of wine, save tonight and fight the break of dawn?"

She giggled at her own cleverness, but the song reference was lost on him. "I don't think so. Easier to deal with it tonight and get it over with," he continued in the same even tone, taking the glasses from her and setting them down on the counter.

Annoyed, she rolled her eyes. "Fine, go on then, let's get it over with. Where shall I bend over? The chair, your knee, the sofa?" Her tone was all politeness but her eyes flashed impatiently. She wasn't in the mood for this. It had been a long day, a long week. An hour ago she'd been presenting to the board. She was still in

11

work mode and he was about to spank her. All she wanted was a glass of wine and a hug.

"Well I'm certainly not going to deal with you with that attitude." Shaking his head, he took a seat at the counter and looked at her expectantly.

Angry now, she snapped. "Oh for feck's sake, make up your mind, will you? I'd like to get to the nice part of the evening."Almost instantly she regretted it, wondering how he always succeeded in making her feel like she was the unreasonable one.

"You, young lady, are going to calm down and lose the attitude. You know you deserve what's coming, and you will take your punishment and accept it."

She sighed; he was getting on his high horse, if only he'd gallop off on it! Soon he'd come over and look her in the eye... The thought had barely formed in her head when he had actually crossed the room and stood in front of her. The urge to laugh was almost too much, but she bit it back.

Quietly he told her how she had disappointed him, let both of them down, needed to be taught a lesson. She tried to block his words out, tried to twist them in her head and make them sound funny, except she couldn't. She really didn't want to face up to it tonight. Or at all if truth be told. But certainly not tonight. Her head wasn't in the right place.

"Look, it's been a long day," she tried to reason, "work was a nightmare, I had to go to the board and..."

He swiftly cut across her. "Take your shoes off."

"What?"

"I said, take your shoes off."

In surprise she complied, instantly feeling smaller with him towering above her. It wasn't fair when he already had a considerable height advantage. She considered making this point but thought better of it, not sure where this was leading to.

Long moments of silence passed before he gave the next order. "Now your stockings."

She was confused. Heels and stockings always came off last, surely, the best bit of any outfit. Didn't he want to stop admire them? She had worn her sheerest pair and her favourite suspender belt with matching bra and knickers especially, anticipating their evening together. It rankled to have to take them off in the kitchen while he looked on so disapprovingly. It certainly wasn't the time to place her leg on the chair and roll them down seductively as she had practised.

And so it continued, he making her strip, watching impassively, not the slightest bit interested in her, or even her beautiful, lacy knickers. It almost made her weep to have to take them off with so little attention paid.

But he was having the desired effect. With the removal of each piece of clothing, the corporate working woman was being put away, back on the shelf until she was needed again. She was becoming less sure of herself, more worried about what was going to happen. In her achingly high heels and sharp cut suit, a spanking hadn't seemed like that big a deal.

Standing before him, completely naked, she didn't feel as defiant. She studied her toes, trying not to shiver in the cold.

"Are we ready to continue?" he enquired.

Reluctantly, she nodded in reply.

"I didn't hear that," he prompted.

"Yes," she answered softly, still looking at the ground.

He didn't let her off that easily. "Yes, what?"

An unbearable silence, until finally, "Yes sir," and he was in her head. Now she was scared.

"Good girl, that's better." Looking her in the eye, he told her he was going to punish her. She squirmed under his gaze. "Punish you firmly. Enough to leave a lasting impression so we don't have a repeat of last weekend's antics!"

In shame she thought back to it. The 3AM call asking him to pick her up. Explaining that she'd no money for a taxi, wasn't sure where she was or how she'd lost her friends. How worried he'd been coming to get her and how she cried in relief at seeing him.

How mortified she was the next day and the countless apologies she'd made.

"I really am sorry," she whispered.

Of course she knew he was going to punish her. Last Sunday she would have even welcomed it, needed it to help her get over the embarrassment of what she'd done. But there'd been no time. Besides, he had wanted her to wait, to stew over it. Which had been all very well in theory until the working week had obliterated the ability to think about it. Now it all seemed a bit crazy that she, a grown woman, was going to be spanked for having a few drinks and being a bit silly. There were certainly worse things a girl could do.

The thought niggled uncomfortably. She couldn't really convince herself that it wasn't a big deal. Couldn't forget how worried he'd been. Or how confused she'd been the morning after, unable to piece the whole night together. Not for the first time, she had promised to drink less when she went out.

The last time, he'd warned her there would be severe consequences if she drank to the point of losing control. The last time, he'd just spanked her, gently over his knee, his displeasure enough to make her cry. It was the first major shift in their dynamic, where she began to be accountable to him outside the world of play.

She hadn't questioned it then, merely enjoyed how safe it made her feel that he cared enough to make such threats. She'd loved how his forgiveness gave her confidence and made her think she wouldn't slip up again.

Now she was back to disappointing him and hating herself for it. Not just him, though; she had let herself down, too. As much of a cliché as it sounded, she knew it to be true.

She wondered, would it be easier if he completely forbade her from going out at all? Or from drinking any alcohol without him there to supervise? Except that it wouldn't solve the problem. She'd never learn self-control, would never grow up.

It was true that such episodes were becoming less and less frequent. She usually came home tipsy but happy and safe to his welcoming arms. He'd forgive her for waking him up to tell him about her night, and she'd make faces as he solemnly promised retribution the next morning. More often than not it'd be a playful spanking, a delicious warm-up to something more intimate and fun. She'd bask in a self-congratulatory glow that she could go out and not be a disgrace. Yet why couldn't it be like that every time?

He broke into her thoughts. "I know you're sorry. You always are, but it's not enough. I warned you last time. It's not acceptable for you to behave like a reckless teenager with no responsibilities and no-one to worry about you."

His words sat uncomfortably with her. The irony was that she'd never been a reckless teenager. When her friends were out being wild and silly and doing the things they'd eventually grow out of, she had had other priorities, acting far older than she really was. Her rebellion had come much later in life, but by then there'd been no-one to rein her in.

No-one to say that partying until 5AM on a work-night wasn't clever. No-one to cut through the 'devil-may-care attitude' to point out she was putting herself at risk. No-one who understood how little she loved herself or how destructive she could be. Until she'd met him.

"I'm not angry anymore," he promised, "but this has to stop. It's not acceptable to treat yourself with so little respect that you don't care what happens to you, and it's certainly not fair for me to have to worry about you unnecessarily. You're not actually a silly, thoughtless girl, so why do you allow alcohol to make you act like one?"

"I don't know!" she wailed, burying her head in his chest, wanting the conversation to be over. "I can't seem to stop myself. Things just seem to happen. I hate that I get into these situations. I really do. I'm not proud of it, honestly."

The sharp smack on her bare bottom made her yelp. She looked up in surprise.

"Things don't just happen; you make them happen, you let them happen! As I keep saying, but you can't seem to hear, you need to take responsibility. Tonight I'm going to demonstrate the real and painful consequences of not doing so."

It was too much to bear. Even though he was right, even though she agreed with him, it hurt to hear him say the words. She wanted to get it over with and be forgiven. For the first time, she welcomed the punishment to come.

It was almost a relief when he sent her upstairs: "Everything you need is on the bed, get dressed and wait for me."

In the bedroom she surveyed with dread the clothes he had picked out for her. It wasn't unusual for him to prescribe what she should wear for play, and at any other time the tight, navy gym knickers were a favourite. Tonight they didn't bode well. He liked outfits and implements to be in harmony. Schoolgirls were caned, cheerleaders were paddled, little girls were spanked, girls in gym knickers were slippered.

Her stomach began to somersault. The significance of what he chose for her to wear wasn't lost on her. She wanted at least to give the impression of being brave and adult, but he wasn't making that easy. The slipper was her least favourite implement: the one that caused the greatest combination physical and mental pain. She has been known to cry before it even landed. Inwardly she both applauded and cursed him; he was out manoeuvring her at every turn, leaving her no place to hide.

She took as much time as she dared getting ready, trying to calm herself in the familiar ritual: splashing ice-cold water on her face, slowly arranging her hair, carefully choosing one of her many pairs of white cotton knickers. To the untrained eye they looked identical, but there were subtle differences that had to be considered. Grudgingly she admitted that he generally noticed, even appreciated the distinctions.

In the end she chose a soft, full-cut pair that fitted perfectly under the gym knickers. Then, she donned a plain white bra and white polo shirt before adding white socks and black gym shoes.

Silently, she contemplated her reflection in the mirror. A worried young girl stared back at her. She blushed, unusually embarrassed by her appearance. Absent was the anticipatory thrill that came so readily with their general play. It was fun to pretend to be a silly young girl who fell heedlessly into trouble, but quite a different matter to have her real-life foolishness reinforced so obviously.

She sighed. Usually she liked wearing the gym knickers, vainly loved how they snugly moulded her bottom. Not for the first time, she bent over in front of the mirror, twisting her head around to see the image she presented. *Not bad*, she allowed herself, *my bottom is perfectly suitable for whacking*.

"Hmmmm," she told the air, smiling wryly at the irony of it.

He'd given no further instructions and so she drifted around the room musing on how this evening could have been. Arriving home to steaks sizzling on the grill, a glass of red wine waiting for her. Undressing in the kitchen for him while he cooked. Undressing in the proper order, of course, with knickers and stockings left until he roughly removed them himself, until she'd teased him so much that he'd forced himself on her, her faux protests and struggles adding to the excitement.

Or maybe she'd be the one cooking. Suffering his hands touching her deep inside her knickers, her nipples tormented and her hair pulled sharply. Arousing her but not allowing her any satisfaction.

She was lost in such pleasant thoughts when he suddenly appeared in the room, making her jump guiltily.

"I hope you've been thinking about why you are going to be punished?" he asked, closing the door behind him. She merely blushed in response and he mistook her colour for shame.

"Come here," he said softly. Sitting on the bed, he pointed to the floor in front of him. Dragging her feet, she shuffled over to him, trying not to fidget as he inspected her clothing. He made her squirm horribly when he tugged her gym knickers down to check what she wore underneath. Then, readjusting them, he smoothed the navy material carefully over her bottom before twitching her vest slightly and nodding his approval.

Her earlier fantasies were far away. She was back to reality with a bang. No titillating spanking was on the cards, and no hot sex either. She knew she'd soon be crying in pain and remorse. Knew that she'd be comforted in his arms after but would only want hugs. Knew that they'd spend the night quietly reassuring each other, she thanking him for punishing her, he showing her all was forgiven.

Tilting her chin up to look at him, he gave her a mercifully short lecture, merely asking her why she was being punished. She searched for the words but couldn't find any, pleading with her eyes for him to just get on with it.

At last, "Because I was irresponsible," she offered, lowering her eyes.

"Yes," he nodded. "Very! What else?"

"And I didn't keep myself safe."

"Indeed, and you worried me sick," he confirmed. "It's not the first time either, is it? Look at me." The last he said sharply enough to make her obey instantly.

Miserably she faced him. "No, it's not, and I don't want to get into those situations. I really scared myself and I hate that I made you so worried. I'm so stupid."

Holding her hands, he corrected her, "Not stupid, just a very foolish young lady. I intend to make you think long and hard about how to avoid getting yourself into another mess like that. I'll do everything I can to make sure of it, starting with tonight's punishment. Because if anything happened to you I'd never forgive myself. Do you understand?"

His words pierced her, and her eyes filled with tears that she couldn't hold back. "Once I've punished you then the slate is clean," he continued, squeezing her hands, "but I certainly don't want you to forget. You will remember this."

"Yes sir," she answered pitifully. She was terrified of what was to come but also longed for it to be over.

Stomach churning, she watched as he fetched the slipper from the drawer. *It'll all be over soon*, she tried to comfort herself. *He loves me and I trust him, he loves me and I trust him...*

18

On his command she slowly bends over, her legs straight, her fingers almost touching her toes, her gym knickers pulled tight against her cheeks, baring her lower bottom. With her skin stretched so tight and uncomfortably, she knows it will hurt all the more.

Tapping the slipper against her, he pronounces her sentence: twelve. Inwardly she panics, afraid she won't be able to take them, but holds her position. She wants to show him that she's sorry, wants to make amends.

From the corner of her eye she watches his arm pull back and braces herself, closing her eyes. When the stroke lands it catches her square on the crease of her bottom, his entire weight crashing behind it. She stumbles forward screaming in agony. It's worse than she even feared, and she starts to cry in earnest, miserable that she has behaved badly enough to merit such pain.

He waits for her to compose herself and to count. When the 'one thank you sir' finally comes, her voice is shaking. He delivers strokes two and three in quick succession. At the third she jumps up clutching her bottom, loud gulping tears spilling out.

Knowing that she's struggling already, he wants to get it over with as quickly as possible, for both of them. His sharp order to get back down and stay in position has the desired effect; trembling, she dares not disobey. She makes it through three more, her counts becoming more ragged, her crying more pronounced. But she strains to hold position, trying not to fall over as the slipper lands; at the sixth her legs buckle, unable to support her further.

He places her over the bed for the second set of six. The bed is solid and reassuring beneath her, and she dissolves at his kindness, marvelling at how he always looks out for her. Weeps bitterly that she doesn't deserve him. Wonders how he can still love her when she lets him down so badly. How he can see her so desperate and broken with her red eyes and swollen nose and yet still want her.

Surveying his work so far, he strokes her bottom gently, feeling the welts that have already come up, astonished at the heat radiating. He knows she'll be sore for days, but it doesn't deter him; the next six will be just as efficacious.

"Good girl," he praises, "taken so bravely. Halfway there now." His words soothe her, giving her courage. *Six to go, five to go...*, she counts down in her head, clutching the duvet as she waits for each to land, willing herself to take them quietly, wanting to make him proud.

When there's only one to go, she finally knows she'll make it. Watching him warily, she holds her breath until it lands. He doesn't disappoint, delivering the hardest yet. She can't understand how she could take so much pain and still be conscious. Collapsing to her knees on the ground, she sobs aloud, almost hysterical. "I really am so sorry, really and truly, please, I'm sorry, please."

Putting the slipper to one side, he sits on the bed in front of her, letting her bury her head in his knees. Stoking her hair gently, he whispers reassurance; it's over, she's forgiven. Long minutes pass before she can face him, but he is patient, knows she needs space. When she's ready for her hug, he holds her tightly, comforting her as she loses herself to the pain and relief.

But despite the pain, she feels lighter. She genuinely thinks she deserves his hugs and attention, that she has made amends and earned a fresh start. Above all she's full of hope that she can change, that she will change, that she can be the person they both want her to be.

Almost in a daze she submits to him undressing her, wincing as he tugs the tight shorts down over her sore and bruised bottom. Welcomes the softness of the nightshirt he chooses. Doesn't resist when he carries her downstairs and gently arranges her under a cosy blanket on the sofa. Quietly regroups under his careful watch as he finishes preparing dinner.

By the time she's allowed her glass of wine she has resurfaced, a young girl no more. The process of atonement is complete. She has faith that she won't slip up again so easily, but finds comfort in knowing he will be there, to pick her up, and set her on her way again if she does.

****

About the author:

Emma Jane Woodhouse describes herself on her twitter account (@lilemmaj) as "a very kinky girl: the type you don't take home to mother." Well the kinky bit is certainly true! Since she plucked up the courage to connect with other like-minded individuals she's been dancing her way through a host of new experiences, meeting many new friends along the way.

Discipline and spanking roleplay are at the core of Emma Jane's kink and she's an experienced roleplayer; whether in school uniform, regency dress or in darker places. She's privileged to count Abel and HH as her closest play partners and her story 'Slipping Up' is inspired by, and dedicated to, both of them.

Based in London, after a recent move from her Irish homeland, she can always be found on her blog, "A Painful Awakening" where she chronicles her kinky journey with great honesty and openness:

apainfulawakening.blogspot.com

Keelin and Shayla

Faye Glass

All was dark.

All was quiet.

And all was lost.

Keelin crouched in the corner of the earthen dungeon... and waited. She was a pixie, and pixies are creatures of the Earth, but the earth that clung in patchy clods to her bare knees was no comfort now.

If only she had talked Shayla out of it! But no, even now, she knew that she would never have been able to do that.

Poor Shayla.

She had been dragged away from Keelin's blind grasp over an hour ago now. Keelin could still hear her last words, whispered feverishly as they'd heard the guards approaching, heard their inescapable tread downwards into the black depths of the fairy mound, *Oh, if only we had wings! Oh, how easy it would be!* She had been almost laughing as she said it and Keelin, suspecting panic, had clutched her hand right up until the very last second.

But now she was gone, long since dragged away, and Keelin was left to sigh over their failed escape attempt in awful solitude.

"At least we tried..." she murmured to herself.

Yes, that was true: but what chance had they ever really had against beings who could fly? Beings with magic at their control? Beings who could twist reality to their advantage, turn day into night and create insurmountable walls out of nothing? From the moment they first heard the bells sound, they had known that it was hopeless. Their only chance had been to slip out, unheard and unseen. But it had failed. Shayla had almost crushed Keelin's hand when she heard them. "I'm so sorry," she had whispered, still running even though it was hopeless. "I'm so so sorry..."

But Shayla was gone now, and Keelin had spent a cold silent unfathomable stretch of time alone in the dark thinking of her, missing her, wishing she could reach out with her thoughts and take away her pain.

Because she knew they would be hurting her. Right now. She knew that somewhere above where she crouched in the dark, Shayla was sure to be crying out in pain. Keelin just couldn't hear her. She didn't know whether to consider this a blessing or a curse...

A distant noise lurched Keelin out of her fevered introspection and she stiffened in sudden terror.

Footsteps.

No, no, please not now... I'm not ready...

Closer, heavier, marching inescapably downwards...

It was the Court Guard.

And, this time, they had come for Keelin.

"Do you know why you are here, pixie?"

Keelin raised her eyes as far as she dared, feeling the hungry gaze of the whole Court upon her. Her bare legs were trembling: she wished they would stop. In desperation, she tried to draw courage from Shayla by picturing her in her mind's eye: Shayla's beautiful deep red hair... her pale pale skin that gleamed like a pearl... the look that flashed through her startling green eyes whenever a fairy addressed her as 'pixie'...

"Well?" The Queen's voice was colder than steel and laced with contempt.

Keelin started slightly. "Yes, my Queen."

"And do you regret your actions?"

"Yes, my Queen," said Keelin at once. It was not really a lie... she certainly regretted that the plan had failed.

"Attempting to escape your natural and rightful enslavement is a very serious crime indeed, pixie. As I explained earlier to your... *friend*..."

She paused, and a ripple of giggles and murmurs swept through the assembled throng. In Keelin's fevered state, they sounded like distant bells trembling in a faraway storm.

The Queen waited for quiet … and then she spoke the words that Keelin had been dreading, words that cut through her like a cursed dagger. "For such a serious crime, only a very severe punishment will suffice."

Keelin shivered, and it wasn't just through fear. They had taken her clothes – and poor Shayla's – when they caught them. And so she was standing before the glittering mass of glimmering finery that was the Fairy Court with not a shred of fabric to shield her pale body from their gaze. Fairies were slender, delicate, all fine cheekbones and dainty ankles… but pixies were a different matter. Keelin was all soft, squeezable curves and though they sneered and laughed, she knew all too well that secretly they liked to look… liked to touch and pinch…

Keelin was suddenly aware of movement up on the raised platform in front of where she stood, alone. Her eyes darted upward almost against her own will, and she had to bite back a whimper as she watched the Queen throw back her shining cascade of black hair and rise from her throne, a birch clasped in one slender pointed hand.

"You will suffer the same fate as your friend. Three-times-three-times-three strokes of the birch and three nights' imprisonment in the dungeons. Unless, of course," and now the Queen raised her voice and addressed herself to the watching fairies, "anyone present will speak for her?"

Keelin was once again aware of every eye in the chamber needling into her bare flesh. She could sense their malice, their lust, their excitement… but she sensed not an ounce of sympathy, nor the barest hint of friendliness.

There was nothing…

…and then a voice cut through the thrumming silence. A burning, scalding voice. A voice that Keelin feared above all others.

It was Brietta, Keelin's Mistress.

"I shall speak, but not to beg you to spare her. Indeed, if anything, I would ask that you double the number of strokes. The stupid little bitch deserves no less."

Keelin swallowed involuntarily and stared down at her bare feet.

"No," continued Brietta. "It is the three-night imprisonment that I take issue with. It is out of the question that I should be without a servant for such an extended period of time. Instead, I would ask that her sentence be reduced to one night only. I can assure you," she added, in a carrying hiss, "that once she is back in my power I shall make sure that she thoroughly regrets her actions."

Keelin could now feel her Mistress's gaze upon her pale, unmarked skin and she shivered more violently than ever.

There was a thick, heavy silence...

... and then the Queen's voice rang out. "It is done."

There was a collective sigh throughout the Chamber... and Keelin feared that her trembling legs would soon cease to support her.

Up on the raised platform, the Queen spread her wings. They were beautiful wings, coloured deepest violet and outlined in glittering silver... but all they evoked in Keelin was bitterness and fear. The Queen took flight, and her tightly structured dress, that was such a dark shade of purple it was almost black, billowed behind her.

Keelin trembled at the horribly familiar sound of rushing wings... but then the Queen reached where she stood, and her tread was as light as a ghost as she landed on the black flagstones of the chamber floor.

With her free hand, the Queen groped in the folds of her skirt before bringing forth her wand. It looked, to all the world, like a harmless twig... but Keelin flinched as though the Queen were brandishing a sword at her. Oh, how bitterly did she wish that she had wings in that moment! Wings she could use to fly far far away from this place... with Shayla at her side...

Striding forwards, the Queen gave her wand a sharp little flick and an ancient wooden bench materialised in front of Keelin. It was worn and creaking through centuries of use, and the condemned pixie shuddered to see the iron manacles glowering on either side: one for each wrist and ankle.

She was not asked, nor ordered, to position herself over the bench. Instead, she was propelled forwards by magic, and there were titters from the sidelines as she squeaked and stumbled in surprise.

Magic tipped her further over the bench than she would have been able to reach by herself; and magic prodded and manipulated her body until her bare bottom was thrust upwards at an obscene angle. Keelin wondered dimly whether this was for her own humiliation or for the delectation of the avid spectators. She suspected both.

Another flick of the Queen's wand and the manacles had clamped themselves around Keelin's wrists and ankles, the cold, heavy iron dragging her shaking limbs further downwards.

She had never felt so keenly the reality of her own enslavement, as she did then; forced across that bench, pinioned and helpless. The dreams than she and Shayla had concocted together in the deepest night now seemed like the height of childish fancy. How could she ever have thought that they would really be able to escape?

"You have forgotten your place," whispered the Queen and, though her voice was soft, the Chamber was so very silent that it carried into every hushed corner. "And now I intend to remind you of it."

Keelin heard a rustle... and then she gasped and squeezed her eyes tightly closed as the first stroke whipped across her exposed cheeks.

The biting sting had barely reached its peak before the second stroke lashed down... and then the third...

Three-times-three-times-three, thought Keelin in rising panic. Oh! How would she ever bear it?

Her only comfort was that, as a magical being, she would heal far more quickly than a mortal ever could. But being magical didn't take away the sting. She had learned this long ago.

And now, as stroke upon vicious stroke rained down upon her helpless bottom, the sting was becoming intolerable. Gasping and screwing up her face in pain was no longer enough, and as a particular vicious lash of the birch caught the soft flesh of Keelin's upper thighs, a sharp, desperate cry escaped her trembling lips.

A murmur of satisfaction spread around the Court as Keelin's cries pierced the keen silence. This turned to titters and giggles as she strained desperately against the chains that bound her, her whipped bottom wriggling and flinching without a single hope of escape.

And now all restraint had dissolved, and each merciless swish of the birch elicited a high-pitched whimpering cry from Keelin…

…and yet, even through the delirium of pain and humiliation, Keelin couldn't help wondering if Shayla was crouching in the darkness somewhere below…

…and if she was reaching out, as Keelin had hours before, to try and take away her pain…

Keelin was back in the darkness again.

But this was a different dark place: she was nowhere near Shayla.

She was still naked, but she found that this mattered less to her now than it had. Indeed, by the time the Queen had finished with her, her lack of clothing had been the least of her concerns.

Keelin trembled at the memory and wished for the thousandth time that Shayla were here with her, so that they might comfort each other. But they had been kept apart: a further cruelty.

But at least it was over now… and Keelin, lying face down in the darkness, could already feel the prickling warmth of her skin healing itself.

Sighing, Keelin felt the cold, hard earth beneath her skin, and the feeling, as always calmed her… calmed her and called to the Earth magic that lay forever dormant inside her blood.

Because, whatever the fairies may say, pixies do have magic. In fact, they are almost brimming over with it. But, like so much else, the tools of magic are denied them. No candles, no athames and, most cruelly, no wands. No instrument through which to channel their powers.

Magic is there but it is wasted, abandoned and can only flutter feebly inside them as a helpless butterfly flutters in a net. Keelin has always felt it as a sort of trembling, almost like panic, the silent desperation of potential squandered.

If only we'd had wings, Shayla had said.

But now, alone in the cold womb of the earth, Keelin was thinking differently: *If only we'd had magic…*

But she knew that magic was not all pretty lights and pictures; it could be used for cruelty too…

Keelin had heard the stories of fairies who used their magic to trap mortals into an endless dance from which they could never escape, though their legs screamed in protest, though they swooned with exhaustion, though vast swathes of time passed, though their feet bled…

But Keelin had no wish to make sport with mortals, and neither did Shayla. But if they could find just enough magic to help them to disappear into the woods, to return to the place from which they had been taken so long ago… well, that would be perfect. They could even live out amongst mortals, if they had to. Just to be free, and together, was all they had ever wanted.

They had almost tasted freedom last night…

…and as slumber finally washed over Keelin's exhausted limbs, she found herself remembering the moon and the stars… and the feel of Shayla's crushing hand…

"You may go."

Brietta's voice was cold and hard.

And Keelin, who was still naked, trembled by the doorway as the guard who had delivered her back into the clutches of her Mistress left, closing the door behind him.

As the sound of his footsteps faded away, silence descended upon Brietta's private chambers.

"Well, well, well," said Brietta softly. "And you thought you would escape me, did you?" And, with that, she swept across the room towards her servant, the hem of her long dress barely whispering against the cold stone floor, magnificent silvery wings almost overwhelming her slender frame. Keelin had thought her lovely once, with her clear blue eyes, fair hair and wings that glittered like ice in a pale winter's sun, but time and painful experience had taught her better.

And, lovely or not, no ounce of fey beauty could disguise the expression of purest rage on Brietta's face as she drew back her hand, slapped Keelin viciously across the cheek and sent her sprawling onto the stone-cold floor.

"You disobedient little bitch!" she hissed, as Keelin pressed a muddy hand to her stinging cheek. "Oh!" she shrieked then. "Look how you dirty my floor!"

Keelin looked down the length of her body and saw the earth still clinging to her skin... and noticed that some was now scattered across Brietta's pristine floor. She swallowed... and then yelped as Brietta yanked her to her feet by her hair.

"I think we need to clean you, don't we? You filthy little creature." And, without waiting for a response, she dragged Keelin across the room and through a side-door.

They had come, Keelin saw, into the room where Brietta liked to bathe and relax and generally preen herself. There was a pool at its centre, fed by a stream that sprang from a cluster of rocks protruding from the far wall.

Magic could make this spring flow as sweetly as the gentlest of brooks, warm and sinuous and enticing. It was always so when Brietta bathed there... when delicate rose petals floated in the soft ripples of the pool and the banks were heavy with sweet-smelling grasses, and dotted with clover flowers.

Now, though, Keelin could see its true form, beneath the glamour and pretty illusion. It was a roughly hewn stone basin, as wide and deep as Brietta's magical pool, but altogether blacker and more forbidding, with dark water frothing and splashing against the sides. And the once gentle spring was now an icy torrent that thundered from a dark gash in the rocks, spewing from the earth with all the violence of nature untamed.

Keelin barely had time to register this unsettling change in form before Brietta thrust her into the pool, directly beneath all that freezing, pounding water. Reeling, Keelin bit back a shriek as the icy torrent pummelled every inch of her exposed flesh like formless fists, making her skin at first shock-white, and then red-raw and tightly stretched.

But she knew better than to shriek in Brietta's presence. Instead she took great gasping gulps of air, short shallow panting gasps like a dying fish, and gripped her own arms so tightly that her fingernails left little red half-moon shapes in her frozen skin.

And just when her skin felt so cold that she almost, paradoxically, felt as though she were on fire, Brietta gripped a sodden clump of her hair and took flight. Keelin's feet kicked and flailed in nothingness, as, whimpering and dripping, she was dragged through the chill air back into the main chamber, before being deposited unceremoniously on an unremarkable spot in the centre of the room.

"You will stand here and you will not move or speak until instructed otherwise. Understand?"

Keelin spluttered out assurances that she did understand but Brietta had already turned and disappeared into an adjoining chamber, as indifferent to Keelin now as if she were a spider trapped in a glass. A spider to be crushed beneath her heel… or set free…

Or drowned, thought Keelin, shuddering at the stream of freezing water now flowing down her back from her tangled mane of saturated hair.

Her bare skin dried slowly in the dizzying cold. It felt numb and rough. She chanced the tiniest glance down at herself and shivered even more violently. How pale her skin was! It was almost transparent – yes, she was sure she could see the faint greens and purples of blood vessels just beneath her skin.

Time seemed to pass, but with no real sense to it. It may have been minutes, hours or even days that she stood waiting. Time inside the Fairy Mound was rarely straightforward, but Keelin had never thought on it much. Now, however, she pondered every passing second, felt the minutes draw out like bitter honey, felt every teardrop of water on her body gradually evaporate into nothingness, into the air. She felt her untended hair dry in stiff, caked clumps. It felt heavy and cold and unpleasant.

She felt her knees begin to tire, begin to ache... she felt the muscles in her thighs begin to tire, begin to ache... and then numbness came, and she didn't feel anything at all for a while.

Her eyelids were finally starting to droop, when Brietta's sharp voice shot through her like a lightning bolt. "On the bed. Now."

Tired though she was, Keelin stumbled forwards at once, albeit on legs that appeared to have forgotten how to function.

Brietta's bed was a vast four-poster, handcrafted from solid oak and decorated with intricate carvings of roses and thorns. Each post was twisted and twined with living vines.

"Lay on your front," barked Brietta, as Keelin hovered uncertainly next to the bed.

She obeyed, and Brietta took out her wand and gave it an absent little flick. At once, the vines about the bedposts sprang to life, and green tendrils slithered across the sheets, coiling around Keelin's wrists and ankles... crisscrossing further and further upwards, stopping only when they bit into the soft flesh of her thighs and upper arms.

Keelin gasped and twisted: she didn't know they could do that.

"Don't you *dare* try to escape!"

Brietta strode towards her, and Keelin could now see the strap in her hand. She knew that strap well: it was an ancient strip of hide, taken from some vicious unnamed creature and it was almost yellowish with age.

Brietta stood beside the bed and allowed the strap to drop at her side. It looked so heavy, Keelin wondered that it didn't drag her arm down, make her shoulder sag. She flinched and the vines tightened, as though sensing her fear and determining all the more fiercely to keep her still, keep her ready, keep her helpless. But no – Keelin inwardly shook herself – it was Brietta who controlled them. How typical of her to take something so natural and blameless, and twist it...

"I don't care for your expression," said Brietta in her cold, hard voice. "You look bold, as if you might insult me."

Keelin lowered her eyes at once. "My mistress knows I would never - " But the rest of her imploration was lost in a great intake of breath as the strap lashed down for the first time.

"I did not give you permission to speak," hissed Brietta.

And then the second stroke seared Keelin's cheeks and she whimpered into the bedclothes. The marks from her birching had faded overnight: her bottom was pale and unmarked once again... and ripe for more punishment...

And Brietta was certainly willing and able to deliver that punishment. More strokes followed, fast and hard, with barely a pause to breathe – or cry out – between them. Keelin pressed her face even harder into the bedclothes...

...and, for what felt like an awfully long time, Brietta's chamber echoed with the inescapable sound of leather slapping against flesh.

Keelin passed the next two days in a sort of waking trance. She went about her duties as normal, but was so distracted by thoughts of poor Shayla all alone in the dungeons, that she kept making little mistakes.

As a result, fast-healing though she undoubtedly was, her bottom was constantly crimson. So, too, was Brietta's right hand.

Nothing stirred her though, until the day of the Ostara Celebrations.

There was to be a Ball, and the whole Court would be there. And, for once, Keelin was even more excited at the prospect of a Ball than her Mistress. Not because she foresaw much pleasure in the event itself, but because this was the day of Shayla's release and she would finally be able to see her for the first time since they had been dragged apart three nights before.

"Unless you want another spanking I suggest you take more care, pixie!" said Brietta peevishly as Keelin's excited fingers gathered up the hairpins that she had just dropped.

"I'm sorry, Mistress," she whispered, flicking a repentant glance at Brietta's reflection, although she didn't actually feel sorry at all. She was also fairly sure that Brietta's threat was an empty one: she would not want to risk being late for the Ball.

Once Brietta's hair had been arranged to her satisfaction, both Mistress and servant made their way out into the already crowded corridor.

Keelin was no longer naked but was now wearing the standard uniform of female pixie servants: a short blue sleeveless tunic.

As Keelin looked about her, she saw many more figures wearing this uniform. And then one in particular caught her eye... and she felt an explosion in the pit of her stomach.

Shayla was mere feet away from her. She looked as perfect as ever, unmarked, and seemingly untouched. *Ripe for more pinching, more slapping, more bruising*, thought Keelin dully.

But as Keelin moved closer, she saw that Shayla's face was bloodless and her eyes were dull: pixies are not meant to spend days and nights alone in the darkness, untouched and unloved. They pine.

But no, Shayla couldn't be pining. She couldn't. A terrible fear bubbled up inside of Keelin and, without thinking, she reached for Shayla and squeezed her hand fiercely.

Shayla's eyes flew wide open and her white face flushed with colour. "Oh, Keelin!" she wept and then she was in Keelin's arms and all thought that they were in full view, in a corridor crowded

33

with court dignitaries no less, evaporated into the stifling air. Keelin kissed Shayla, squeezed her, stroked her face and arms and back with short brisk movements, almost as though she were trying to rub her warm on a cold day. And she wept as she did so, trying with all her might to force that awful dead look to fade from Shayla's face. And Shayla gasped and clung to Keelin, as though she were the only real being left in existence.

But then Brietta grabbed a fistful of her servant's hair, gave a sharp tug and, in a heartbeat, that shining moment of reunion was pierced irretrievably.

"How dare you embarrass me in front of the whole Court!" hissed Brietta, before shoving Keelin in front of her.

Shayla's Mistress Lady Catriona, however, was far too immersed in conversation with Lord Annan to give Shayla more than a sharp poke in the back to start her moving again.

Onwards they went, and this time Keelin looked at the floor, whilst grief and delight shuddered through her body in equal measure.

The Court Chamber was decorated extravagantly for the Ostara celebrations. Spring flowers garlanded every available wall and surface. But here, underground and illuminated only by candlelight, they looked dimmed and out of place. Keelin shuddered, and the Earth magic coursing through her veins lamented the sight of so much life trapped in this place, twisted into artificial bundles and condemned to wilt slowly in the shadows.

Finally, after much fussing, Brietta and Catriona were both seated, and Keelin and Shayla took up their places knelt alongside one another, as they always had. It was almost as though nothing had changed.

Keelin longed to reach out for Shayla again, but she didn't dare. Instead, she gazed at the side of Shayla's soft, heavy breast, clearly visible through the paper-thin fabric of her tunic. The plain dark blue of this tunic did nothing for Shayla's beautiful fair complexion, her startling eyes, her hair. In her mind, Keelin would often fashion her in shining emerald greens, silvers, golds, purest whites and deepest blacks. If it must be blue, she made it a soft, dusky blue, trimmed with gold…

She contented herself with gazing, until the music started, and then she addressed Shayla in the tiniest of whispers.

"How are you?"

"Much better for seeing you," murmured Shayla, her face carefully impassive. "Oh Keelin, I am sorry you know. It was my idea and - "

"Don't be sorry," soothed Keelin, her hands positively twitching with the desire to reach out. "Listen, Shayla, I did a lot of thinking when I was…" she faltered, took a deep breath. "…when I was down *there*. And I've realised that the only way we'll be able to… to… I mean, the thing we'll need is - "

"- magic," Shayla finished for her, and her voice trembled, just a little.

Keelin blinked. "You think so too? Oh Shayla, I was so hoping you would!"

But then their conversation was interrupted by the arrival of dinner, and both pixies leapt to their duties at once. Pixies all about them were doing the same, and for a while, they busied themselves supplying their respective Mistresses with glass upon glass of velvety strawberry wine, delicate platters of vegetable tartlets and exotic fruits, and endless buttery cakes.

Keelin wondered if it was all real food. It seemed too brightly coloured to be real, too perfectly delicate and aesthetically pleasing. Pixie magic called to real, honest earth-grown food but these dainty delicacies left Keelin cold. She had never doubted the stories that told how fairy food would crumble into dust and ash if taken out of the Fairy Mound. Still the authenticity of otherwise of the food on offer made no difference to Keelin or Shayla: as mere servants, they were not permitted to eat any.

Finally, it was time for the dancing to start and, as she once again knelt in her allotted place, Keelin caught a fleeting glimpse of Shayla, who had an oddly triumphant look on her face, before she was obscured by the sweep of Brietta's elaborate golden dress.

Soon, the Court Chamber was filled with the opening strands of a merry fairy melody and dancing couples twirled and glittered and sparkled in the candlelight.

Keelin spoke again, her voice so low it was almost inaudible. "So, do you... do you wish to try again?"

"Of course," Shayla murmured, her pale lips barely stirring, her expression bland and unmoved.

"But how?" whispered Keelin, turning ever so slightly.

Shayla's arm twitched, giving Keelin the tiniest glimpse of a fragile split of wood hidden in the folds of her skirt. One blink, and it was gone again. "Lady Catriona seems quite distracted by Lord Annan this evening, do you not think?" Her tone was as expressionless as ever but her lips curved in a small smile.

There was a flicker then, an odd trembling in the air.

Keelin's eyes widened.

Shayla's hand was suddenly crushing hers... and pulling...

And the fairies danced...

...and danced...

...and danced...

****

About the author:

Faye Glass is a woman in her mid-twenties who has been merrily churning out kinky fiction on and off for the past four years.

Aside from her obvious interests in spanking, debauchery and the fiction thereof, she enjoys scrummy food, the seaside and anything that makes her laugh.

She is happily coupled up with the lovely Richard Farthingdale, who has taken on the unenviable and arduous task of turning her into Acceptable Wife Material. Nobody genuinely expects him to succeed but it is very fun trying.

She really hates writing about herself so is going to stop now.

Watching Xanadu

Paul Bailey

Stop.

Rewind.

Play.

...

Stop.

Rewind.

Play.

...

Stop. Rewind. Play. ...

Stop.

It's all digital, of course, so there isn't really anything rewinding. It just jumps back to the start. I can even set it to loop endlessly — see?

Although you might not even be able to see that it's looping. Xan is standing so completely still in the corner — as I'd told her to do — that the end of the loop is exactly the same as the beginning. She would be standing there forever, if I let her.

I suppose you could argue that I'm lucky, in a way. Most times things start to go wrong, for most people, they sail past the moment, not noticing. By the time things are bad enough for them to try to work it out, it's too far gone, so they never really know what happened; just that it happened.

Figuring out what happened between me and Xan might still be all tangled up in my head, but the when is right in front of me. If I turn the volume right up, you can actually hear it. I'd just moved the camera, and zoomed right out to get all of Xan in frame. Once the framing was right, I took a step back to watch her. I leaned back against the wall, and after a minute or so there's a sort of sighing, crumpled sound on the video. What I felt then was a bone-deep weariness — it comes back to me now, watching it.

I'd just punished her. The word comes with so many scare quotes in my head now, so many layers of encoding, that I can barely even write it. Looking at her standing there in the corner, still and straight and noble and completely fucking *beautiful*, there was a moment of perfect clarity. I might have spanked her, said all the right things and hit all the clichés, but she was so far beyond being *punished* by me it wasn't even funny. We were dancing the right steps, but it was all fake. Xan's capacity to give — need to give — was so much greater than my capacity to take, and I couldn't sustain it any more.

After that, it did get messy for a while, but not unkind. I think she sensed the same thing I did, so we tried to be gentle with each other, even while our lives were wrenching apart. There was no particular goodbye moment, maybe because we both hoped that it wasn't that sort of goodbye. One day she moved the last box out of my place, and that was that.

It's important to be clear that I don't regret it. This wasn't a rejection of something that could have worked. Our eyes were wide open. It was healthy, in a way.

Four dull months later, I was tweeting something about heading into London for a weekend convention, and there she was:

xan_a_duu
@S_T_Coleridge Fancy dinner Sunday night, loser?
M. is away on business. I'll cook you something nice.
See the new place?
1 day ago

No hellos, no goodbyes. That's really where we'd left things, a friendly but careful detachment taking the place of any real feeling. She hadn't been following me — I'd have noticed — and still wasn't. The account looked new, and there wasn't much in it, just some oblique references to a new job, and a new squeeze, and followers I didn't recognise.

S_T_Coleridge
@xan_a_duu Sure. Meet where/when?
3 hours ago

xan_a_duu
@S_T_Coleridge Waterloo at 5, by the clock? It's a short train ride in/out. I'll come get you.
1 hour ago

S_T_Coleridge
@xan_a_duu Cool. See you then.
10 seconds ago

The con was flagging by three, so it was easy to bail and head across town to the station early. I wanted to see Xan from a safe distance before we met, so I could get my bearings a bit first. The sandwich place across the concourse was still open, even though the rest of the station had the lonely windblown feel of a city Sunday, so I got something and sat in a corner. People came and went. A girl in high DMs and heavy eyeliner got a coffee, sat for a

40

while at the next table, smoking and poking nervously at her phone, then hurried off. A two-carriage workhorse diesel made a big huff and puff of disgorging just a few passengers, who ran into the arms of those waiting, or no-one.

But it passed five, and there was no Xanadu, by the clock or anywhere else. I carried my things to the barriers and looked down the track as if that would help.

"So," she said, from behind me. "How many today?"

I turned. She'd changed her hair, but there she was. "Just three, I think," I said. "A newbie girl at the con, doing cosplay. She was so into it, but she looked a bit lost all the same. And another one earlier, over there, the full goth thing."

Xan smiled, god love her. "Always the waifs and strays with you, you hopeless fucking case."

"And then another one, just a few seconds ago."

"Don't do that."

"Although I wouldn't call this one *love*, exactly."

"Don't."

"I know," I said. "I'm sorry." Okay, so it hadn't taken me long to show that I hadn't changed much. Well done me. "Your hair's different."

She smiled again. "It is. I like it, I think."

"Suits you. You were late, by the way."

"No," she said. "I was early. Because I knew you'd be early and I didn't want you watching me."

"Okay. I think you just won."

"How are you, loser?" She gave me a quick but tight hug.

"Good. I'm good."

"Oh," she said, suddenly remembering something she'd clearly at no point forgotten. "Mark is eating with us tonight. He switched his flight for a later one so he could meet you. Is that okay?"

"Of course. Absolutely."

Mark. *Right.*

Three stops south was far enough to take us deep into Surrey. The house was solid Victorian redbrick on the outside and sleek Scandinavian on the inside. Mark met us at the door — confident, poised, firm handshake, tasteful tie and overdone men's magazine cologne. A drink was fetched, and they both busied themselves in the kitchen while I was left to do the conventional dinner party audit of the hosts' stuff. It was a picture of lives in balance, comfortable without being showy or precious. I didn't see anything of Xan's that I recognised.

They emerged, Mark smiling and wiping his hands. "Just another ten minutes and it'll be ready." He turned to Xan. "You should go and change, baby. There won't be a lot of time after dinner." I saw a flicker of surprise in Xan's eyes, and the beginning of an objection. "You hadn't forgotten that we need to talk about your behaviour before I go, had you?"

"No, sir, I just thought that..."

"What?"

Xan's chin actually dropped a little. "No, sir, I hadn't forgotten."

"Good girl. Off you go."

She disappeared upstairs, leaving the two of us to some clumsy male bonding over cars (I don't drive), jobs (he doesn't know anything about web programming; I don't know anything about marine insurance), and the convention (yeah, right). We were rescued by tentative footsteps on the stairs, and Xanadu reappeared as a perfect schoolboy, bare legs between grey school shorts and knee-socks, an old-fashioned stiff Eton collar keeping her neck straight and chin high, her new boy-cut neat and apt. She stood in front of Mark, arms folded behind her back, as he needlessly straightened her tie.

"Well then," Mark said. "Shall we eat?"

The food — pasta with chicken and garlic and sundried bloody tomatoes — was obvious but tasty. I just wasn't hungry. I watched them both, and barely even needed to pretend that I wasn't. It's not that they ignored me, or that I wasn't welcome. I just wasn't even really there. Mark had done his small talk; Xan was in his orbit. Towards the end of the meal, some cream sauce fell from Xan's fork onto her starched white shirt, but barely even visible. Mark laid down his own fork, pushed his chair back from the table, patted his lap. She draped herself across it, without hesitation or argument, had the backs of her legs smacked for a good minute, and sat back down, flustered and blushing.

I was interested in the fact that I didn't feel very much. It was all as distant as the moon through the wrong end of a telescope. Frankly, it was a relief when I was able to correctly interpret Mark's mention of his need to finish his packing as my time to go.

Another firm handshake from him.

"Thanks for coming," Xan said, with a smile and a quick hug. "It was good to see you."

"You too."

And that was that. It didn't feel like I was coming back, but we don't really do goodbyes.

"Wait for me in the study, baby," Mark said to Xan as he took me to the door.

21:12.

The departures screen on the station platform beamed out brightly in the dark. I wanted to bat myself against it like a moth, as if it could take me away like that. I was cold and tired and ready to be home. There was a train at 21:40, and another — the last — at 22:55. My laptop had plenty of battery left, fortunately, so it kept me company for a while. I played some bits of TV I'd torrented, but didn't really pay attention; they were just moving shapes on the screen. I started the last video of Xanadu, without really meaning to — just muscle memory, I guess. I stopped it and started it a few times. I moved it to the trash. I moved it out of the trash.

The 21:40 slid quietly onto the platform. Through its open doors the train looked warm and inviting, an end-of-weekend mess of newspapers and junk-food wrappers strewn around, but almost no-one travelling. It seemed to wait far longer than necessary, then the doors closed and it chugged on without me.

I packed my machine into its case, and into my bag, lifted the bag onto my shoulder, and headed back to the house in the cold and dark.

The Jag was still in the drive when I reached their house again. I sat on the low wall in front of the house opposite, watching. There wasn't a plan, exactly, but I suppose I thought I'd wait for Mark to leave for the airport, then figure it out from there. I wanted to be gone, to be far away, but being gone seemed to presuppose at least a moment of *being there* first, a moment of real connection. And yes, fuck it, a proper goodbye.

I'm not sure anyone else would have heard it quite the way that I did, but on top of the carrier wave of the light wind among the trees there was a distinct *thwack*, and then, maybe thirty seconds later, another.

I crossed the road. The path along the side of the house was loomed over by mature Leylandii, which bought a lot of privacy for them, and for me. The end of the path opened out into a patio, onto which light spilled from the room at the back of the house through French windows, and widened across the lawn, as if projecting something. On the patio, a wide table and chairs were still covered in wintering canvas covers, which made a perfectly shadowed spot to sit and wait.

Thwack. Much louder this time. And...

Play.

I couldn't see the whole room from where I was, but I could see enough. Tall shelves of fat showpiece books lined the far wall, behind a working desk — a big old fuck-off one, not the IKEA restraint of the other bits of the house I'd seen. A few lamps here and there provided a warm light. A second desk had been set in the centre of the room, facing the first, this one small but high, with a sloping surface. Xanadu was bent across it, her toes and

44

fingers pointing towards the carpet, and the rest of her taut and poised, like a bow about to fire.

Mark paced backwards and forwards behind her, gesturing rhetorically with the long cane in his hand. The rumble of words that came through the windows was blurry, but I understood the familiar rhythms. It's always the same script — we just either believe in it or we don't. I could see Xan nodding, her head low. Mark settled himself to her left, drew back the cane in a slow, wide arc, and brought it down perfectly square. After the sound of impact, Xan tightened still further for a few seconds, then relaxed.

It felt like I could just reach out and touch her, she was so close. But she wasn't. And I couldn't stop, or rewind. I wanted to be there, and I wanted to be anywhere but there. Another two strokes, just as careful and precise. To a simple command, Xan stood, took down her short trousers and the white underpants underneath, then bent across the desk again, red stripes burning across her bottom.

I started to feel the weariness again — the weariness of everything being so impossibly fucking difficult, so out of reach and right there in front of me, everything blurred and completely in focus. In between the cane strokes — harder now, on Xan's bare skin — the sounds from this garden, and the gardens surrounding, fizzed in my ears: owl hoots, and cat howls, and distant traffic and bins being emptied and a whole world in which I was sitting here watching Xanadu being beaten by someone who wasn't me.

And then Mark dropped the cane and unfastened himself and pushed apart Xan's cheeks and he was fucking her. He was pushing himself deep inside her thrashed backside and pushing and fucking and fucking and fucking her, Xanadu still bent across the desk, her legs finally kicking and shuddering, the desk rearing up on its front legs with each hungry stroke.

And there was an end. Mark stepped back to dress himself, face blank, as if fucking Xanadu had been just part of a punishment to administer, cold and regretful. Xan wasn't much more than a ragdoll draped over the desk, but she gathered herself at another low rumble, stood and walked carefully to the corner behind the big fuck-off desk. Mark took a minute to gather himself and pull a few things together into a brown travelling bag. He stepped behind the desk, tapped at the keyboard of the PC, turned the screen towards himself. Then he bent over Xan, completely covering her body from view — whispering in her ear, kissing the back of her neck, I couldn't tell. But he swept out of the room, leaving her there. I heard the Jag's contained roar as it prowled away.

Suddenly there was real, deep silence, Xanadu and me. I wasn't sure how long to wait, so I just waited, watching her in the corner in the warm room, still and straight and noble and beaten and completely fucking *beautiful*. Five minutes, ten minutes, maybe fifteen, I wasn't looking, but she hadn't moved, so I came to the windows, tapped lightly. Nothing. I tapped again, and tried the handle, which turned.

"Hello," I said quietly, not wanting to startle her. "It's just me."

Nothing.

"Hello? Xan?"

She didn't say anything, but there was a movement of her back which signalled she'd heard. I stepped in.

"What are you doing here?" she asked, with an edge in her voice. "Did you forget something?"

"No. No."

"What are you doing here?"

"Can we talk?"

"Talk about what?"

"I don't know," I sighed. "Just talk."

She seemed to realise something, and the edge was much harder this time. "Did you come here to watch us fucking, you fucking loser?"

"Jesus, Xan, *no*." And then I suddenly had an edge of my own. "Did you invite me here to make me watch you fucking?"

"What?"

"Over dinner. He doesn't need to put his cock in you for you to be fucking, you know."

"That was two people into each other being into each other," she said. "I know that's not something you're used to." There was a bit of a moment, and she sighed. "I didn't plan it that way."

"I know," I said. "I'm sorry. Will you turn around and look at me?"

"No."

"Please."

"I can't."

"Please."

"I can't. He's watching."

"Who? *Mark?*"

"On the desk," she said. "There's a camera. It's on, and it's pointing at me. His phone is sitting on the dashboard of the car, and that's on too. He's watching me."

I stepped towards the desk, and there it was, clamped to the top of the screen.

"Cameras can go wrong, Xan," I said. "Cables can get unplugged."

"No," she said. "*No.* And this is why: I want him watching me. I like it. I like doing what he tells me, and I like him beating me, and I like him fucking me, and I want to be with him. So I stay here, and the camera stays there. Understand?"

"For how long?"

"Until he calls. However long that takes."

I looked at my watch. 22:34.

"Xan, the last train leaves in twenty-one minutes. I'm going to be on it, and I'm not coming back. Will you please turn around so I can say goodbye?"

The 22:55 slid into the station at 22:56. I got on it. It slid out again, and the lights of the station curved slowly backwards into the night. The convention hotel room minibar welcomed me back with expensive chocolate and lukewarm Coke, and there was a message:

47

xan_a_duu
@S_T_Coleridge You put me on a pedestal, and
then told me I was too high up for you. That
was a stupid thing to do. Be happy, Sam. x
6 minutes ago

We don't really do goodbyes.

Stop.

Rewind.

Play.

Another train, this one taking me home. Fields of green grass and
bright yellow rapeseed flash by under a spring sky. Xanadu is on
the screen, on the laptop, on the table, standing in the corner, and
it's me behind the camera.

It occurred to me this morning, making the most of the warm
bed before I needed to get up and pack, that Xan's webcam has to
send content to a server somewhere. Even if it's a machine in their
place, it still needs an IP address if Mark can get to it with his
phone. So with an address, a username, and a password, I'd be in,
and I could probably figure those out sooner or later.

And then I laughed. Once upon a time it would have been
something to hold onto, but now the ridiculousness of it just made
me laugh. Fucking loser. This is a good thing, I think. *Be happy.*

Stop.

Rewind.

Play.

...

Stop.

...

Delete.

...

Empty Trash.

****

About the author:

Paul Bailey is the real face behind some online masks that have been around for a while. Stories and other writings by him — under the screen-name "Pablo" — and his partner are collected at thetreehouse.net; he's also been involved in the running of the Usenet newsgroup soc.sexuality.spanking as Pablo since its creation.

You can find him on Twitter and FetLife as PaulAtNorthGare, and he blogs — very slowly — at northgare.net/blog.

Go and find the Mull Historical Society track "Watching Xanadu", which in many ways was the inspiration for this story. Besides, it's good.

Staff Handbook: Chapter 5
Discipline and Punishments

Henry Higgins

Disciplinary problems are addressed with a graded system of punishments. The general scale to be applied is as follows:

- Impositions are appropriate for lax schoolwork and minor breaches of discipline. A pupil is commonly required to write out an educational or improving sentence 100 to 500 times. Impositions should not normally take more than 3 hours to complete.

- Detention is used for more serious breaches of discipline and for minor repeat offences. Pupils may be instructed to report for up to five 90-minute detention periods.

- Corporal punishment is appropriate for serious matters or where detention has proved ineffective. Corporal punishment is also administered for misbehaviour of any kind that occurs while in detention.

Corporal punishment may be applied to the hand or to the clothed or uncovered seat. It is most common to use a strap or tawse on the hand or a cane on the seat, but exceptions to this are permitted when appropriate.

Punishments on the hand

Teachers are responsible for procuring their own straps. Suitable implements may be purchased from a variety of suppliers, including John J. Dick of Lochgelly, who offer a reliable mail-order service. John J. Dick supplies 2-tail and 3-tail tawses graded M (medium), H (heavy) and XH (extra heavy). All these are approved for use in the school. Straps and tawses purchased from other suppliers must be approved by the Headmaster before use.

Punishments on the hand may be applied either in class or in private. In a classroom situation, the pupil should be instructed to come to the front of the room for punishment.

It is very important for teachers new to the profession to acquire proficiency in the use of the tawse. The usual procedure is to instruct the pupil to raise his or her hands with the instruction "Cross your hands". The hands should be held out at or below the teacher's chest level, one resting on the other. It is important to insist that the fingers be straight and together. The teacher measures the stroke lengthways on the hand, then raises the tawse over his shoulder and brings it down with full force on the outstretched palm.

Two to six strokes of the tawse are commonly applied. It is usual to distribute these between writing and non-writing hands. The pupil should be told to "swap hands" either half-way through the punishment or at intervals throughout.

The weight of the tawse used should be graded to the severity required. It is better to use a full-force stroke with a lighter tawse than to use reduced force with a heavier one.

Inexperienced teachers may find that their arm extends further on the downstroke than when measuring position. Care should be taken to compensate for this and avoid striking the wrist. A well-aimed stroke lands with the tip of the tawse approximately level with the base of the thumb.

Strokes of the tawse are generally most effective if "followed through", but inexperienced teachers attempting this for the first time must take care to position themselves out of the line of the stroke.

Punishments on the seat are usually administered with a cane, though the tawse is an acceptable alternative. Suitable canes may be purchased from James Duckworth in the High Street or by mail order from Eric Wildman of City Road, London.

Canes vary greatly in severity, and teachers new to the profession should seek advice from experienced teachers. Canes from 1/4" to 5/16" thick and from 28" to 36" long are appropriate for general use, though the Headmaster keeps more severe implements for application when necessary. In general, "dragon" cane is denser and more severe than "kooboo".

The cane should not usually be used in class, except for punishments administered in detention. The pupil should instead be instructed to report to the teacher's room at a specified time. It is usually beneficial to specify a time at least a few hours (and perhaps as much as a day) in advance.

If more than one pupil is to be punished at a specified time, it is usually best to admit them to the room one at a time. However, there may be occasions when it is beneficial for one pupil to witness another's punishment.

The Headmaster and Housemasters are authorised to administer up to 18 strokes of the cane for serious offences. Other teachers may administer up to 6 strokes. Offences warranting more severe punishment should be referred to the Headmaster.

Experienced teachers often develop a personal style of caning and prefer a variety of positions. However, teachers new to the profession are well advised to use one of the "traditional" positions: touching toes, bending over a chair, or stretched out over a desk. It is important to position the pupil's seat high enough that the cane can strike evenly across both cheeks.

The cane is most effective if the seat is well stretched.

Clothing can make a big difference to a caning. A boy's trousers can sometimes be left in position, especially if they are tight. However, loose trousers or a skirt of any kind should be removed. Trousers should be lowered at least to the knees. A skirt should be raised and tucked into the waistband, or if too tight should be removed completely.

Blazers and jumpers should always be removed.

The following points of technique should be noted:

- It is not essential to use full-arm strokes: proficient caners often develop a wrist action that is equally effective.

- The cane has a tendency to strike hardest at the tip. To achieve evenness, it is often beneficial to take a half-pace to the left (or to the right for left-handed caners) after initial positioning.

- The cane should not wrap around the far cheek and strike the hip. The tip should land just beyond the crown of the far cheek. Novice caners may find that their arm extends on the downstroke, and should compensate for this when addressing.

- Cane strokes should usually be distributed evenly across the seat, from a point just below the cleft to the junction of the thighs. However, occasional doubling-up of strokes can be very effective.

- Most cane strokes should land straight across the seat, not diagonally. This is mostly achieved by correct positioning as described above. An exception to this is the "five-barred gate", where the last stroke is deliberately aimed to cross the first five.

Novice caners should inspect the results of their cane-strokes carefully to perfect their technique.

A caning should always be carried out slowly. The fact that the pupil is required to adopt and hold a position designed for punishment is an important element. The pupil should be allowed time to absorb each stroke and prepare themselves for the next. Ritual elements such as requiring the pupil to count each stroke add considerably to the disciplinary effect.

The cane is a severe punishment, and it should be applied with sufficient force for the recipient to dread a repetition. It is better to punish thoroughly the first time than to hold back and invite a repeat offence.

Not all pupils can remain still during a caning. Moderate kicking and vocalisation should be tolerated. Nevertheless, the teacher should insist that the pupil returns promptly to the required position and is properly presented for each stroke.

The teacher should insist on respectful behaviour at all times, from entering the room to leaving. Many teachers insist on the pupil thanking them respectfully for each stroke and again before leaving the room.

It is entirely appropriate to add extra strokes if the pupil fails to adopt the proper position promptly when required or displays disrespect of any kind.

Punishments on the uncovered seat

There are times when punishments are best applied to uncovered skin. These include occasions when a previous punishment has left marks that should be avoided, and cases where an additional element of embarrassment is intended to be part of the punishment. Teachers new to the profession may simply wish to see the effects of a punishment as it progresses.

It is a matter of personal choice whether the teacher lowers underpants or knickers themselves or requires the pupil to do it. In either case, however, the lowering should be carried out formally as part of the punishment ritual. It can be very effective for the teacher to lower the undergarments after the pupil is bending over, but inexperienced teachers should remember that a chair or desk can get in the way at this point.

All the issues of technique described in the previous section apply equally to uncovered punishments.

Punishments on the uncovered seat should *always* be administered in private.

Over the knee

The traditional over-the-knee position favoured by many parents is not usually appropriate in a school context. However, there are exceptions to this, especially in cases where the teacher has established a parental relationship with the pupil, as is often the case between Housemasters and members of their houses. It can be particularly appropriate for domestic offences, such as talking in the dormitories after lights-out.

Over-the-knee punishments may be administered with the bare hand or a variety of domestic implements including hairbrushes and slippers. They are usually most effective applied to bare skin. Such a punishment is less formal than a caning, and it is not appropriate to count strokes. Instead, the teacher simply continues until he feels the lesson has been learnt. Two to five minutes of spanking is usually sufficient. It is then often beneficial to send the pupil to stand in the corner for a period of reflection, and to enquire of their attitude afterwards. Further punishment may then be administered if the pupil is not sufficiently contrite.

Over-the-knee punishments are usually best applied in private. However, an exception to this may be made for offences committed in the dormitory, where punishing one or two pupils in this way often has a salutary effect on the others.

Punishment Books

All punishments in which a cane or strap is used must be recorded in the official School Punishment Book. Each teacher is expected to maintain a personal punishment book, from which entries must be transcribed to the School Punishment Book within 7 days.

The School Secretary maintains an alphabetic index of punishments recorded in the School Punishment Book. This index should be consulted in any case where a teacher suspects that he may be dealing with a repeat offence. It is usual for punishments to be increased in such circumstances, and a note should be made in the Punishment Book where this has been done.

Legal Position

Teachers are deemed to stand *in loco parentis* and enjoy the rights and protections of parents and guardians in applying reasonable chastisement.

There have been a few cases in which teachers at other schools have been prosecuted for excessive severity in corporal punishment. It is extremely unlikely that punishment applied within the guidelines above would be viewed as excessive by the courts. Nevertheless, it is school policy to obtain a photographic record of the results of any punishment that leaves visible marks. It is of course necessary to lower undergarments for this purpose.

An album of photographs is maintained by the school secretary and may be consulted by any teacher or member of the Board of Governors. Teachers new to the profession may find it useful to consult the record in order to establish the level of severity that is considered appropriate.

H. Higgins, MA (Oxon)
Headmaster

****

About the author:

Henry Higgins (HH) is a mean old top in the North of England, who likes to photograph damsels in distress and blogs very occasionally at:

artofpunishment.blogspot.com

He specialises in intense roleplays involving carefully crafted backstories, evocative documents, and authentic historical flourishes. Somehow they usually involve spanking or other abuse too.

His other fetishes include old oak beams, cryptokink, and quantum physics. One day he will track down the miscreant who described him as "adorable".

Penitence and Mercy

Graham Grey

"Confess. You know you want it."

"I… Let's slow down here."

"This moment's all we've got."

"We should think this through. Talk it out."

"Oh, we can think it over and under and around the block, sugarsnap. But I'd prefer the action."

"Sorry, I'm just not sure I'm — prepared."

"Come on. It's not that big a deal."

James flung a plaintive appeal to a stained-glass window. "Not a big deal? Ingrid, we'll get caught!"

But stained-glass Mary wouldn't help him. I didn't blame her. The kid could try a saint's patience.

"Yeah… Haven't you been listening? Eyes on the prize, choirboy. Getting caught is the point."

It was hard to sound assured at a whisper. Strain had crept into my voice, and this was problematic. Hysteria would not do. Not crouched in the shadows of the chapel an hour after curfew. *Keep calm, keep quiet.*

But in here, I always wanted to scream.

"They'll kick us out," James muttered, not so much to me as to the faux-marble floor.

Hail fuckin' Mary.

"Again. The point."

"For you, fine. I can't get sent home." His words were clear this time, and his eyes weren't on the floor.

"What, you actually wanna stay? Sure. I guess that's a valid lifestyle decision."

"It's got nothing to do with what I want!" I'd never heard him sound so hostile. He could get quite the little frown going, for such a cherub. "I hate it as bad as you do."

I pushed my face close to his. "Well then. Win, win."

The Good Friday House had, I divined, been thus named not simply for its affiliations with fanatic fringe-Catholics, but for its expertise in slow, crucifying torment. It was a prison with incense and altars. It was rehab with crosses and thorny crowns. And for twelve weeks each summer, its inmates were grace-grasping, rehabilitation-ready teens whose crime was being gay.

Like James and me.

"It's not that simple."

"Isn't it? We get frisky, Jesus and the angels look on, Sister nabs us, hello sweet freedom. Is that not simplicity itself?"

"I want to help you, Ingrid."

Of course he did. That's why I picked him.

James shook his head. "But if I get expelled, my parents will kill me."

"For hooking up with a girl? You sure they won't throw you a parade?"

James was different from the other boys in Good Friday's Consecrated Love Program for Young Sinners. He had the quiet-and-gentle act mastered so well that at first I thought he was one of the Believers, driving out the demon gay with all the sincerity of his Jesus-happy heart. But then I caught him hidden in the mop closet during daily confession. Reading James Baldwin.

A genuinely nice kid who was both smart and sane? At GFH, that was like finding a five-leafed clover, or the lost heir to the Russian throne

I'd know. My sanity, intelligence and goodwill toward man had undergone a righteous shredding since my internment at the Lord's halfway house began.

Ingrid, open your heart to the beauty of natural, godly love. I had tried to be patient. College was so close, I could almost smell the free condoms. All I had to do was grin and fake and study and sweat and seethe for a few more months, a few more weeks... But Leah found me first. *Ingrid, close your eyes and think of hell.* Leah was paradise. I'd been sure I was the only specimen of my doomed species in our high school, possibly county — and it turned out that every time I checked out the captain of the women's swim team, Leah was checking out me. And she could tell my gaze was not one of wrath or envy, but honest Lust. *Feel the flame. Hear your parents weep.* When Leah offered to drive me home from Eco-Justice Club via the scenic route, Carrie Adams and all her lithe teammates fled my fantasies faster than you can say "breaststroke." Leah had hips that curved right into the palms of my hands. All I had to do was wait. *Be released. Wash yourself in the blood of Christ. Be cleansed.*

Confession: I lack a saint's patience.

Unfortunately, I also lack a seasoned sinner's prudence, and when my parents caught me bound to my headboard with Leah's ties, they refused to believe we were practicing for the school play.

How long will you suffer them to weep?

It was two weeks til graduation. My parents didn't come to watch me walk the stage. Too busy packing my things.

Welcome to the Good Friday House. It is a place of hope and healing, of Christ's all-enduring mercy.

Good Friday House was like scooping your eyes out with the business end of a crucifix.

"Trust me, they won't give a damn," James was protesting. "I get kicked out, they eviscerate me, the end. Why didn't you ask one of the girls, anyway?"

"Are you joking?"

The Good Friday Girls. I'd comforted myself, in the days of disgust leading up to my incarceration, with daydreams of the cute oppressed dykes I'd bond with at Jesus Camp. How we would snicker behind the backs of Authority. How we would... console each other.

Oh, how I was blind. There were only four of us in this year's Consecrated Love class – teen lesbians being rather less conspicuous than high school gay dudes. There was Bethany, an uber- zealot who had enrolled voluntarily, and seemed convinced she was an earthly martyr chosen to battle the devil's desires as proof to God and His Children that one really could pray away the gay. And Alexis, who belonged in actual rehab, but whose parents considered their daughter's dependence on narcotics a trifling matter compared to her penchant for girl-on-girl porn. Alexis was not pleasant to talk to. And finally there was Natalie. She was just fourteen, hadn't even started high school, never spoke, was terrified of everybody and definitely wasn't going to be locking lips with a desperate delinquent beneath the Virgin's mournful eyes.

"I get your point," James conceded.

"Besides. I need some hetero cred. It's the only way my parents will take me back."

"I'm sorry. I know this place makes you miserable. But I can't get thrown out, I just can't."

Miserable. Misery sounded almost romantic, something a saint suffered. Like all those words: Passion, agony, martyrdom. But I did not feel venerable or blessed.

I was surrounded by psychopaths. At GFH, we spent most of our time listening to descriptions of hell, knelt on hard floors in prayer, watching the bloodiest portrayal's of Jesus's last hours that had ever been captured on film and reciting coerced confessions of our sins. We spent the rest of the time in cold showers, eating cold slime or shivering in solitary – I'm sorry, the "Reflection Corridor" – for asking a priest to cite the Gospel verse wherein Christ prohibits cunnilingus.

Sister Assumpta, the enforcer, prowled the halls day and night with a hawk's glare and lips redder than saints' wounds. She headed the operation with Father Tristan, who was fond of telling us that "choosing a gay lifestyle" would result in dying of AIDS and/or making baby Jesus cry. The two of them ran the joint like a hyper-morbid Shawshank.

"You won't be sent home if you don't want to."

James looked perplexed.

"Well I don't want – "

"Then you won't. Christ's all-enduring mercy, remember? Haven't you read through the policy handbook? As long as you repent, you can stay. That's all it takes. Get on your knees and repent. When Sister comes, throw yourself at her feet, tell her I'm a temptress and you know it was sinful but you thought Jesus wanted you to be straight and look at her with those angelic eyes of yours, and your mom and dad will never hear a word about it."

In its current expression, James' face could not be described as angelic.

"They'll still rake me over the coals, Ingrid! Isn't there a better way?"

Footsteps sounded on the stairwell. I clutched James' wrist.

"Please." This time I invited the hysteria. "You're the only one I could trust."

Oh yes. I'd observed James closely. I had his contraband copy of *Giovanni's Room* as leverage just in case, but I knew he couldn't refuse a direct appeal for help.

The sigh that escaped him was definitely angelic. "You owe me."

"More than you know."

Sister Assumpta would be here any second. Acceleration time.

I grabbed the back of James' head and planted my lips on his. "You're the best, choirboy." I shimmied out of my shirt and thought of Leah.

I had James pinned beneath me when a glowering light spilled into the chapel, followed by the screech of a livid nun.

"How dare you desecrate the chamber of the Lord!"

We had time for one more kiss, which I landed on James' forehead, before Sister's claws wrenched us apart.

"Get up this instant!"

She was quaking with rage. I'd rate it a 6.2.

"Breaking curfew? Out of bounds? *Fornicating* on the floor of our chapel?" For a few moments, the blasphemy overwhelmed her and stalled her tongue. "These are unspeakable acts. In all my years… You can both expect to be thrown out of here by morning."

The time had finally come.

"Please sister, I'm sorry – forgive me!"

I fell prostrate at Sister Assumpta's feet and clasped my hands in contrition.

"I know I've committed a terrible sin, I know, but I was weak, I was confused, I didn't want to be wrong anymore, I couldn't stand being wrong, I didn't want to go to hell..." I began to sob. High-pitched, stained-glass-smashing hysteria. "I'm a weak and terrible girl, I'm evil, a sinner, please let me stay, I'll do anything, I have to get better – oh, please have mercy on me, Sister!"

Sister backed away as my hands grasped for the hem of her garment. James stared at me, speechless and unblinking.

"Well..." Sister started in a grim tone. I heaved another sob, nonverbal this time.

"Well, penitence can be restorative... You, boy, what have you got to say for yourself?"

James just gaped.

"Are you prepared to repent as well?"

He didn't make a sound. *Oh, honestly.*

"Yes, Sister. He'll repent. Just don't make us leave."

Sister Assumpta yanked my hair and James' ear. "Come with me."

One of the perks of being nearly 18 was that I was very rarely forcibly dragged anywhere. Or so it was in my innocent, un-reeducated days. Sister pulled us along the corridor like a pair of squirmy kindergartners. Or convicts. The top brass at Good Friday House treated us as a strange hybrid of both. The fine print in the GHF handbook echoed in my head and soothed my raw nerves: *Discipline tempered with mercy... Repentance rewarded with justice...* Choirboy was waking from his catatonic state. It wouldn't be long now.

Sister Assumpta lugged open a heavy oak door with bronze locks and shoved us inside. It was Father Tristan's study. (In good Wackolic Tradition, the pomp and circumstance was reserved for men.)

"I trust you understand the punishment you've brought upon yourselves?"

"Yes, Sister," I said meekly.

"You may think what you've done is some kind of progress, but that is the devil's logic. And the devil shall be beaten."

James' eyebrows lurched.

"Wait here and pray. I shall return."

Sister swiveled away, and I dropped my head. The pattern on Father Tristan's rug was really quite fascinating.

"What. The. *Hell.*"

Each fiber so minute, and the sum so magnificent!

"I mean, what the fucking hell, Ingrid? You said – you said you wanted to get thrown out!"

"Don't be ridiculous," I muttered. "Can't get thrown out, or it's *nein* to college. Authorities were very clear on that."

James couldn't keep still. He was twitching with anger, he was pulling his hands in and out of his pockets like an obsessive-compulsive.

"You lied to me. Did you see her face when she said the devil shall be beaten? Somehow I don't think she was speaking metaphorically!"

He was nearly shouting. Definitely beyond hysteria.

"Will you be quiet? Yeah, I heard her. Don't forget you already agreed to this. It's not my fault you haven't read the handbook."

"I agreed to help you get out of here," he shot back. "Mind telling me why in God's hell I'm even here?"

Is it possible he'd believe I was just trying to get into his pants?

"It's been a long summer, okay."

"So? What, completely screwing me over is your sick entertainment?"

"No!"

What'd he take me for, a sociopath? For the first time I met his eyes. Big mistake. *Such intricate weaving...*

"Well?"

Screw it. Screw James and his innocence and his goodwill toward man.

"Look, I'm not patient," I snapped. "I'm not good. I'm trapped in a dormitory with three of the most unrelatable females I've ever seen and if I have to take another cold shower or write another Sin Log I swear I will perpetrate a felony. So if I'm going to maintain any semblance of sanity, I've gotta have something, *some*thing to...

And while I'll be first to admit Sister's reincarnated from the Stasi, let's face it, she's kinda got it goin on for a full-time celibate, and if the only action I can get this summer is bending over for a dose of her 'discipline,' then goddamn it I'm gonna take it."

I caught my breath, or rather, my breath caught me. James didn't say a word, and I fell back from his glare, rolling my shoulders forward and clutching the edge of Father Tristan's desk. A lovely carpet. Truly lovely.

"Psycho. *Bitch.*"

"Yeah, well."

Well, yeah. The Good Friday regime had left me a few beads short a full rosary. James didn't deserve this, we both knew it — I wasn't callous enough not to care, nor was I in any condition to conduct myself like a sane and thoughtful human.

"Look, I'm… I'm sorry James. I'll do all your journals for the rest of the summer."

"Damn right you will."

"Come on, don't be dramatic. Don't act like you don't understand. Like I haven't seen you ogling Father Tristan at Mass."

"Shut up, Ingrid."

"Dark, sweeping hair… Rugged old-school handsomeness… Betcha don't all that mind getting down on your knees for him…"

"Ingrid, that is…" James hands swung out of his pockets and he started pacing frenetically. "I mean, what the fuck does that matter? Do you think that's the same as this? I could never understand this. How you could be so selfish… There is no reason for me to be here other than you're deranged. You could have broken the rules on your own!"

"Not with a girl. And the non-sexy sins would probably have earned me a court order."

"You could have marched up to that altar and masturbated under the Host, so don't give me that."

Point. My thumbs set to twiddling. "Well… " My shame set to pulsing. "It was true, before. I need some hetero cred. Haven't exactly made a great impression on the hierarchy."

"Go to hell."

"Look, I'm sorry!" I wasn't bothering with quiet anymore. "You're a good kid, James, and I'm a psycho bitch, but you can resent me for an eon and a day or you can accept my offers of appeasement and let what's done be done! I mean, haven't you ever gotten desperate? You have your books, your Baldwin, what do I have?"

"Reading doesn't hurt anybody else."

Well aren't you just Mother Teresa. But my defenses would not hold for long. Could Sister please come back now? "I mean, when was the last time you... You know, when was your last time?"

"I don't follow."

"Oh, Christ, you know, the last time you got any, before they sent you here – who'd you get caught with?"

James stopped mid-pace and stared. Dumb as cardboard.

"Who'd I get caught with?" he repeated.

I nodded, my patience fraying.

"Shakespeare," he said flatly. "Oscar Wilde. James Baldwin. Stephen Sondheim. My dad laid down the deposit on this place when I signed up for the school play." His stare could cut steel. "Not all of us had such a fun time in the closet as you apparently did, Ingrid."

My turn to go cardboard.

"So you're a... So you didn't even..."

A grim shrug.

"Christ, James."

I shivered, but there was no breeze.

"I hope she beats the crap out of you," he muttered.

"All your journals. And when we get out of here, I swear, I'll buy you a freaking library."

"Whatever. I just want to get this over with."

My immunity to normal human emotions had shattered. I spent every day listening to rants about my depravities, and I'd never truly felt guilty until now. The plan had seemed like such a good idea last week in Morning Scriptures, when I'd mentally muted Sister Assumpta's Job lecture and leered at her chest for twenty minutes. It seemed fair, then: *If I'm going to be repeatedly punished for being gay, I might as well enjoy it.*

James hugged his arms close and glared at Tristan's bookcase. He'd been willing to meet this fate when he thought it was an act of kindness.

The plan no longer seemed fair.

The trod of watchful disciplinarians echoed in the corridor. Despite my better angels, ripples of excitement flared down my legs like 1970's blue jeans. The knob twisted, and in strode Sister Assumpta, a wide leather strap in her hand and Father Tristan at her side. I donned my best "I've just been praying" face.

"These are our miscreants, Father."

The priest surveyed us with stony countenance.

"Sister Assumpta has informed me of your impiety in the chapel."

"We're sorry, Father." I bowed my head like a novice. James stood uselessly.

"What you have done is in no way righteous. One does not fight one sinful desire by succumbing to another."

"We know, Father. I – " Maybe it wasn't too late. "Please, it was my fault. I told James I could… fix him. I told him it was God's will. You shouldn't blame him for my offense."

"Is this true, young man?"

The boy was absolute cardboard. It might have had something to do with the way Sister's talons curled over the strap. "Uh…"

"Nonetheless, we are all responsible for our actions," intoned Sister Assumpta. The look she gave James contained zero mercy.

"Yes," continued Tristan. "And punishment is necessary. You know that at Good Friday House, we believe in the power of godly love over human frailty. We practice a discipline that is not cruel, but just; not hateful, but sustained by our Savior's enduring mercy."

Just get on with it. Sister's knuckles tightened on the strap. My lips moistened.

"Sister Assumpta, it's time to begin."

A-freaking-men.

"Certainly, Father."

I bowed my pious little head again, this time to hide a smile. James let his arms drop listlessly to his sides. Father Tristan took a step forward, and Sister Assumpta placed the strap into his hands, then disappeared into the dark of the corridor.

What. The. *Hell.*

The sound of James' and my jaws hitting the floor should have made a sound, but silence rang out in the priest's study.

"Turn around, lambs, and place your elbows on my desk."

James scraped his chin off the carpet quicker than I did. I turned to him in full confused dismay. He pivoted around to Tristan's desk with a shrug that was positively jaunty.

Son of a bitch.

"*Now*, Ingrid."

I turned with the creaky movements of a clockwork ballerina. As I lay my arms on the smooth wood of Father Tristan's desk, my body gelatinized. The bell-bottoms of desire no longer clung to my lower body; my internal fruit-punch bowl of pleasure was drunk dry; my mental porno – *Dirty Nuns and Catholic Schoolgirls XXX!* – went snowy with static.

Maybe there was still time to change course. Isn't college overrated?

"I'm sorry, first you must remove your trousers and underpants. Then return to position."

The speed with which James managed to vacate his pants did not escape me. I peeled off my undergarments with the slow shame of the rightfully condemned.

I stared determinedly at the pine, but it did not good. I could feel James' delighted, mocking eyes; they were practically emitting their own army of cartoon clowns.

Should have known. Dabbling in heterosexuality never leads to anything good.

Father Tristan and his Ominous Leather loomed over us.

"Bless these children, most merciful Father," he prayed.

Bless us with an early apocalypse, please.

"Since you claim greater responsibility for this misconduct, Ingrid, I shall begin with you."

69

I made a sound like "gruhr."

He drew the strap across my backside to take aim, and I willed myself to a happy place, of Smurfs and Skittles, of the swim captain's calves and infinity tongue rings.

"Holy Father, have mercy on this lost lamb."

Then the prayerful priest thrashed the Lord's justice into my backside with all his might.

I made a sound like "fucking Christ!"

The good father did not take kindly to this, and his strap even less so.

It hurt like a feral goat attack, and I would have committed nineteen deadly sins to stop it, and I hated Tristan and all he stood for – but all the same, I knew I deserved it. Without a doubt. Not for the dyking or the macking or the chapel-desecrating, but for swindling the one person who could have been a real friend.

That didn't make it easier to take.

I squeezed my eyes shut and imagined Sister Assumpta, her domineering voice, her svelte curves. I envisioned Leah and Carrie and Jennifer Connally, but no go, all I felt was pain; ugly, sexless, Tristan-inflicted pain.

Maybe it would have been different with Assumpta. Maybe it was all in my head, or maybe I drastically underestimated the effects of a big slab of leather hitting you over and over.

"Lead her not into temptation," Tristan droned. "Deliver her from evil." He sliced the strap into me again. It was unholy.

It was fair.

After a lengthy bout of whimpering, the rite concluded, and Father Tristan moved aside to administer his services to the next lamb. I heard James draw in a tense breath. I vaguely heard Tristan blather about punishment as an act of love, but ignored him. I popped open a misty eye and sneaked a glance at my partner in sin.

Was my vision overwatered, or was he actually arching his bottom upwards?

The first lash landed. A somehow far more elegant gasp fled James' lips, and he staggered forward, startled by the weight of the blow. I couldn't watch. The second fell, and the third — and let's not kid ourselves, of course I could watch — I stared agape as James winced and hissed, as Tristan dealt out "love" in ever-harder portions, as James' neck snapped back and his gasps reached for the heavens.

Look what thy thoughtless deeds hath wrought, o horny depraved one!

Miserably, I looked.

And it was unmistakable. James' bottom was not the only thing pointing up.

"Will you be led by discipline unto the righteous path?" Tristan boomed. "Will you learn from the ordeal of punishment, and renounce temptation?"

He smacked the strap full-force into James' waiting backside.

"Yes, Father!" he cried.

Jesus.

Tristan and James were too engrossed in the Sacrament of Homo-Spanking to notice my slack jaw and bugging eyes. James wasn't gasping, he was *sighing*. Those weren't winces – that was straight-up O-face! Indignation burrowed in my breast like a rabid squirrel. Oh *really*, Mr. Decent-Pants?

Choirboy indeed.

Mid-moan, James twitched his head toward me. He winked.

Pervy little bastard.

I watched his knuckles clench, his knees buckle and his face contort, but I felt no compassion. And as I listened to his flustered breaths, I no longer felt resentment. A drop of clear, certainly unholy water had cooled the fire of my wrath. As the ripples spread, all I could think was, *go virgin go!*

Bless his sick heart.

When Fr. Tristan lowered the lash for the last time, I had the wherewithal to cast my eyes contritely to the ground and hold still.

But when he stood behind me and raised the lash again, I had no wherewithal at all.

"But, Father – "

"Penance must match the sin, child."

Then the strap screamed across my skin, and I screamed with it.

Throw me in the shower and turn the knob to freezing. Screen Technicolor crucifixions on repeat. Double my Sin Log quota and shove gruel down my throat and make me listen to Bethany warble sexist hymns and tell me again why Jesus wanted girls to wear lipgloss and make babies – just please, JesusMaryJosephJonBonJovi, make it stop.

My parents never hit me, their preferred torture method being the silent treatment and De-Gaying Jail. The sweet nuns who taught me catechism gave us cookies and juice, not ruler-whacks. School was a civilized place of detentions and "mandatory extra credit." Society had not prepared me for the searing anguish of a sound thrashing. My only solace was my guilt. I wallowed in it, my inner squirrel beast shrunk to a piteous wet mouse.

I wasn't gasping, I was sobbing. They weren't winces – this was straight-up gnashing of teeth. I bucked like a horse. Correction: I bucked like a horse being beaten with a wicked strap.

Wretchedness, pain and shame closed over me like a coffin lid. These were the lowest weeks of my life, and I'd never felt so low as this.

I opened a wet, stinging eye and caught James looking at me. *Oh, great.* But he didn't wink or smirk. He just held my gaze with his still blue eyes. He gave a nod, as if to say, *all right, almost there.* Then he reached across the priest's desk and grabbed my hand.

"Let the lamb know your mercy, Lord."

Father Tristan slammed down a final stroke, which sent my knees crashing into the desk and my elbows nearly drilling through it. But I didn't scream. I might've broken some of James' finger bones. Tristan mumbled some more penance-Lord-baby-sheep gibberish and I fumbled through a passable response. By the time the priest stepped over to James, his hand had retreated to his side of the desk, and he was waiting in position.

James took his beating much better than I did, for reasons that best remain between him and his god.

Sometimes in life you find yourself biting your lip through the whipping of your fellow sexual deviant in a priest's office with your underwear tangled around your ankles, and the moment rapidly turns awkward. Okay, never in your life will you find yourself in this situation, but trust me, it's awkward. I hung pointlessly in the air, taking up space. My body, so extremely distracted this long evening, finally called up complaints as it realized it was the middle of the night. My eyelids sagged. Since Father Tristan was quite preoccupied, I quietly slipped my undies back into place.

It finished. For the record, James did not *finish* finish, but if you asked me he looked like a mighty satisfied cherub. He avoided my eyes, but a smile lingered at his mouth.

Then there was the business of getting on our knees and praying and pretending to listen to Father Tristan and nodding earnestly, and Christ's wounds and the GFH Handbook and sex-is-a-holy-sacrament and our immortal souls, and finally we were told that we could go to bed. (Separately! Prayerfully! Alone and totally hands-free!)

"Only harshest love can defeat the devil, my lambs."

With that, the man of god dismissed us.

We stepped out into the dark hall, and it seemed like the arms of night itself accosted me. What a mess. A complete wreck. And I didn't know if I meant my clumsy scheme – or my far clumsier self.

James turned to me.

"Oh, go ahead. Say it."

"Say what?" And with the perfect pitch of innocence, too.

"Whatever it is you're dying to say, we both know I deserve it."

"I wasn't going to say anything, Ingrid." His hand strayed to his backside, where it paused for a light rub, and his eyes glazed ever so slightly before blinking back to reality.

I guess nothing more needed to be said.

"Well. I got mine, you got yours, fair is fair, go Jesus, long live ponies and cupcakes. Night, James."

Before my heels could twist me away from further humiliation, James reached out and grabbed my wrist. I stared at the hand that held me, and then at the face.

And then I knew. It was written right there.

My master plan hadn't won me a session of irreverent pleasure, but it had given me something far more valuable. An ally against the devils. A friend.

"You don't have to do my Sin Log," he said.

"Fuck the Sin Log."

The remaining weeks of the world's worst summer camp loomed long before us, and yet, from here – the dark hall, with James, our asses smarting from the same strap – the weeks didn't seem quite so long, nor quite so looming.

"Night James," I whispered. "You pervy little homo."

He grinned. "Night, psycho dyke."

We parted and made for our respective dorms. As I approached the end of the corridor, James called back.

"Hey, Ingrid?"

I turned. "Yeah?"

"Hang in there," he told me. "It's just five weeks. And I wanna see you on the other side."

"I'll be there, choirboy."

"Good." He smiled. "Cause I've heard it gets a whole lot better."

****

About the author:

Graham "The Girl" Grey, 24, was born and raised in the midwest. (She's proud of this.) In addition to her CP fetish, she has a perverse love for unpaid labor, and so contributing to a kinky charity anthology brings her the greatest glee. Who says kink can't be a force for good in the world?

For some of Graham's not-so-altruistic writings, visit her blog "The S Word" at:

grahamgreyblog.blogspot.com

The Punishment Room

Martha Linton

The drive home, when it eventually came, was conducted in stony silence.

I hate it when this happens, when the silence lies thickly between us. It feels crushing, enveloping and, now that I know well enough what it preludes, deeply ominous. Not that it has been often, don't get me wrong – I am not that stupid! Or maybe I am, because if I wasn't then surely it would only have happened once? Not the peppering of occasions that it had done over the years. But anyway, today, this time, I *was* stupid: full-on, high-scale, undeniably stupid. A frightening weakness from my past, rearing its ugly head… And, all too soon, I was going to pay for it.

I stole a glance at Adam, jaw set in profile as he concentrated on the busy roads. Even after nearly four years together, the last 18 months of them so happily married, he could still make my heart flutter just from the sight of him. I loved that; that he could still give me reactions like a hot young lover just at the handsome sight of him! Analysis can't really explain that chemistry, I just know that, for us, it's there, always has been – and I am thankful for it every day.

Just now, though, that handsome face was clouded and, even allowing for his focus, his eyes were flint hard. I had learnt pretty early on in our relationship that, for Adam, discipline went beyond the boundaries of the bedroom and our sexual predilections. We may've met online via, for want of a better description, a kinky personals website (true story!) but, for him, for us, it went deeper than that. Of course, for our mutual pleasure, he would happily turn me over his lap and spank me into a warm glow with very little excuse wanted or needed – at the least! Creatively evil and delightfully rude, he had carefully pushed my limits further and further over the years, exploring a world of kinky fun beyond anything I had experienced before. Drawing out my submissive nature whilst feeding his own dominant desires kept us healthy, strong and content as a couple. That we had proved equally compatible as life partners had fulfilled my wildest dreams. But still, for all that, there was a flipside to this man I loved deeply, which right now I was being forced to recall vividly…

If – when – I messed up in life, in a big way that couldn't be excused or overlooked, Adam would punish me.

With love, yes. With care and consideration and fairness, certainly. But also unswervingly, remorselessly and, if merited, hard. I felt a tremor run through me, whether of shame or grim anticipation I was unsure.

Of one thing, though, I was sure: this time it *would* be hard.

I decided against pleas of mitigation, at least for now. Experience had taught me that there would be a time, if I had things I needed to say, and that this wasn't it. Adam's face conveyed his own emotions more than eloquently, and I had no wish to provoke him even the slightest bit further. So the blanket of silence remained in place throughout the journey, each of us left to our own uncomfortable thoughts of what had happened, and what was still to come.

We swung up the drive and scrunched to a halt; emptied the boot; went inside. It wasn't until we were indoors that Adam finally looked me in the face, and then it was I who couldn't return his gaze, had to drop my eyes. Guilt… I waited for the inevitable order, dreading it. He sucked in a breath.

"You're in a lot of trouble, Mrs Elliott."

I managed barely a nod in response, from my position of studying the hall tiles. He reached forward and tilted my chin up with his forefinger, forcing me to look back at him and feel the heat of disapproval; the disappointment, sadness, registered there.

"Upstairs, now" he said very softly, intently. "Take a quick shower, then go and wait for me in the Punishment Room, in position. Don't bother getting dressed again, you won't need to. And you can think very hard about how to explain what just happened in Jubilees. Because, believe me, I want to hear all about it. Go."

He released my chin with a jerk in the direction of the stairs, and I went. Sometimes, when I'm facing a punishment, I am not so meek; if I dispute the sentence or am just plain bolshie with it. Today I knew that any disobedience on my part, when I was already so horribly in the wrong, would only inflame a bad situation. And anyway, I didn't have the will: this was one of those times when I accepted to the full that, having done the crime, I would now have to do the time.

Oh God though: the Punishment Room…

It's amazing how much significance that title could lend to what was, in essence, a spare bedroom, I thought, as I stripped off and stepped into the shower in our en suite. Our friends and family stayed in there on occasions without the least suspicion of its alter ego (I hope!); washing got hung there, stuff dumped or stored up at times; it was just a room, like any other. I'd granted its moniker half-jokingly, after the first time Adam had taken me in there to be strapped for swearing at him. It had struck me how he'd deliberately steered us out of our own bedroom, where we'd been, and punished me next door instead. Instinctively we both knew why he'd done it; moved us to neutral, less emotive territory, separated the spanking fun and intimacy of our bedroom from the more formal, no-fun discipline of real life. Which gave the spare room, at such times, a character all of its own, unique to us and this facet of our relationship. Powerful… The name stuck, and I'd paid it several more visits since that first time. I guess if we were American then we'd have a woodshed instead, but they weren't so prevalent in suburban middle England!

So I mused, as I let the warm water flow over me comfortingly, grateful at least to have been spared a cold one. Yet I shivered for all its warmth. The Punishment Room sent its own message even before Adam entered, without an implement in sight. Its name alone could be invoked as a threat: "Do that again and we'll be discussing it in the Punishment Room…" If it was serious, if it was a big deal for us as a partnership, if I had to be really taught a lesson, then it would be dealt with in there.

Today it was all of those things.

Towelled dry, hair tidied, I pushed the door and went in. Luckily, I suppose, the room was clear currently. It was simply furnished, just the double bed, small tables either side, a compact desk and one sturdy, straight-backed chair – innocently useful, to lay out your clothes on, for example. All the storage was built-in, out of the way. The curtains had been drawn, I noted, although I would have realised Adam had been upstairs anyway by the magnetic presence of the items now lined up neatly on the duvet. In an otherwise plain and neutral setting, they leapt out as a stark premonition.

The dragon cane. A two-tailed tawse, our heaviest: it rarely appeared during play. A pair of cuffs. Nipple clamps. What the…?

Gooseflesh rose all over me as I took it all in. To know that you deserve to be punished, to accept it, is one thing. To see the evidence of how much it will hurt, what form it is likely to take, moves it to another level. For several long seconds, I could only stare at the horrible collection and frantically speculate as to how my fate would pan out. Then I had to tear myself away, partly to stop mentally torturing myself and partly because I was very aware that, whenever Adam returned, I needed to be where I'd been told to wait, in position, or things would get off to a very poor start.

In position, in this context, meant the corner. As he'd intimated downstairs, Adam believed in giving the offender, i.e. me, some thinking time, to consider what they'd done to get themselves in their current predicament and why; to consider what this meant for both of us, and to contemplate the impending penalty for such behaviour. It could also allow me time to calm down if I was mad, or him to calm down if he was too angry to deal with me. The former wasn't an issue this time; the latter, I knew, was. It had been all he could do not to haul me over his knee and spank the hell out of me there and then in the store detective's office. But he hadn't, and we both knew that he wouldn't come back into the Punishment Room and address this until his temper was fully under control. Sane and safe, of course. But also so unnerving to know that, in cold blood and after calm consideration, he would be physically punishing me for my wrongdoing. The twinge that sent through my insides was intense.

I went to my corner and, cringing inwardly, took up the expected pose. Facing into the apex of the walls, nose pushed close enough to brush the paintwork, hands placed on top of my head, elbows curling round to fit into that space. A humiliating situation as always…the first of many to come. And heightened by my total nudity today, not unprecedented but more unusual than not. Another deliberate message from Adam: this is major, let's be clear from the outset. Even though it wasn't cold, I shivered.

Time passed, I've no idea how much. Maybe five minutes, maybe 20. As always when in the corner, it both dragged and raced, a weird paradox I'd long ago given up trying to explain. The waiting was an agony of its own: please just get it over with…Yet getting it over with will be awful, horrible: please put it off, please don't come…

I thought about what I'd done. And about other times… I didn't like the person I saw when I made myself face those truths. And now I'd been caught, and couldn't pretend it wasn't me any more even if I wanted to. There in my corner, I vowed that I would tell the truth at last, that I would confess a past I wished wasn't mine.

Footsteps on the stairs heralded his approach. Time up! Adam shut the door behind him and it had an air of finality about it: there really was no escape now. Let the music play.

Let me be strong…

"Come here, Christina. Hands down."

I turned, flexed my shoulders to relieve the stiffness, and walked the short few paces to where Adam waited by the bed. When I'd halted before him, he told me to look at him. This time, when I did, he raised his hand and slapped my face hard, both cheeks in quick succession, stinging blows.

"You stupid, stupid girl! I just can't believe what you did!"

Involuntary tears sprang to my eyes, my hands went to my face but he caught them instantly and yanked them back by my sides, forcing me to remember that I didn't get to touch when it was a punishment, not even there. I could whimper or wail or cry if I must, but there would be no comfort, not till it was over. And that was, literally, just the opening salvo.

"You were actually going to steal that perfume, weren't you? I mean, that wasn't an accident. I'm not misunderstanding here, am I? Because please correct me if I'm wrong. You've no idea how much I'd like to be wrong, despite the evidence stacked against you."

I wished he was wrong too. But, as he wasn't, and as I felt so ashamed not only about what I'd done but about the anguish he clearly felt over it, I couldn't do anything other than nod my head through the smarting pain.

Adam grimaced, but still insisted I confirm it. "So you put it in your pocket, of your own free will, and just walked away with it?

"Yes, sir," I whispered.

"Right. That'll do for now. We've a lot more talking to do, believe me. But since you've confirmed that we are dealing with a shoplifter, I can start to treat you as one. Turn around."

As he spoke, he picked up the cuffs from the bed, and I knew with a thud what he was going to do. I turned as instructed and immediately he grabbed a wrist and drew it behind me, setting one of the cuffs around it. They're made of soft leather, beautifully crafted and usually a pleasure to wear for some sensual scene or another. Today they symbolised something very different as I was buckled into them, before Adam fastened them together, securing my wrists firmly in the small of my back.

"You're damn lucky they're not the real thing," he growled. "They'd be way more uncomfortable for starters. But since that's how a criminal should be treated, it's clear you need a taste of them. Get back in the corner!"

He smacked my arse in dismissal and I scuttled back there, grateful for its sanctuary to hide my blazing face. Knowing I deserved this treatment didn't make it any easier to bear. I sniffed furiously, I couldn't cry already. I wasn't naïve enough to think I'd stave off the tears completely, but was desperate not to just succumb. I still had some pride...

Time ticked by. I wriggled against the sensation of the handcuffs, understanding their significance, just as I was meant to. Aware that I was having the message hammered home. Concurring over my idiocy, over the risks I'd taken, the fool I'd been. As ever, there was little in the way of comfort to be found in that corner.

Eventually, Adam called me back to him.

"So, Christina, let's talk about why you shoplift."

I chewed my lip. It's all very well to sound conversational, but when one of you is innocent, plus fully-dressed and at ease, whilst the other is naked and bound and guilty as sin, it's not so simple. At least, it wasn't from my perspective, but that didn't cut a lot of ice with my husband.

"Well, I'm waiting."

"It's, um...I...I'm sorry," was all my first attempt really amounted to.

"Are you? Well good, so you should be. But that doesn't answer my question, nor does it excuse your behaviour, nor does it alter the fact that, one way or another, you're going to pay for that perfume now. So: why did you do it?"

I shot him an agonised look, willing him to understand about weakness and mistakes and wanting stuff, and unsurprisingly failing given that no actual words came out. His expression hardened.

"I can see you're going to need some incentive to talk to me. Okay then, so be it."

He took the clamps from the bed and the "Noooo!" had escaped my lips before I'd even formed a conscious thought.

"Yes I figured these might help you to find your voice," he said grimly.

"Please don't..."

"I'm all out of sympathy for you right now, young lady, so I'm afraid 'please' isn't going to work. Stand still."

Adam could sense I was preparing to back away, his command forced me to battle the instinct and hold my ground. The instinct to cover my breasts at this point was, however, denied me. With my hands tied, I was completely vulnerable, and their position behind my back also had the effect, I remembered, of pushing out my breasts in a particularly inviting manner. All very well in the bedroom, but this could not have felt more different. Now I was not aroused, just completely exposed and close to panicky at the thought of the imminent pain. I wasn't good with clamps, a fact we both knew well and which was about to be put to frightening good use.

Meeting my gaze with one of implacable awareness of all he was about to inflict, Adam grasped my right nipple, squeezing and twisting it as I squealed and almost danced on the spot. When he took his fingers away, it was forced erect, but the relief was only momentary before he fitted the clamp and it bit home. The breath hissed through my teeth, I gnawed down on the scream longing to emit. My left nipple was then subjected to the same brutal regime, and the pain doubled as it too was cinched with a crocodile clip. The two were linked by a chain which added to the overall sensation by dragging at my breasts, and which jangled when Adam slapped one of them for good measure as he sent me packing to the corner again.

This time rational thought was much harder. There are some ways, at the right time, when I can cope with a fair amount of pain - which is fortunate for the games we play, I guess. But this was anything but a game, besides which I found nipple clamps a trial at the best of times.

Now my breathing was laboured. I tried to focus on coping with the vicious biting sensation, scrabbling for some control or, failing that, some way of trying to block it out. As a punishment technique, clamps were new to me: I had never done anything to earn their deployment before. The realisation that this meant I had probably never let Adam down so badly before either, when it dawned, marked a new low in the day's proceedings. A tear leaked from one eye and rolled slowly down my face.

There came a point, in the blur of time, when the edge of pain started to ease a fraction, the beginnings of numbness I expect. I'm not sure if Adam knew from observing me or was just timing the exercise, but I had barely acknowledged it myself before he asked if I was ready to talk to him now. Yes, oh yes, I babbled desperately: anything to rid myself of the clamps more quickly! So we met face to face again, only his face was studied calm and mine felt twisted in agony. An agony which reached new heights when, without warning, he reached out and released both clamps simultaneously, whipping them off.

Then I did scream.

Blood raced back to the nipples, searing them. I doubled over, longing to nurse the tender nubs but unable to. Adam let me indulge the pain for a few moments, to get a grip. When I straightened up, my eyes were properly wet. But the wicked flash of fire had at least eased enough to see beyond. Cruel indentations marked my nipples, they looked red and raw. Similar to how I felt.

"Why did you steal that perfume?"

The same question, and this time I answered him, as honestly as I could. Because I liked the fragrance but knew he would object to me buying yet another one; because I wanted it anyway and figured that, if I just swiped the tester, it wouldn't be tagged and no one would twig; that it was nearly full so just as good, and that he'd never notice once it was ensconced in my collection on the dresser.

Because, ultimately, I had thought I could get away with it.

"But you didn't, did you?" he reminded me needlessly, having allowed me enough rope to hang myself with before responding. "Clearly it *was* tagged, hence our embarrassing scene at the door. And the further embarrassing scenes in the security office."

"Yes, sir," I muttered, acknowledging it.

"And you, young lady, are extremely lucky that you don't have a criminal record now, as a result. By rights, you deserve one."

"I know...thank you for persuading the guard not to call the police."

"You are damn lucky I was able to. And do you know what: I'm sure the sole reason I was able to was that he knew I would sort you out myself."

I looked at him, eyes widening.

"Oh yes," he continued, "I'm pretty sure that was it. Unless I'm very much mistaken, Mr Brian Palmer, Head of Security at Jubilees department store, is a man with good old fashioned values when it comes to petty theft and the like – all that crap he has to deal with day in day out. Given the choice of packing off another shoplifting brat to the local nick or actually having her dealt with, in his view, 'properly', it was pretty clear which he'd opt for."

"I'm not a brat!"

"No, actually you're worse: you're a well-brought-up young woman who should know better," Adam snapped. "You're not some problem case who's had a deprived childhood, who doesn't know any better, or who even stole out of necessity. You just thought you'd help yourself to what wasn't yours, and you got caught," he added bluntly. "So now you can pay for it in *my* currency."

So saying, he reached behind me to disconnect the cuffs, then very deliberately picked up the cane. I felt every bit as small and ashamed as he intended me to, because I couldn't actually deny any of what he said. When he spoke again, it was quietly but firmly.

"You know the rules, Chrissie. Our rules. For serious transgressions, corporal punishment applies. I'm still struggling to believe you did this, but I'm not going to shirk my responsibilities in our marriage in order to remind you of yours. Move right over there and touch your toes."

My responsibilities…what a mess.

As I bent over, I felt so deeply in need of my husband's salvation that I almost welcomed the forthcoming thrashing. We may not have used the old service at our wedding, but I still understood fully how we both embraced its tenets in our relationship. Today, in my weakness, I hadn't shown Adam much in the way of love, or honour, or obedience. How had I let this happen to myself, and to us?

The cane tapped my inner calf and I shuffled my stance wider, as it demanded. Often the utter humiliation of displaying myself like this, stretched taut and open, appalled me. I knew that Adam would be able to see my vulva as well as my bottom; that my recent wax left no room for modesty. And whilst on the one hand I cringed at the thought, in another way it was only right that it should be this way between us. Total openness, no secrets...

He took up his own position, away to my left. I felt the tapping of the cane being lined up, full across the crown of my backside. When it lifted away, I had barely time to brace my mind for the blow before it came, flying down in a singing rush of air, cracking home. I wobbled forward with the force of it, steadied myself and gasped as the pain broke and bloomed in a line of fire across me. There was little time to collect my senses before the next landed just above the first. Again I rocked, gasping, as a second scalding weal rose up. I realised that I didn't know how many strokes I was going to receive, that he hadn't said. When the third one struck, I didn't know how many I'd be able to take.

The fifth one broke me.

An odd sort of number to break on. In the crease, of course, where any form of resistance is hardest, where even the brave can falter. I didn't merely falter: I wept. I cupped my hands around my bruised flesh, crouched upon the carpet in our Punishment Room, and wept tears of bitter sorrow. Adam let me, knew I needed to, but didn't intervene. When I was able to get up again, I didn't turn around and I didn't plead; I resumed my splayed position before him and waited for him to continue caning me. He did.

Harrowing. I suppose that's how you'd describe it. Cleansing also, perhaps. Necessary, certainly. But harrowing.

I think even Mr Palmer, with his old-fashioned values, would have approved.

Somewhere in the middle, in the stillness before unleashing a stroke, Adam said matter-of-factly: "You've stolen before, haven't you? Like today, from stores."

A heartbeat passed. I remembered my vow, in the corner.

"Yes..."

"And got away with it." A statement. I'm pretty sure he'd already worked it out for himself anyway. But I could still only croak my miserable confession.

"Yes, sir."

The cane whipped down, branding a new ridge into my flesh, and I howled.

"Later we will discuss those other times," Adam's voice informed me through the haze of pain. "But for now, we will focus on today."

Although I wasn't made to count the strokes, I think there were 16 of them in the end. But I may be mistaken. It's not what you'd call a round figure, but I wasn't in the best position for accurate score-keeping. However many it totalled, it was the hardest caning of my life, certainly the most traumatic. And also, a plain truth I couldn't escape from, the most deserved.

Those strong hands helped me up from the floor when it was over. My backside was pulsating, a mess of furious welts, and my face, in its way, was just as red and swollen. I held back from Adam's arms, resisting at first, not wanting to be hugged, not feeling worthy. But, having taken me apart, he was now picking me up and putting me back together again.

And I *was* allowed back. I had been punished. It was done, over. Sure, we had things to deal with, there was fall-out, we had a lot of talking still to do. At the least... But, for today, I had done my time. When I cried out all my pain, there was now comfort. I let his arms wrap around me and, as the tears flowed, mine clung right back. The man I adored, whom I had so badly let down along with myself, was prepared to forgive me and help us both move on. He stroked my hair as I sobbed my relief, held me tight for as long as I needed, mopped my face and wiped my nose, put cooling gel on my stripes and helped me back to our bedroom to dress. I felt very blessed to be so loved and understood.

It wasn't for some hours, after life had resumed a degree of normality, that I recalled the unused tawse in the Punishment Room and Adam's comment about previous offences, to be discussed 'later'… He hadn't said anything since, but it wasn't a particularly comforting thought either. My backside still throbbed from this morning, my nipples remained tender against the chafing support of my bra. Surely this was enough? At least for one day…

I decided not to go back up to the spare room and see if the tawse was still there. If 'later' ever came, I would find myself back there plenty soon enough.

Bridges. Crossings. One at a time.

I went and put the kettle on.

****

This story © Martha Linton 2011

About the author:

Martha is in her 30s and lives in Surrey, England. Lifelong leanings towards both kinky (submissive) fantasies and creative writing led to her earliest forays into cp fiction as a teenager, when she addressed her desires for more naughty reading material by producing her own stories. This was long before she enjoyed the delights of a sound spanking or caning herself, and sadly these fledgling efforts do not survive, but the fascination which sparked them certainly does!

During the 'Noughties', Martha was privileged to write as an occasional guest for spankingwriters.com/blog and her Easter adventures with kinky couple Abel and Haron form an appendix of their first published anthology. She was also one of the original writers for boarding school blog lowewood-academy.co.uk and remained a regular throughout its three year lifespan. Contributing to the Spanking Writers' Anthology is Martha's first public writing foray since 2009.

'Out' in the scene for over 11 years, these days Martha enjoys regular doses of hearty, well-earned cp from her partner, and is blessed with a wonderful social circle of friends and fellow kinksters who combine to make her very content. When not huddled over a keyboard, she is at her happiest either talking about, reading about or playing her favourite games!

Follow Martha on Twitter via @St_AnnesSchool

Suite Two

Bonnie

"I can't believe it." Gayle mouthed the words again and again as if trying to convince herself this predicament was simply impossible.

"C'mon, hon. It'll be all right. We'll figure it out." Roland shifted his attention from the highway just long enough to flash Gayle a confident smile.

"Just look where we are," he continued. "It's so different from home." Gayle paused to take in the majesty of the Sonoran Desert spread before them. As they drove north toward the Colorado Plateau, the giant Saguaro cacti began to thin out in favor of scrub and sagebrush. The broad afternoon sky above was brilliant blue and painted with just the faintest cirrus clouds.

"It is beautiful," she conceded.

"You're going to love this, I promise," Roland assured.

"But what about...?"

"The baggage guy said he'd send our suitcase up from Sky Harbor tomorrow afternoon."

"Do you believe that?"

"Gayle, it does not much matter what I believe. We're headed for Sedona and our suitcase got sent to Newark. Either it will find its way here or it won't. Regardless, this is our vacation."

"But it had all our..."

"Yes, and I can only imagine that the TSA in Newark is paddling suspected terrorists even as we speak."

"That's not funny."

"Especially for the terrorists..."

"I'm serious, Roland. What are we going to do?"

"We're going to take in all the glorious desert around us and imprint it on our memories. Just enjoy this red rock canyon we're driving into now."

"Yes, sir." Gayle's somber tone contradicted her acquiescent words.

"There's no need to feel dejected. We're going to have so much fun. Just you wait."

April was an ideal time to visit Oak Creek Canyon. The weather was clear and mild. Gayle couldn't help being impressed by the rugged Arizona landscape as she and Roland climbed the steep road to their resort.

"Look at that," she exclaimed and pointed at a sign for the Sedona airport. "Why couldn't we...?"

"It's a general aviation airport. Unless we have a plane, it isn't much help."

"But what about our suitcase?"

"We're not going to charter a plane for that dumb suitcase."

"It's not dumb," Gayle whined, "It holds every one of our favorite spanking and sex toys, plus my brand new bustier, garter belt, and panties."

"All right. I'm sorry I said it was dumb. But we're almost there."

On cue, Roland turned their rented silver Lincoln into the parking lot of the resort.

"Ooo, look at this place..." Gayle said. "Look. Look at that. It's a roadrunner, right here in the parking lot."

Roland simply grinned.

Moments later, they strolled into the two-story lobby. Roland pulled their lone remaining suitcase behind him. They both froze just inside the entrance. The far wall of the lobby was almost entirely glass and exposed the expansive canyon and red sandstone towers beyond. Gayle admired the Hopi artwork adorning the walls.

"This is cool," Gayle observed.

The couple checked in at the desk and received card keys for suite number two. "Have a nice visit," said the smiling young man behind the counter.

Their suite featured the same amazing canyon vista they had seen from the lobby. It was decorated in an Old West motif that seemed to ideally fit the setting.

"I feel like we just walked into a cowboy movie... A really luxurious one, that is." Gayle was obviously pleased with the accommodations her partner had arranged.

After removing his shoes, Roland rolled in one continuous motion onto the spacious king sized bed. It had been a long trip – a two hop flight into Phoenix, negotiating with the airline's baggage manager, and the two hour drive up to Sedona. He was hungry as well, but fatigue won out.

Gayle was less tired so she decided to take her book out to the balcony. As soon as she sat down, she was distracted from her reading. The late afternoon air was alive with the sounds of birds and the fragrance of piñon and juniper. At this time of day, the aptly named Capitol Butte and Coffee Pot Rock stood like dark sentries on the far side of Oak Creek Canyon.

She instantly loved this place, but what of her real love? Her whole reason for being out here? He was dead to the world. There could be no play tonight because all of their toys were in Newark or buried on some equally filthy airport loading dock. Everything was ruined. Being in paradise and not being able to enjoy it seemed worse than sitting at home.

Gayle leafed through her novel, but it failed to hold her interest. She eventually decided to wake Roland. When she opened the patio door leading from the balcony, she saw him stretched out and relaxed. He looked very sexy in his khaki pants and forest green golf shirt.

"Honey?"

"Huh?"

"It's after six o'clock and I'm hungry. Can we maybe go and get some dinner in a little bit?"

"Uh, yeah, sure." Roland slowly rose from the bed looking more dazed than rested.

After composing himself, he took Gayle to an upscale Mexican restaurant in town. Their meals arrived quickly and were artfully presented. Better still, the food was fresh, flavorful, and satisfying. They discussed whether travel makes everything taste better and decided that it does.

The sun was descending as Roland and Gayle drove back up the airport road to their resort. Upon their return, they caught the last rays of the day while seated on the balcony. The massive rock formations across the canyon were now displayed in silhouette against the violet sky. Roland took Gayle's hand in his own.

"I love you, Gayle. I'm so glad we did this."

"I love you too, dear, but what do we do now? We don't have any of our toys?"

"I believe we can make do. Let's go give it a try." With that, Roland tightened his grip on his partner's hand and led her back into the room.

After securing the sliding door, Roland suggested that they test the double shower. Intrigued but wary, Gayle pulled her dress over her head.

"But what about...?"

"I said we will manage." Roland's voice registered frustration for the first time on a day filled with complications. "Go turn on the shower and I will be right in."

Now naked, Gayle scurried into the well-equipped bathroom. She didn't want Roland to be upset with her. And yet, they had no implements, no vibrators, no restraints, and worst of all, no condoms. She saw nothing but unfulfilled promise in this night. She had no idea what Roland had in mind, but he didn't have much with which to work.

"I don't hear any water..." This was all the encouragement Gayle needed. She turned on both sides of the double shower and selected a pleasant temperature. After feeling slightly chilled from the desert evening air, the warm water tumbling over her body was like a soothing caress. She closed her eyes as she placed her head beneath the delightful cascade.

Suddenly, Gayle became aware of another presence. Roland had slipped into the shower beside her. His firm, strong body tantalized her. He was now just inches away. She gasped softly as his hands traced her slippery curves. They embraced as water fell upon them like precious rain in the desert. She held him tightly. Her inhibitions rinsed down the drain with the grime from a thousand mile journey.

She washed her lover using her delicate hands to distribute the suds. His solid frame felt like sculpted steel under her fingertips. He bent down so she could shampoo his wavy auburn scalp. The tactile and olfactory sensations of being so close to her clean, handsome man excited Gayle.

When Roland returned the favor, he did so with great vigor. Where Gayle's washing style had been meticulous and gentle, her lover spread the soap using broad, sweeping motions. Gayle let out an involuntary moan as he brushed her nipples. Her utterance dropped in pitch when his attention dropped to her crotch. He knew her well. He knew just how to drive her libido right off the cliff and into the sky. She wanted her man and she wanted him right away.

But how?

Gayle dropped to her knees, deciding that Roland had one appendage that could benefit from additional cleansing. Roland placed his hands beside her face as she demonstrated her affection. She lovingly kissed and lapped her lover to satisfaction. His growl testified to the effectiveness of her technique.

But what of Gayle?

After another sweet embrace, the couple decided to finish their shower. They dried each other using extra large, white, fluffy terrycloth towels. It was wonderful to be warm, comfortable, and together.

Yet, Gayle ached for more. Yes, she was the submissive in this relationship, but her needs had to count for something.

"Will you spank me?" she inquired.

"Why, of course, my dear! You didn't think we were going to skip that part, did you?"

"Well, I didn't know. All of our fun stuff is lost in New Jersey."

"Stuff? What stuff? I can take care of you with this stuff right here." With that, he turned on the television and selected a noisy action movie. "There's no sense asking for interruptions."

Still naked, Roland sat at the edge of the bed. He beckoned his woman to join him. Without further invitation, she lowered her still slightly damp torso onto his thighs. Roland was the first man to ever spank her in earnest and she couldn't imagine anyone else doing it better.

And yet, he had no paddles, no straps, no canes, and no hairbrushes.

"Ow! Ow! OW! What is that?"

"That, naughty girl, is my belt. How dare you think I wouldn't spank you!"

The braided leather scorched Gayle's soft skin, but the resulting burn was one she welcomed. The doubled belt cleansed her soul as even the double shower could not. Before long, she was greedily raising her bottom to meet each impact. Over and over, Roland laid crimson stripes one upon another. Gayle's entire body shook with pain, thrill, and lust. Whether erotic punishment or punishing eroticism, she drank in each fiery sensation.

"Ouch! I'm sorry!" She wasn't entirely sure she was sorry or why exactly she should feel sorry, but it seemed like an appropriate sentiment when being spanked.

"Sorry? Let me tell you. You're going to be sorry tomorrow every time you sit."

Gayle found this dire pronouncement oddly exciting.

Roland then slipped his left hand beneath his partner until he made contact with her nexus. The arousal the spanking had generated was immediately evident. Stroking as he swatted, Roland soon lifted Gayle to a shivering, bucking completion. The intensity of the moment and the elevation left her panting for oxygen.

Gayle felt a little wobbly as she raised herself from her man's lap. They found each other again moments later beneath the bed covers. He kissed her lips tenderly.

"That was good... Really good."

"Didn't I tell you?"

"Do you wish we could make love now?"

Roland smiled. "Of course I do."

"But we don't have..."

"Shhhh..."

Roland jumped from the bed and pulled a long strip of condoms from his carry-on bag. "There are some things that are too important to be entrusted to baggage handlers."

"But you didn't..."

"I told you not to worry. Had we really been out of condoms, I would have stopped in town."

"OK, I've stopped worrying."

"Good. Turn out that light."

****

This story © Bonnie 2011

About the author:

Bonnie is a writer, blogger, wife, and lifelong spanking enthusiast. Her blog, My Bottom Smarts, is a crossroads where spankos of every stripe are invited to join the conversation or just relax and read. It can be found at:

bottomsmarts.blogspot.com

Finished

Rebecca Williams

"Honestly James, I don't know what father was thinking!" Annabel complained to her butler for the umpteenth time.

"I'm sure he has his reasons, Miss." James answered politely, wondering if this finishing school would be any more successful than the previous two. Privately he thought that Miss Annabel might think she was a grand young lady now, but no proper young lady threw bowls of soup at the footmen or ordered her maid birched for failing to procure cosmetics that her father had forbidden in the first place.

"You *would* take his side," Annabel pouted. "Does service render you totally incapable of independent thought?"

"I wouldn't know, Miss. Why don't you just lie back and enjoy the rest of the journey: we'll be there soon enough?" he responded through gritted teeth. The Honorable Annabel Riverton was beautiful with her slim figure and long auburn hair but it was a pity that her temperament was far less charming, at least where her perceived inferiors were concerned.

Annabel sighed and glanced dourly out of the window. They were already miles from London, which to an eighteen year old on the cusp of her debut felt like the centre of the universe. Silently she reflected upon her father's words about this being a special institution that would ensure she was properly prepared to take her place in society, and that she might find it difficult, but he trusted she would try. Good riddance to that, she thought to herself; she would show them she wasn't some little girl to be trifled with, and with any luck she'd be heading home in time for Lady Grey's summer ball.

The coach drew to a stop, which shook her from her reverie. In the late afternoon shadows Carrington Hall appeared grey and forbidding, and she looked around disdainfully as James helped her to the ground.

"The Honorable Annabel Riverton, I presume?" A stern-faced, silver-haired woman greeted them. "I'm Miss Tarryton, the Headmistress, and you'll be coming with me." Then she nodded to a navy-clad footman, "Thomas here will deal with your bags."

"Nice to meet you," Annabel replied, attempting a smile. "You can be on your way home to my beloved father then, James," she added as an afterthought, following Miss Tarryton through the door and up a narrow flight of stairs.

"This will be your room for now, although - as you will learn later - we move you girls from time to time. I shall send Mary to help you unpack, and then you may rest until six, when you will meet the other girls before dinner," Miss Tarryton explained, and with that Annabel was left alone with her thoughts. It seemed a dour place, to be sure, but at least they recognized that someone of her status befitted proper staff. She made her mind up to stamp her authority upon the staff and other girls as quickly as possible, to make it clear she was far too old for such an institution.

There was a knock at the door, and a plump blonde girl in maid's dress entered shyly.

"Miss Tarryton sent me to help you with your unpacking, Miss," she explained, looking down at the carpet nervously.

"Well, unpack then!" Annabel retorted. If this girl thought she was helping, she had another thing coming to her. She smirked as the girl blushed and set about opening her trunks and setting out her belongings. She idly reclined, issuing the odd order or correction whilst examining her reflection in her looking-glass.

"Please, Miss, cosmetics are forbidden at Carrington Hall: should I leave these in your vanity?" questioned Mary, holding up her powder and rouge.

"What a stupid rule! No, leave them out on the dresser!" Annabel commanded, failing to notice the look of mild amusement on Mary's face.

"As you will, Miss," Mary replied. The unpacking process seemed to take an age, Annabel thought in irritation. By the time Mary had finished arranging Annabel's things, close to an hour had passed, and it was time to dress for dinner. She changed into one of her favourite dresses, a striking green colour that contrasted beautifully with her fair skin and dark hair. Mary returned to help her with her hair, but to Annabel's fury was none too competent.

"Carefully, for goodness sake: do you want to leave me bald?" she complained as Mary brushed the tangles left by a day's travels from her hair. "Honestly, Mary! What are you thinking with this awful style? Are you trying to embarrass me in front of the other girls?" she demanded. There was, in fact, nothing wrong with the hairstyle, but Annabel noted that the maid seemed near to tears, and commanded her to begin again.

"But Miss, it's five to six, you don't want to be late to dinner and the hairstyle will more than pass Miss Tarryton's approval, I'm sure," Mary said anxiously, knowing all too well what befell young ladies who were late to dinner.

"Late to dinner be damned, I'm not going down looking like this, and you shan't talk to me like that, you common slut!" Annabel declared, wrenching the hairbrush from Mary's hand, standing up, grabbing the girl's hair and using it to propel her across her lap. Angrily she smacked the hairbrush down several times upon the girl's ample bottom.

"Please Miss, you're not allowed to do this, and you're going to be late," Mary pleaded, her cheeks flushed red with embarrassment.

"I'll do what I like, you're just a maid!" Annabel hissed and yanked Mary's dress up to reveal her drawers. Mary didn't fight her but lay resigned as Annabel pinned her arm to the small of her back and bought the hairbrush down hard on her left cheek, eliciting a quiet gasp. For a slight girl, Annabel was strong, and by the time she'd given the girl half a dozen, Mary was already sobbing quietly and squirming across her lap.

"Crying like a baby," Annabel sighed, "well, babies get it on the bare - don't they, Mary?" she continued, pausing to work the girl's cotton drawers down over her curvy backside. Her skin was already pink in places and pleasingly warm to Annabel's touch. She thought in pleasure how nice it was to have such a pretty girl over her lap as she started spanking the girl in earnest.

Mary's pale skin quickly turned from cream to pink to red as Annabel systematically applied the hairbrush from the top of her bottom to just below the crease. Annabel found the whimpering oddly erotic, and thought it would certainly teach Mary to defy her again; it was a shame she didn't have a belt or cane, though. Growing tired, she decided to give her six more for good measure, and ordered Mary to count. Making sure to put all her power into the strokes, she took quiet pleasure in how the impact made the other girl shudder.

"One, thank you, Miss," Mary whispered dutifully, obviously used to this sort of treatment.

Annabel aimed the next stroke right where Mary's thighs met her bottom, and smirked as the other girl shrieked.

"Two, thank you, Miss," Mary counted. Annabel was just contemplating where to place the next stroke when the door creaked open, framing an angry looking Miss Tarryton.

"Annabel, Mary: what on earth is going on?" she questioned, not waiting for them to respond. "Annabel, you should have been downstairs twenty minutes ago, and you most certainly are not in a position to be chastising Mary like this."

"But she..." Annabel butted in, but was silenced.

"Never mind what she did or didn't do, you have no place punishing her. Mary, report to Mr White, he's been waiting for you to help with the drinks. " Mary rearranged her clothing and scurried off, wiping her eyes on her sleeve. "Annabel, there is no excuse for this sort of behavior; I guarantee you will quickly come to regret it. Your father had warned me of your ill manners, but not your apparent idiocy. You will come down to dinner with me now, and we will discuss this later." With that she turned and headed swiftly down the stairs before Annabel had a chance to argue.

Pouting, Annabel followed her downstairs and into a small drawing-room. There appeared to be five other girls, all about her age - although none so grandly dressed, she noticed smugly. With any luck she could persuade one of them to do whatever lines or embroidery Miss Tarryton intended to punish her with, she thought. A flushed Mary handed her a glass of wine but Annabel ignored her, already planning her revenge on the girl for getting her into trouble.

A tall gentleman entered and rang a bell, and Miss Tarryton ordered the girls to gather round and take a seat. Oddly, the butler and maids were present too.

"Good evening, girls, and welcome to our new arrivals: Annabel, Louise and Hermione," the Headmistress started. "As those of you who have been with us for some time will know, Carrington Hall prides itself upon turning out young ladies who are not only pearls in society, but capable of managing their households efficiently. Many of you have come to us from other finishing schools with more relaxed discipline, and find our routine something of a shock, so I will explain now. In order to be Mistress of a household and manage your staff well, you must understand what it is to serve yourself. Therefore, as well as your lessons in dancing, etiquette, calligraphy and music, you will undergo a most rigorous course in household management. This will involve undertaking the role of a maid to fully comprehend the responsibilities your staff must bear. To aid with the discipline in the hall, although you will all serve at some point, each day the two girls whose behavior has been most lacking will move to the maids' quarters and join the staff for the following day. During this time you will be subject to the discipline of our butler Mr White, and also myself, should the girls make any complaints about your service," she explained.

Annabel felt herself turn white; she couldn't quite believe what she was hearing. Glancing across at Mary, she could see her smirking slightly, and quickly looked away.

"You will all, of course, also be punished for poor behaviour or performance in addition to this. This will take place before dinner each evening. In something of a record-breaking performance, it seems I already need to deal with young Annabel, so we will retire to my study whilst the rest of you finish your drinks," she added. "Now come along, Annabel: follow me."

Annabel weakly raised herself to her feet and followed Miss Tarryton, suddenly feeling rather afraid. What sort of institution had her father sent her to, that they thought it appropriate to punish her, a grown-up young lady? Although her hands were trembling, she resolved to put a stop to this nonsense once and for all.

Miss Tarryton closed the door behind her and stepped behind her desk.

"Now, Annabel, I'm sure you have a hundred and one excuses and explanations for what happened earlier on. However, Mary has already spoken to Mr White, and I overheard much of your discussion, so I would suggest you don't try to lie - or it will be more painful for you," she stated quietly.

"It was all that awful girl Mary's fault," Annabel complained, "she made a mess of unpacking, a rat's nest of my hair, and was fearfully rude to me."

"Your room appeared in perfect order to me, as did your hair," replied Miss Tarryton, "and that explanation doesn't cover why you were late for dinner, had prohibited cosmetics, or thought it acceptable to deal with my staff. I fear you will have some apologizing to do to poor Mary if you want to make a friend of her for the rest of your stay."

"Why would I want to be friends with a common maid?" Annabel questioned in fury.

"My dear, Mary is no common maid, she's Lady Mary Sandringham, the daughter of the Earl of Sandringham. Thankfully, her temperament is somewhat sweeter than yours, so I am sure if you ask nicely she will forgive you. So, we have to deal with your rudeness, your lateness, your contraband and presuming to deal with a member of staff without permission. I will deal with the former issues and then I shall call in Mr White to deal with you taking it upon yourself to punish Mary," she explained.

"Well, what are you going to do?" Annabel asked reluctantly.

"Young lady, there is only one way that we deal with infractions at Carrington's, and that's with a good dose of corporal punishment. I'm sorry that you have to experience this so early in your stay - but really, you've bought it upon yourself."

"Don't be ridiculous, I'm eighteen, you can't do that!" Annabel protested, fighting the burning sensation that signaled she might begin to cry.

"Nonsense, we have your father's blessing. In fact, he said it would do you a world of good. Now, are you going to be sensible, or am I going to have to go and get Thomas to hold you down?" Miss Tarryton asked, feeling the discussion had gone on long enough.

Annabel had no desire to allow Miss Tarryton to chastise her, but still less for a mere footman to witness her shame.

"Fine," she pouted, "but I shall write to Father tomorrow morning, demanding that I leave this place immediately!"

"Very well, we shall begin with the rudeness, for which, I think, a simple spanking will suffice. Place yourself over my lap, hands on the ground."

Annabel complied, feeling utterly ridiculous and cursing her stupidity in placing Lady Mary in that position earlier on. If she'd only told her who she was, this whole mess could have been avoided. She felt herself blush as Miss Tarryton raised her skirt and petticoats, commented on the scandalous nature of her undergarments and started spanking her bottom like a little girl's. It had been a long while since Annabel had been over anybody's knee, and she found herself fighting to keep still. Determined not to give the other girls next door the pleasure of hearing her cry, she bit her lip and locked her legs as the Headmistress set her bottom on fire. Finally she could take it no more and started to cry quietly, feeling sure that nobody had ever been spanked this hard before.

Looking down at Annabel's pink cheeks, Miss Tarryton smiled. The girl was making an awful fuss for a mere spanking; still with any luck it would ensure that she learnt her lesson more quickly. Noting that Annabel was starting to cry, she stopped.

"Very well, Annabel, that concludes part one. As you seem so fond of the hairbrush, you can fetch mine from the top drawer of my desk, and then we will deal with your lateness."

"Part one! You must be joking! I'm sorry, now can we end this nonsense?" Annabel demanded in horror.

"I will let your rudeness pass on this occasion, Annabel, but you will thank me for punishments from this point onwards. Now, unless you want me to call Thomas, bring me the hairbrush." Sensing that she was unlikely to win this battle, Annabel dragged herself up from Miss Tarryton's lap, stomped across the room and procured the hairbrush, noting with a shudder that it was much larger than the one that she had used upon Mary.

Grumpily she returned to the Headmistress's side and held it out.

"Very well, Annabel, over you go," Miss Tarryton proclaimed, guiding the reluctant girl over her lap and pinning her legs between her own thighs as a precaution.

"Now, Annabel, you were twenty minutes late, so twenty strokes with the hairbrush seems more than fair. I won't make you count them on this occasion but you will thank me when we are finished," the Headmistress declared, not waiting for poor Annabel's agreement.

From the first stroke Annabel was convinced that her bottom was on fire, surely she would never be able to sit down again. Desperate not to make a scene, she dug her fingers into the carpet, but couldn't help gasping and then crying out in pain as each stroke landed upon her delicate bottom. Halfway through the punishment it seemed unbelievable that there were another ten strokes to go, and Annabel began to squirm and beg for the spanking to end. However, the Headmistress's right thigh held her kicking legs firmly in place as she delivered a blow to each thigh and admonished Annabel to stop behaving like such a baby. After a lifetime it was finished, and Annabel lay sobbing across Miss Tarryton's lap.

"Very well, Annabel, it seems the message is at least beginning to get through to you. Now we will deal with your possession of cosmetics that are clearly forbidden by the school rules. I think we will have you up and over my desk for these, to give me a little more swing with my strap, and you can take your ridiculous drawers off."

"No, no, I won't!" Annabel sobbed, "You can't take my knickers down, I'm too old!"

"I can, Annabel, and I will, unless you would prefer I called Thomas in to assist me. You didn't seem to have such a problem with punishing Mary's bare bottom earlier, so stop being such a moaning little hypocrite. A lady takes her punishment with grace. If you move, we will repeat the stroke," Miss Tarryton stated, gently helping Annabel up.

Sniffing, Annabel laid herself across Miss Tarryton's desk, reflexively reaching out to grasp the far side.

Inwardly smiling at the girl's obedience, the Headmistress lowered Annabel's drawers to her knees, noting that her bottom was already nicely pink in contrast to the porcelain white surrounding it, yet didn't show any real damage.

"Four, I think, Annabel, as I believe that's the number of items you brought with you. I am being lenient on account of this being your first punishment here, so you should be grateful. You will count these and thank me for each stroke, do you understand?"

"Yes, Miss Tarryton," Annabel ground out between gritted teeth.

Annabel felt horribly vulnerable bent over the desk with her bare bottom presented for the strap. She couldn't quite believe the pain of the first stroke; as it landed on her tender bottom, she was sure it must have branded her. She yelped and kicked her legs, and only just remembered to count. Annabel gripped the desk desperately, remembering the threat of repeated strokes should she rise from her position. The second and third strokes exploded her world in pain; she could hear a voice counting, but wasn't sure that it was really her own. The Headmistress expertly placed the final stroke across Annabel's crease, and unable to stop herself the girl leapt up, clutching her bottom.

"Back down, Annabel, and we'll try again." Miss Tarryton commanded.

"But please, I didn't mean to..." Annabel sobbed.

"But you did, and you did mean to break the rules. It's just one more stroke: please try to bear it with fortitude."

Painfully, Annabel resumed her position over the desk and tried to remind herself that she was the Honourable Annabel Riverton, not a little girl. Holding her breath awaiting the final stroke, she felt like a little girl, though, and a sorry one at that. Her knees buckled and slammed into the desk as the strap scorched her cheeks, but she managed to stay down.

"Four, thank you, Miss." she uttered tearfully, temporarily too dazed to rise from the desk.

"You are welcome, Annabel. Now we just have the affair with Mary to deal with. I will fetch Mr White, and you can have a moment to recover, but no rubbing your bottom please," Miss Tarryton declared, leaving the study in search of the butler, whom Annabel presumed to be the tall gentleman from dinner. Furtively Annabel reached round and rubbed her stinging cheeks, confident that there was time before they returned. Hearing footsteps she returned her hands to the desk, feeling smug that she'd outwitted them, at least in that respect.

"So, this is the girl?" questioned Mr White. Annabel attempted to regain her knickers, but a slap on the thigh from the Headmistress warned her against the endeavor.

"Indeed, it's a rare case that you deal with them before they serve as maids, but in this case it seems appropriate," the Headmistress explained. "She's been dealt with quite severely already, and appears new to formal discipline, so I suggest a junior cane would suffice."

"Very well, I think it had better be six of the best, young lady. It is entirely unacceptable for you to presume to punish the household staff, especially when it was entirely unwarranted. You will stay in position, you will count, and you will thank me. Then you will apologise to Mary: do you understand?"

"Yes, Sir," Annabel answered miserably. The day really had gone from bad to worse: if you'd asked her this morning if she would have submitted to a thrashing from some awful butler, she would have laughed.

"Very well, let's not waste time," he declared.

Annabel resumed her grip on the desk and hissed as the first stroke landed. It felt as if a red-hot poker had been pressed against her skin, and she could barely get the words out to count. She bit her lip, waiting for the next one and willing her legs to stay locked and her body in position. The pain was unbearable as the stroke fell just below the previous one, lighting another line of fire across her delicate bottom. She tightened her grip and determined not to beg: to take it gracefully, like the Headmistress had said.

"Three, thank you, Sir," Annabel sobbed miserably, wishing the drawing-room and the other girls were further away, as they must surely be able to hear her humiliation through the wooden door.

The fourth stroke made her shriek again and stamp her feet, but somehow she counted and thanked the butler as she added to the pool of tears seeping into the desk. Unable to stop herself, Annabel found herself kicking her feet as the penultimate stroke landed upon her poor bottom.

"Five, thank you, Sir," she cried, feeling genuinely sorry for herself and the situation. She'd had no idea how painful such punishments were; recollecting the many times she'd ordered them for her maid at home, she felt utterly ashamed of herself.

"Now, Annabel, what do they say about the last stroke?" the butler asked quietly.

"That it's the hardest," Annabel whispered fearfully, remembering being told so by a governess in another life, when a punishment consisted of maybe half a dozen spanks over her dress. She closed her eyes, gritted her teeth and clutched the desk in desperation, and then yelped as the final stroke landed across the others, leaving her bottom a mess of painful welts.

"Six, thank you, Sir. I'm sorry, Sir." Annabel sobbed, collapsing upon the desk.

"Now, Annabel: take five minutes to collect yourself, and then come through to dinner. I think we've delayed quite enough for one evening," Miss Tarryton commanded.

Five minutes later a red-eyed Annabel appeared in the dining room and thanked Thomas for helping her to her seat. A smiling Mary commented that her hair looked a little out of place, before giving her a squeeze on the shoulder in sympathy. Apologising had been embarrassing, but Miss Tarryton had been right: Mary was a sweet girl at heart, and had accepted Annabel's apology gracefully.

Annabel found herself with little appetite and virtually unable to sit still, as Miss Tarryton reprimanded her several times for her poor posture. The starter and main passed without event, and then before dessert the butler once again rang the bell.

"Girls, as you know two, of you are chosen each day to serve as maids based upon your behavior and deportment. Tomorrow Clarissa will wait upon Louise, Hermione and Maura; Annabel will wait upon Mary, Hannah and Amelia. You will both report to Mr White after dinner to clear the trays and ensure that you are up in time to prepare the breakfast tomorrow morning. Remember, a lady must bear all her trials with grace," Miss Tarryton announced with a smile, as Annabel felt the blood rush from her head.

****

This story © Rebecca Williams 2011

About the author:

Rebecca Williams is an English dilettante currently chasing kangaroos in Australia. She has been active on the spanking and bdsm scenes in London for four years, but still proclaims herself entirely sweet and innocent!

Rebecca loves few things better than dressing up and misbehaving, especially when her misdeeds are found out and severely punished. Other interests include travel (her work provides for multiple misadventures overseas), music, martial arts, theatre, rowing, cocktails and cupcakes.

Previously the writer of 'Cassie' for Lowewood Academy, her ramblings can now be found in the Twitterverse as @bex_williams or at:

rebecca-breakingtherules.blogspot.com

The Library

Casey Morgan

She was a sensible girl. Everything about her was sensible: her hair, her wardrobe, her reputation, her name. She couldn't change her hair, as there was little you could do with anything as straight as hers. She couldn't change her wardrobe; true, other girls adjusted pieces of their uniform, but she had no desire to lower her neckline or raise her hem. Her reputation, once a burden, had reached the point of paying dividends. Thus, she resolved to change her name.

Some teachers addressed them by surname, and those who employed Christian names had known her too long to accept a change as anything but affected. But when asked her name by Mrs. Salte, the new art teacher, Charlotte was at last able to introduce herself as Charlie.

She was the first good reason he had for getting caned. She was in the fifth form at St. Agatha's, and ever since her team had trounced his at the debate skirmish, he had been unable to sleep properly. St. Agatha's was too far away for College boys to interfere with its pupils, but after the debate, St. Agatha's captain had cornered him outside the toilets and told him two things: 1) she had a dentist's appointment near his College the following Thursday; 2) her name was Charlie. Then, she had grasped his wrists, held them against his hips, and kissed him.

Jeremy was not the kind of boy who kissed girls. He liked girls, certainly, but until his encounter with Charlie in the village hall, no girl had ever paid him attention. At the Christmas ball, St. Agatha's girls always fluttered around the athletic boys, who inspired confidence, or around the willowy ones, who inspired affection. They never fluttered around Jeremy, who was dark but not handsome, active but not accomplished at Games, bright but not verbally clever—in short a non-entity. Why St. Agatha's captain should have kissed him, he had no idea. He decided not to ponder it but to seize the opportunity. He considered it likely he'd never get another.

He had double chemistry Thursday afternoon. If he cut lessons, he would probably be caught; if he claimed he'd been in the San, he would certainly be caught; if he turned up to chemistry and then slipped out once the experiment began, there was a chance, albeit slight, that his absence would go unnoticed.

The cane at College was usually dispensed with ceremony and always with force. *Shakespeare, Plato, Swift, Aristotle...* Once you learned the names, you never forgot. *Donne, Demosthenes, Milton, Herbert...* Old boys could recite them without a breath's hesitation, ten years on, twenty years, forty. No College boy who'd had those names imprinted on him could ever leave them entirely in the past.

College was known for three things: its version of fives, its Tractarianism, and its library. Resembling the larger and more extravagant library at a rather more famous institution, College's library featured two open stories and a collection of busts lining the hall on the main level. When boys first arrived at College—thirteen years old and easily intimidated—they were ushered directly to the chamber and greeted by the body of school prefects, called collectively the Library (not to be confused with the room itself, represented in the lower case). The eye was drawn first upwards—to the vaulted ceiling and to the upper floor of open shelving along three sides of the room—then forwards down the center aisle lined with nooks, each nook guarded by a marble bust on a pedestal. There were twenty-four of them, and new boys had twenty-four hours to memorize the names and positions of each bust.

Jeremy had heard all about the library before coming to College. It was the chief thing people told you about College that proved true. Therefore, twenty-four hours after arriving, Jeremy stood before Astor, a Library prefect, palm outstretched.

"Shakespeare...Plato...Swift...Aristotle...Donne..." The first five were easy. The first hurdle came next: could he say

Demosthenes without mispronouncing it or breaking his rhythm?
"Demothsenes—"

Crack. He gasped as the tawse fell, sharp, fiery, breathtaking
across his palm.

"De-MOSS-tha-nees," said Astor with crisp pronunciation.
Jeremy clutched and unclutched his fist. "Again," Astor
commanded. With great reluctance, Jeremy returned his hand to
position.

He tried to clear his head. It was important, they said, not to
let the Library rattle you. They would try, but you must refuse to
be rattled. Jeremy closed his eyes and tried to imagine the trees
alongside the science block where he and the other new boys had
practiced together.

"Eyes open!" Astor barked.

Jeremy opened his eyes and took a breath: "Shakespeare,
Plato…Swift, Aristotle…Donne, De-moss-thenes, Milton…"
Milton meant you'd passed the quarter-mark…but he had to
concentrate. He had to keep from getting rattled. "Herbert,
Johnson, Keble, Augustine…" And he'd pronounced that one
right! "Pusey, Sophocles, Rossetti…" After Rossetti came…?
Concentrate. Keep the rhythm. You weren't allowed to break
the—

Crack. Gasp. A hack of fire. "Again."

They said your chances of passing diminished drastically each
time you had to start over.

"Shakespeare, Plato…"

The throbbing-burning-sting in your hand distracted you. It
was harder not to get rattled—

"Aristotle, Augustine—"

Crack. "Again."

Harder to put your hand out before Astor, a giant in prefect's
clothing.

Crack. "Again."

Harder to return it to harm's way, holding it under the tawse
which loomed like the sword of—

"Damocles—"

Crack. "Last chance."

After six, they sent you away. The next day you had to return to the library, but instead of reporting to the table in the middle of the hall, you reported to Swift. Third statue, three strokes of the cane.

That was how punishments worked at College. Four black marks in a week? An Aristotle. Caught smoking? A Donne. Out-of-bounds? Milton. Cutting Games? Demosthenes, first offense. At the start of Prep, you were expected to be waiting beside the bust corresponding to your sentence. The Third and Fourth forms would file in to their places at the upstairs tables. The duty prefect would arrive and arrange his things on the center table. The bell would ring. You would continue to stand where you were—beside Swift if you were lucky, beside Pusey if you weren't—facing the shelves, hearing sounds of Prep behind you, awaiting the arrival of whichever member of the Library was to administer your punishment.

"Shakespeare, Plato, Swift, Aristotle, Donne, Demosthenes, Milton...Sh-Shakes—"

Crack. "That will do," Astor said quietly. "Swift, tomorrow, Prep. We'll see if the cane can't sharpen your memory, or at least your concentration."

The cane had concentrated both, and Jeremy had passed the Library Test the next evening. The experience had been unpleasant enough that he'd done everything possible to avoid repeating it. Until now.

"You came," she said.

His heart thudded. Her eyes were blue, the kind of blue that made him want to break every rule to be in her presence.

"I didn't think you'd have the nerve," she said.

"I did."

Those blue eyes glanced down the high street, and then her astonishing hands gripped his wrist and pulled him into the doorway.

"What will happen if you're caught?" she asked.

He affected a shrug, heart beating up his windpipe. "Just the cane."

A smatter of pink across her cheek. He could smell her shampoo, which must that morning have cascaded through her heavy blonde hair. She tilted her hat back, pinned his wrists to his sides as she had before, and as before, she kissed him.

He never wanted to take his tongue from between her lips. He never wanted to stop drinking from her, breathing her, pressing against her.

"Charlie?"

She flinched back and glanced around the doorframe. "Coming, Mrs. Salte."

He was going to lose consciousness if she departed. There was no way he could survive it. "Charlie..." he breathed.

She adjusted her hat and wiped her mouth with her sleeve. "Cross country tomorrow," she whispered hastily. "I'll be at the old mill from two until five past." With that, she darted away to rejoin her chaperone.

"Charlie," said Mrs. Salte on the way back to the car, "I would rather not ask what was going on in the doorway back there."

Charlotte blushed to the back of her eyeballs. She hoped her hat would conceal her face.

"You're such a sensible girl."

"Thank you, Mrs. Salte."

"At least that's the consensus in the Common Room."

What in the name of St. Agatha was that supposed to mean?

"To be perfectly honest," Mrs. Salte continued in confidential tone, "there's a certain discrepancy between this sensible Charlotte everyone goes on about, and Charlie who makes the rather extraordinary drawings I've seen in Studio B this term."

Had Mrs. Salte just paid her a compliment or accused her of being a fraud?

"At any rate," Mrs. Salte continued, "I'd advise Charlotte to keep an eye on her friend Charlie, especially when it comes to College boys, or I shall be forced to discuss their joint sensibility with their housemaster."

Charlotte's housemaster had only come to St. Agatha's that term to cover for her housemistress, who was away having a baby. Charlotte didn't know her housemaster very well, but she did know two essential facts: his name was Mr. Salte, and he was married to her art teacher.

Jeremy's only hope was the Lucky Dip, a College tradition which offered the chance of being let off your first Library offense if you could answer a question the Library put to you about the figure who matched your sentence. Jeremy was caught coming in the kitchen gate after the kiss outside the dentist. The prefect had given him a Herbert for being a) out-of-bounds, b) during lessons. Jeremy had not been summoned by the Library since his Library Test the year before. He wasn't sure how a Herbert would compare to a Swift, but he knew it would hurt. A lot.

"Gaston," said the prefect holding the cane, "you had the cast iron cheek to be out-of-bounds during lessons. Have you anything to say?"

She was the first good reason he had for getting caned, but standing before Astor, now Captain of Games, contemplating an eight-stroke sentence, Jeremy was losing his nerve. "No, Astor."

Astor fixed Jeremy with an athletic glare, flexed the cane, and then turned to the duty prefect. "Is this a first offense?"

The duty prefect looked up from his exercise book and seemed to consider the matter. It was all an act, of course. Jeremy knew the Library had not only researched the punishment ledger but researched the Lucky Dip. He had even researched the Lucky Dip, at least glancingly. Herbert had written a great many poems, and the pages of his biography ran over five hundred. Standing now in the library, all Jeremy could remember was a poem called "Discipline," which was far too obvious for the Lucky Dip. This was going to hurt.

At length the prefects concluded that it was indeed Jeremy's first offense (Library Test notwithstanding). Was Jeremy aware of a little tradition in the Library, the tradition of the Lucky Dip? Jeremy was. Then perhaps Jeremy would care to consider the question, in hopes of being let off his well-deserved punishment? Jeremy was eager to consider it. A long shot indeed, but anything offered in the shadow of the rod…

Astor set down the cane, unbuttoned his jacket, and removed a card from his inner pocket. "Complete the stanza," Astor told him, "and off you go. Get it wrong, two extra strokes."

Jeremy nodded and forced himself to breathe. It was essential not to let yourself get rattled.

"Then," Astor read, "let wrath remove…"

She was the first good reason he had for getting caned, but some power—Herbert, the Fates, or Eros himself—conspired against it! "Discipline" he had read, and "Discipline" he received. Jeremy squared his shoulders and visualized the page before him:

Then let wrath remove;
Love will do the deed:
For with love,
Stonie hearts will bleed.

It was ridiculous to imagine she loved him, but something about the dark, gangly College boy made it impossible to concentrate, even during Drawing. Especially during Drawing. Mrs. Salte was clearly unimpressed and called her aside at the end of the lesson.

"I asked Charlotte to keep an eye on young Charlie, not take her art lessons for her."

Charlotte burned with shame.

"Please send Charlie to the studio on her own tomorrow."

If she were a phoenix, at least the flames would consume her, until she turned into something else and could fly away.

Dear Charlotte, her father wrote, *You are the one person keeping me from the brink. How I'd survive without a daughter as sensible as you, I'll never know.* Her twin brothers, it transpired, had been thrown out of their third prep school. Aunt Nancy was back in the hospital. Her father would be unable to come to her debate at the weekend, but he knew she'd be successful. *My best, most sensible girl.*

It was ridiculous to claim he loved her, but something more than hunger for her lips drove him to cut cricket practice and tramp cross-country to the mill. Who was this girl with the razor mind and the cool, shackling hands that always pinned his wrists to his side, imprisoning him before her mouth? She had a boy's name, and he felt she'd make a sensational boy, with the right hair-cut. Confident, vigorous, resourceful, renegade, she was the type of boy he could never hope to be. She was probably as clever at Games as she was behind the debating podium, as audacious under the cane as she was in the dentist's doorway.

He couldn't claim to love her, yet, but if his heart wasn't bleeding, then he had no explanation for the restless, aching sensation that afflicted his chest with each breath.

It was all working out like the best argument: well-researched, well-structured, executed with unflinching nerve. She feigned cramp, fell back from the middle pack, and cut briskly across the stream before the back group had a chance to top the hill. Who said sensible had to mean Sensible?

She arrived at the old mill as the hands of her wristwatch passed two. He was there, dressed in the old-fashioned cricket costume College boys still wore, pulling himself up to the platform above the water wheel. The stream rushed beneath them, masking her footsteps. He'd rolled his sleeves above the elbow, revealing arms on the verge of a man's. She thought he was younger that she was, but it was hard to tell. The only things she knew for sure about him were his name (Gaston), his debating style (self-effacing and cheeky), his mouth (expressive, addictive), and the sound of her name on his tongue... *Charlie...*

She whistled as her brothers had taught her, with two fingers. He startled and then broke into a smile that would melt icebergs. In an instant, he had clambered down and was standing before her, offering his wrists.

He'd expected only to have five minutes with her, but she stayed half an hour. Even after they'd pulled apart, lips and jaws sore, she'd remained behind to question him. Had he been caned last time? Would he be today? His pretend indifference only fueled her curiosity. Shakespeare, Plato, *what?* He'd expected girls to find Library customs boorish, but Charlie cross-examined him more rigorously than she'd rebutted his arguments last Saturday. He was sunk for cutting Games, a Demosthenes at least. *Shakespeare, Plato, Swift, Aristotle...*She devoured his account almost as she'd drunk from his mouth; then, after announcing she had to leave, she took his wrists and began kissing him again.

The Games prefect running sweep did not believe that she had taken a wrong turn and got lost. She did not believe Charlotte's excuse because it was a) untrue; b) implausible; c) delivered with a pathetic lack of conviction. Thus Charlotte found herself in her housemaster's study, still in running kit and feeling as if she were at her novice debate but lacking even a shred of preparation.

"Charlotte," exclaimed Mr. Salte when the prefect had left, "what is this all about?" Surely there was a logical explanation? Charlotte, self-conscious with her muddy shins and sweaty clothing, could think of nothing to say. "The captain of our debating society struck dumb? Come, come, Charlotte."

"Oh," said a voice behind the standing lamp, "I expect you'll find an explanation if you ask Charlie, rather than Charlotte."

Charlotte's heart pounded in her throat as Mrs. Salte emerged from the wing-chair, sketchbook in hand.

"Since I doubt she's begun wearing lipstick, I imagine she was detained by an abrasive force applied repeatedly to the lips. Something like that, Charlie?"

Mr. Salte made the kinds of noises a housemaster was expected to make under the circumstances. He conducted a half-hearted inquiry, which seemed to pain him as much as it did Charlotte. It was a strange relief when he moved on to the consequences.

"Out-of-bounds and...let's just draw a veil over the rest. This can't be allowed to continue. It'll have to be a week's gating."

"Oh, but sir!"

"*But sir*, what? I should have said a fortnight, but as you're normally so sensible, I thought some clemency—"

"But, sir, the district debate finals are tomorrow, and I'm captain."

"You should have thought of that before canoodling with a College boy."

"But, sir—"

"Perhaps," inserted Mrs. Salte, "we could find a more expedient solution?"

Mr. Salte flapped at his wife like an agitated water fowl. "St. Agatha's doesn't—this isn't Wingfield Hall! I can't simply—"

"One mustn't be rigid, darling. Your debate captain is telling you she strenuously prefers not to be gated."

"Most strenuously," Charlotte said.

"But one can't begin dealing with these girls as one dealt with Wingfield boys. It would be—"

"A discreet exception," Mrs. Salte said. "Why not ask Charlie which punishment she prefers?"

And so, as Charlotte stood speechless on the carpet, her housemaster presented her options: a week's gating or twelve strokes of the slipper, administered there and then. She had never had the slipper. She had never even been smacked as a child. Her heart beat in her tongue, in her lips, everywhere.

Mr. Salte rummaged in a drawer and produced a large, worn plimsoll. "And don't expect any less than the boys at Wingfield used to get," he told her gruffly.

"Oh, it's all very fierce," Mrs. Salte winked, "but nothing Charlie can't survive."

Her husband turned, exasperated: "*Will* you let this girl make up her own mind?"

Suppressing a kind of smirk, Mrs. Salte retreated to the armchair and resumed her sketching tablet.

"Well, Charlotte?" Mr. Salte asked.

"It's Charlie. Sir."

The district finals were held in the Hall of his College, a different world entirely from St. Agatha's or any school she'd ever known. Twenty-four hours after kissing him, she stepped down from College's carved podium and carefully took her seat. He was watching from the fourth row, his gaze steady but inscrutable. Had he been caned after all? He didn't look any different, except that his cheeks showed more color and his eyes possessed a kind of electricity she'd not noticed before. He didn't look ashamed, defeated, or chagrined. What would he think if he knew the price she'd paid? What would anyone think?

If she had accepted the gating, her team would have performed well enough without her, but under no circumstance was she willing to miss a visit to College and the chance to see its library for herself. *Shakespeare, Plato, Swift, Aristotle*...concentrate. She had to concentrate or she'd miss a turn in her opponent's rebuttal. She couldn't lose now, not with him watching.

Demosthenes had indeed been a more formidable trial than Swift, especially when delivered by a Library keen to avenge a Lucky Dip. Astor had given no quarter, and it hurt to sit in chapel Friday evening. Saturday afternoon in the Hall, it hurt to sit down and it hurt to get up. Feeling the effects of his punishment while watching Charlie gracefully demolish the team before his, Jeremy feared he would be unable to contain his desire. If he couldn't see her alone that day, he doubted he'd be able to think straight again. No one ever told him love could feel like panic.

It was easier than he expected to slip away with her during the interval. Refreshments were served on the West Lawn, where several hedges gave way to doors, which led to passages, which led to staircases, which led to the library she so wished to see. She made him recite the names as she walked past each bust. *Shakespeare, Plato, Swift, Aristotle, Donne*...She paused at Demosthenes and ran her hand across the face of the Greek, caressing it until Jeremy thought he would burst.

"Was it a Demosthenes after all?" she asked.

"Sure," he said.

"Was it bad?"

"I didn't enjoy it."

"Is it always the cane?"

"Usually."

She resumed her inspection of the busts. "At our school, it's the slipper."

"Did you get caught?" he asked, the idea exploding in his mind like a slow-motion film of the atom bomb.

"Well," she said causally, "what do you expect?"

"How many did you get?" Surely she could hear the pounding of his heart, even across the room.

She ran a finger across the base of Milton and continued down the room. *Herbert, Johnson, Keble, Augustine, Pusey.* She stopped there and turned to him with an unfamiliar, lip-chewing expression. He could contain himself no longer. He strode down the hall, seized her wrists, and under the gaze of Dr. Pusey, he kissed her.

****

This story © Casey Morgan 2011

About the author:

Casey Morgan is a writer living in New York. caseymorgan.org or via email cdm@caseymorgan.org

What the Butler Saw

Jessica Davies

The bright afternoon sun shone through the small, high windows of a tiny, nondescript room, grey-painted, wooden floorboards, empty but for a row of bells mounted on a board, neatly labelled by name. The motes of dust in the dry, dead air floated serenely, sparkling in the strong sun like tiny diamonds. This was a place between two worlds, with a green baize door on one side of the room that led to the main house with no sound to be heard from beyond and on the other side a strong oak door that led to the servants quarters from which floated the noise of clattering pans and people talking and laughing.

A single bell on the board began to ring.

The noise increased exponentially as the oak door opened and a maid sallied forth from her kitchen lair, short, round and with a face as rosy as an apple. She glanced at the ringing bell.

"It's the Mistress" she muttered and rushed back through the door. A moment later, another maid came from the kitchen and through the green baize door to the house beyond it. This one was taller, slimmer, fairer of face and neat in demeanour with movements like quicksilver. The dust motes whirled and jumped as the wind of her passing disturbed them, before settling back into their slow dance to mark the march of the afternoon.

In another room, the sun shone into the long dining room, busy with footmen as they laid a long mahogany table, buffing glass, polishing cutlery and filling salt pots. The head gardener, neat in his apron but in stockinged feet so as not to drag mud on the Turkish carpet, arranged hothouse flowers to his satisfaction in two fantastic centrepieces. The first footman anxiously prowled the room, correcting a knife here, turning a glass there a fraction more

123

to the left. The air was one of suppressed excitement, because soon he would come to check their work. There must be no mistakes.

The sun had dropped beyond its zenith and was making its stately progress towards the west. It shone through the long windows of a bedroom, lighting the heavy red walls and temporarily lifting the somewhat sombre mood of the bedchamber which was all heavy mahogany tallboys and a massive four-poster bed. Here, the neat maid of earlier stood behind her Mistress, who was naked apart from her stays. The maid, Violet, was carefully brushing the long golden tresses and laboriously, one golden strand at a time, fastening them into rag paper to curl them. The only sound in the room was the tap… tap…tap…of the Mistresses' nails on the marble top of her dressing table. Then the silence broke.

"Ow! Be more careful!"

"Sorry Madam" came the conciliatory reply.

"If you can't be more careful, you can look for new employment" was the sharp reply. Then, with a brisk motion, she brought the ivory backed hairbrush round in a swift arc, catching her maid accurately and painfully on the knuckles, making her suppress a squeal of pain and drop a pin on the floor. She smiled at herself in the mirror, enjoying the chastened face behind her.

"Get on with it." she snapped.

The room was a careful symphony in the preparation of a woman for her public, with a full hip bath of rapidly cooling water, scattered with herbs, a fine cerulean blue dress ready on the bed, a locked jewellery box on the dressing table ready to spill its valuable secrets to the world.

"Is everything in hand below?" said the Mistress.

"I would think so Madam. Mr Mortimer is very thorough."

"Indeed."

"You can lie on the bed now Madam, to give the curl papers time to take. I'll bathe your face with rosewater in the meantime."

The Mistress made her way carefully to the bed and lay prone, wincing as the uncomfortable curl papers came into contact with the pristine satin coverlet. Tonight was an important night. Tonight, her new husband, The Honourable Hugh Maynard, would have to dinner the important and influential people who would decide whether or not he was the right kind of man to become the Member of Parliament for Aylesbury. Already a successful barrister, fourth son of an Earl, reasonably rich in his own right, but richer from his wife's dowry, he wanted public recognition and this nomination was the first step on the road that surely led to the office of the first Lord of the Treasury. Or at the very least, the Cabinet. Much hung on it. This his wife, the Honourable Constance Maynard, knew perfectly well. She'd seen enough dinners in her father's house to know how important a good hostess was in the advancement of her husband. Tonight would be her first test. And she was nervous.

In a small spare room on the ground floor of the house, a shaft of late-afternoon sunlight shone through a blood red-claret, held up to the light to check for imperfection and for residue. It was lowered and then lifted to the mouth of the man that held it. He tasted. He nodded. It would do very well.

This man was not tall, but imposing, with a lean strong frame, grey hair above a high brow and fine arched eyebrows, a stern face and a strong chin. He wore the clothes of a gentleman, a neat black striped coat from which snowy white cuffs peeked, a plain grey waistcoat and neat watch chain. Only a gaudy handkerchief on the wrong side of his chest marked him out as not a gentleman. Because he was not: this man was butler to the house and was known to all in the house from the Master to the lowest scullery maid as Mr Mortimer. If he has a first name, no one knew what it was or would have dared to call him by it.

Satisfied that the claret was what he had expected, he rang the bell to summon the still-room maid to the room to take the claret and Madeira barrels to the butler's pantry and then made his way to the dining room. As he passed along the entrance hall sunlight dappled his black suit, making him for a moment frivolous. But only for a moment, for frivolity was not in his nature, whatever nature itself might think about it.

As he entered the dining room, the chatter fell silent, hands redoubled their efforts, the Head Gardener impaled his thumb on a rose thorn, the first footman drew himself up for the inspection and a nervous new housemaid dropped a cruet dish to the floor with a clatter. All eyes swivelled to her, then swivelled back to Mr Mortimer for his reaction.

There was a pause.

"Pick up the dish Rose, wash it and then put it in its proper place. Look sharp." was all he said.

Mr Mortimer, focusing his attention like a wolf with a juicy doe in its sights, advanced on the table. There would be no mistakes here. This was his domain. There were never any mistakes. He made sure of that. He didn't suffer fools gladly and fools quickly found themselves disgraced and walking out of the gate. But he was a fair man. A genuine accident was overlooked once corrected. It was only the deliberate accident or a lack of consideration for one's duty that drew his wrath. This, after all was his house and he ran it to his lines. Nobody was allowed to forget this. Owners came and went. But the house and its traditions endured.

In the bedroom, Constance was now ready. The dying rays of the setting sun illuminated her golden hair and breathed fire into the diamonds at her throat. There was a small knock at the door and her husband's valet entered.

"Is he ready?"

"He is, Madam."

"When did he get back?"

"Around an hour ago."

Constance frowned. Then she understood.

"I take it he's been with Mrs Pomfrey?"

The valet looked embarrassed. Not at the fact that his Master had a mistress, a scarlet woman tucked away in a villa in St John's wood, but that his Master's wife knew about her and worst of all admitted to knowing about her. The talk in the servants quarters was all about the lack of propriety of the new Mrs Maynard, her boldness, her fondness for a drink, her lack of inhibition. How would the Master cope with her? By ignoring her, said the wiser heads. The Master was focused on two things, his career and his lady-friends. His wife was unimportant.

Constance took pity on the man who looked like an awkward schoolboy as he sought the words. "You don't need to explain. I'll be down in a moment. Tell Thomas to bring us both a glass of champagne in the drawing room."

"Yes Madam".

Constance looked at her reflection in the full-length mirror, noting without vanity her long golden hair now arranged in pretty curls, her full, womanly figure with its narrow waist and generous hips and bosom, her deep blue eyes the colour of a gentian, her milky-white skin.

Frustration flooded her as she chafed against the restrictions of her position. This was no marriage, to be so disrespected by her husband who, regardless of his behaviour, expected her to perform like a puppy whenever he called. But she had little choice. It was her role to fulfil and one which she was expected to perform.

The sun slipped below the hills, leaving only the pink and blue light of dusk; not dark, but not day, a strange light that smacked of anticipation. And as the light dimmed, the house lit up like a Christmas tree, windows blazing with light. The house was ready.

In the drawing room, they were met with the champagne and Mr Mortimer came personally to pour it for them. He had noticed the dangerous *froideur* developing between his Master and Mistress, but, good servant that he was; it was not his place to comment. But he did observe. Observation was his job and he was very good at it. His own opinion, had it been canvassed, was that the Master was a weak man, and used to giving way: an understandable habit in the youngest son in a family of boys. Mrs Maynard, by contrast, was the eldest and used to ruling the roost over seven sisters. So the Master, rather than tame her, let her go her own way, becoming wilder and wilder like a horse in need of a curb.

He poured her a second glass and shook his head slightly. Her taste for champagne was well-known and understandable, but this was an important evening. Ever discreet, he withdrew. He had work to do.

Dinner was in progress and going well. The twenty guests were convivial, influential and expansive. The dinner was delicious and the staff seamless, a balletic procession of service moving with perfect precision. From his eyrie at the sideboard, Mr Mortimer watched. The Master and Mistress sat at opposite ends of the table, she with one of her old beaux, now the Member of Parliament for Middlesex, on her right. They were intimate together as she all but ignored the man on her left, and as he signalled for her glass to be refilled again and again, they grew gradually louder and more careless. Mr Mortimer frowned. He was not close enough to hear their whispered conversation. But Mrs Maynard's next words dropped into one of those inexplicable lulls in conversation. She had perfect clear diction and her musical voice rang like a bell into the sudden silence.

"Oh yes, my husband is a dreadful dullard. His mistress only finds him interesting because of size of his monetary endowment, it's the only endowment he has of any decency!"

Silence.

A nervous titter from one of the younger ladies, whilst an older matron snapped open her fan with the sound and fervour of a gunshot. An elderly gentleman with a seat in the House of Lords who was also an avid member of his parish council choked on his wine. Mr Mortimer watched as the Master's face turned white and his wife flushed an ugly, unbecoming red.

And that was where Mr Maynard's hopes of a parliamentary seat drifted away like leaves on the water. This was, after all, a decent, God-fearing crowd. They all understood that adultery was rampant in their midst. It was just *terribly* bad form to talk about it. And from a lady's mouth! Shocking!

The marital row that followed the guests' departure was audible all over the ground floor, because Mrs Maynard used her musical voice to scream like a virago at her husband. No, she was not sorry. No she did not care. He had no regard for her feelings. She would not be his puppet. It would be over her dead body!

Mr Mortimer, stationed in the hall to divert any maids trying to eavesdrop, brooded. This would not do. It was not what he ran his house for. He would have to make a stand.

Constance sat at her dressing table and rested her head in her hands. It was spinning from anger and drink and her corset was uncomfortable against her stomach after the rich meal. What could she do? Hugh would probably never speak to her again. *"I don't care"* she thought defiantly.

The knock at the door startled her.

"Come in!"

Mr Mortimer opened the door and came inside, shutting it gently behind him. The lock clicked.

"Madam."

"What's the problem Mr Mortimer?" She always called him that, never just plain Mortimer. She wouldn't have dreamed of it. She knew his value, as did he.

He didn't beat about the bush. He never did. "I regret Madam, that tonight, you were the problem. You let us down. You disgraced us, your husband, your staff, your house – everyone."

Constance was scarcely able to believe her ears. "Do I hear you correctly Mr Mortimer? Are you, a mere employee, criticising me, your Mistress? I assume you are drunk, to speak to me in this manner. How dare you!"

His face was impassive. "This is my house *Madam* and I won't have it disgraced by a chit of a girl. You, *Madam* need to develop a little bit of discipline and self-restraint. I think you need to learn how."

With a swift movement he advanced on her and grabbed her by the wrist, his hand tightening with an iron grip, drawing her towards him. She struggled and tried to pull away, gasping with shock, flailing at him with her free hand, her pretty nails scratching at his hands and neck.

Moving methodically, with no undue sign of exertion, he transferred his grip to her golden hair, yanking it hard, and forced her over the end of her own bed using his hand on her neck and his knee on her back to pin down her wildly flailing figure. Then with his free hand he hauled up the blue silk and the light petticoats and brought his hand down on her drawers with a tremendous slap.

Constance screamed her outrage, and received another hard spank.

"How dare you!"

"Oh, I dare Madam"

Then, grimly (although not blind to the delectable sight of her snow white bottom peeking through the open back of her drawers) he methodically started to spank her, his hand heavy, drawing shrieks from his Mistress as she attempted to kick and bite.

"Do you want to be tied down?" he asked.

"No!" she wailed.

"Then have a little dignity for heaven's sake. This is something that you deserve and you'll get a whole lot more if you keep misbehaving!"

He started to spank her again, his hand slamming down on her, hard and fast. She kicked, choked, whined and then burst into a flurry of sobs throughout which he kept spanking, ignoring her laboured gasps for breath. Eventually, the pain of the spanking and the humiliation of the tears was just too much and she lay limp, weeping into her coverlet. Her mind raced as she lay sobbing. How could she, the Mistress of the house be treated this way by a servant? And yet....and yet....something deep inside yearned for the strong hands, wanted the reins to be drawn tight. She felt ashamed.....

"I'm soooorryyyy...." Once the words were out, they didn't seem so terrible.

He stopped and gently stroked her hair. She lay still, allowing him to caress her head.

"That's better. You've been a very naughty girl, haven't you?"

"Yes." she said quietly.

"You deserve a harsh lesson."

It was like being back with her tutor. "Yes" she said, slowly and reluctantly. He was right. She didn't hate her husband. He disappointed her, but what had she expected from an arranged marriage? Love? Intimacy? Eroticism? "I've been very naughty."

"Reach behind you and pull your drawers apart properly. I want to see the whole of your bottom."

Blushing, chewing on her lower lip, she reached aside and pulled her drawers open. Her glorious rear sprang into view. Full and firm, peppered with red marks from his earlier spanking, it was a beautiful sight. Sitting on the side of her bed, her drew her over his lap and she went willingly, balancing herself on her arms and knees, pushing up her bottom into the optimum position for a spanking. He watched her wriggles with wry amusement.

"Does this bring back memories?"

She was silent, still chewing her lip. They both knew the answer was yes. Slowly, he raised his hand and started to spank her again, firmly, then gradually growing harder with each slap. The hand that was so delicate when decanting claret felt like it was made of iron as it smacked hard onto her naked flesh, which grew rosier with each whack. At first she remained silent, willingly raising her bottom to meet his hand. But as the pain grew and the smacks became harder she started to wriggle, her legs, at first demurely together, drifting apart, giving him a wonderful view of her delicate parts, which even he could see were growing as rosy as her bottom. He paused to thrust his hand between her legs, teasing his fingers between the soft lips and seeking out her centre of pleasure, circling his dextrous fingers on her clitoris, teasing her labia – and then, with a meaningful thrust, penetrated her pussy with a firm finger, causing her to arch like a cat and thrust herself back on his questing fingers.

"Oh no Madam" he said. "I'm afraid we'll have none of that yet. Stand up."

She stood, her skirts falling about her feet and temporarily restoring her to decency. Her eyes were downcast and she still blushed with confusion and passion. Drawing her to him, he unbuttoned her dress as easily as her maid would, allowing it to pool on the floor, her petticoats following, then…and oh how she blushed…her drawers until she stood before him in her corset, cerulean blue like her eyes, and her white stockings and little slippers. He ran his eyes over her, assessing.

"I see my Master made himself a fine bargain. Perhaps if he made use of his property more often, she might not be quite so wilful…."

Gripping her hair again, he led her to the chaise-longue and bent her over it. Her bottom was now the highest part of her. From his pocket, he drew a thick leather razor strop. "Oh no" she protested, attempting to rear up.

"No Madam. You deserve as sound a flogging as I ever gave a girl and by God, you will get it. You'll rue the day you made a commotion in my house." Quickly undoing his tie, he rapidly bound her wrists together, running the other end under the leg of the chaise-longue. She was stretched out, her bottom tight and waiting for the strap to descend. She gave a tiny whimper of fear.

Mr Mortimer smiled.

Then, with a swish that made her jump like a nervous mare, he brought the strap down hard across her backside, making her yowl with pain. A second stroke followed, then a third. She kicked her legs and he strapped her sharply across the calves.

"Keep your control Madam and keep those legs down."

And keep them down she did. The strap rose and fell with regularity, each stroke sounding like a pistol shot in the candlelit room. Methodically and firmly, he covered her bottom with red and purple welts and when her bottom could take no more he moved onto her tender thighs, wealing them from bottom to knee despite her squeals and protests for mercy. But despite the yells, it was unquestionably true that Constance was much aroused by her harsh treatment.

"Spread your legs nice and wide for me Madam"

She obeyed with alacrity. Would he make love to her? Suddenly, she longed for a cock, knowing that her rare nights in Hugh's bed were worth the waiting for. His hand stroked her bottom.....she arched towards his hand....and then the strap came down on the delicate white flesh of her inner thighs, provoking such a scream that it was a wonder no member of staff came running to their Mistress's aid. But none did, because all over the great house the staff knew that Mr Mortimer was dealing with a matter. And deal with it he would.

The tawse came down again on her inner thighs and then continued to strap her until her head was just one huge sensation of pain. But deep inside, she knew she deserved it and she welcomed the discipline he provided.

He flogged her without mercy until she lay limp and almost senseless, broken and obedient.

A pause.

He removed his jacket, fussily folding it onto a chair, followed by his waistcoat and shirt. Turning her head, she could see he was lean and muscular under his clothes. A charge of lust ran through her. He casually unbuttoned his breeches and she knew what he intended to do. But she yearned for it, yearned for him to take her. He moved behind her and she whimpered.

"Do you want something, my little slut?" he teased.

Wordlessly, she thrust herself at him. He pretended not to understand until she cried out with frustration for him to take her.

"Oh no Madam," he whispered. "I can tell you're greedy for pleasure. But you've been a very naughty girl and naughty girls don't deserve pleasure. Besides, it's not for me to sully the spot where my Master takes his pleasure."

She felt his hands on her bottom cheeks, drawing them apart, exposing her most secret hole to him. She cowered away, for never had she been taken in that place. But then his finger started to tease the shy hole, dipping in and out of it whilst other fingers played with her wet pussy. She revelled in the sensation of the forbidden pleasure as he worked the juice from her pussy into the tight hole of her anus. Then she felt his cock press against her and his hands grip her hips.

"Don't be too hard…." she whimpered.

"This is a punishment fuck Madam. It will be as hard as you deserve." With that, he thrust forward, filling her back passage to the hilt with his stiff cock as she yowled with shock. Then he began to work her properly, his cock moving roughly in and out. He gloried in the sensation of both the pleasure and the power as he fucked his Mistress's bottom, revelling in the exquisite tightness of the passage, until he could bear it no longer and with a groan of pleasure, he exploded into her rear, filling her with his cum as she writhed and moaned and begged for her own release. He rested against her trembling, yearning back.

"Not until I say you may, Madam" was all he said.

She whimpered her acquiescence.

Outside the room, Hugh Maynard rose from his knees, smiling with satisfaction. He would, he thought grimly, have no more trouble from his wife. She, like every other female in this house, would be perfectly obedient to Mr Mortimer. He pressed a hand to the front of his trousers, enjoying the sensation that it caused. The sight of his wife's naked rear impaled on Mr Mortimer's cock had excited him greatly. Luckily the pliant Violet, his wife's maid was waiting in his bed for him to slake his lust.

He smiled grimly. He had no pretentions as to who the Master of the house was.

Nor, now, did his wife.

****

About the author:

Jessica has just hit her thirties and lives in London with her lovely dominant husband, He-Who-Must-Be-Obeyed. She has been into the wonderful world of BDSM since leaving rural Wales for university and discovering that there was life beyond sheep and farming.

Jessica and He-Who-Must-Be-Obeyed live a life of unreserved hedonism, exploring everything from smacked bottoms to electric shocks – all in the name of pleasure. They also inhabit several different time periods – not because they are Dr Who – but because they enjoy roleplay and get excited about history. Not being the jealous types, they both have different partners and playmates of both sexes, which leads to a wonderful merry-go-round of spanking, submission and sex.

Jessica firmly believes that whilst good girls go to heaven, bad girls go everywhere. In her ten years on the scene, she has explored enough to make your eyes pop, whilst maintaining that she still has a long way to go and a lot to learn. Anybody who thinks they can help her with her quest is welcome to contact her via Fawcett Hall (fawcetthall.co.uk) or at Rapunzel@Fawcetthall.co.uk.

*And singing in choirs

Knock-knock-knockin' on Mr Batts' Door

Zille Defeu

She looked at the door in front of her, and decided not to knock on it. What was she thinking? What the hell was she doing? What would her friends think if they caught her coming here, coming here of her own volition?

She could lie, and say Mr Batts had summonsed her here. But then she'd have to make up some trouble she'd been in to have warranted it. And that was the thing. The first time Mr Batts had insisted she come to his room after school, she *had* been in trouble – but she'd been very careful not to get in trouble (or at least not to get caught!) ever since.

Then why had she been to the caretaker's room twice since then? And now, a third time … each time it became slightly harder to deal with the turmoil in her own mind. The first time, she hadn't even really had any conscious thought about it – she just found herself in front of the door, knocking, The second time, it was after weeks of torment, fighting a lure she couldn't explain to herself, that if she thought about confused her, disgusted her. And the same this time, but worse, stronger, more insistent. Instead of learning her lesson and staying far away, it was only a matter of time before she found herself looking down the hallway to the caretaker's door, feeling the inexplicable urge to go and knock on it.

But this time – no, she would turn away, and go find Laurel to do some studying with. Or maybe Nicola, to do one of her workout DVDs together.

Resolved, she turned around and almost got away. But at the end of the hall she stopped, and found herself again being pulled back to Mr Batts' door. She might as well knock, and get it over with. Once it was done, she would be safely appalled with herself –

with the whole situation – and, well, satisfied, in some terrible way, for some weeks to follow. On the whole, best to just get it done and out of her mind, for a while.

And that's how she found the strength to lift up her hand and knock....

He was quick answering the door. There was Mr Batts, peering down at her from eyes topped with over-grown, bushy eyebrows, a bit like an owl. "Ah, Edith. What brings you 'ere? No, no, I'm not busy, come in, come in."

Now, she really regretted knocking. And knew she'd be regretting it worse, shortly. But at least now it was out of her hands. Mr Batts could – and would – steer the rest of this dreadful situation through its conclusion. Oh, best not to *think* of the conclusion....

"Well, you're just in good time, Edith, as I've got the kettle on. I'll 'ave a cuppa tea for us in a tick." The kettle popped, and he kept talking, as he made two teas, in chipped mugs which wore the stains from years of tannin saturation. "Now, then, Edith, 'ave you got youself in a spot of bother? That why you've come to see me, eh? You in trouble again? "

It was just once she'd actually been in trouble – but from the way he'd made it sound, she was the sort of girl who'd be asking him to help sort out problems several times a week. But there was just that *one* time – and it wasn't like she was the only girl who'd ever flirted, a bit, with older guys. It's just that then one of them wouldn't leave her alone, was actually *stalking* her, and all the girls said that if you got into trouble, the best thing to do would be to ask "Old Batty" to help you, because he was the one you could really go to for help at Chasforth College.

However, Mr Batts did exact his price. He would make your problems go away. *But.* But he would need to "assure himself" that you learned your lesson from the situation. "Discipline," he would say, "is what you young ladies need. There's no need for a girl to get in trouble, and suffer consequences. No, I take care of you girls – you lot all deserve to have someone looking out for you! But I can't just have you thinking you can get off scot free, can I? You wouldn't learn your lesson then, would you? No, a bit of discipline's what's called for. That'll fix everything up, right as rain, that will! Best of both worlds, really, that!"

"Best of both worlds." Edith could seriously see the irony in that. It was quite obvious that the person who had the best outcome in these situations was Mr Batts. But she really couldn't complain, because her problem with that stalker guy had magically disappeared. On the other hand, she was left with a whole new problem. First there was the matter of satisfying Mr. Batts that she'd learned her lesson. But then, there was the rather worse problem that she kept returning to his doorstep....

"No, Mr Batts, sir – I'm not really in any trouble...." And that was all she had to say. If she couldn't explain to *herself* why she had returned like some pathetic homing pigeon, it was extremely unlikely she could explain it to *him*.

"Ahhh, I see, Edith, yes I do." Did he? *Did he?* And if he understood this, was that somehow worse? "You 'ave some more trouble with discipline. Wise of you, young lady, to come back to Old Batts. Very wise. Finished with your tea?" No, she'd faked having a couple sips, but her tummy was in no state for having anything put into it. "Well then, good enough. Let's have you over here, now, young Edith...."

And Mr Batts, sitting on his battered old settee, gestured her over from the uncomfortable upright chair beside the small table that held the kettle, tea caddy, and (chipped) sugar bowl. She froze, unable to take the next step towards the inevitable.

"Alright now Edith, I know it's not pleasant, but let's not make it worse than it has to be. Show me you remember what I taught you last time about discipline, and I can go a bit easier on you, can't I?"

It was a lie. Well, a bit of misdirection. He'd find some excuse to *not* go easier on her, she knew that from experience. But she clung to it like some great shining truth, to make it possible to become unstuck from the chair, and move over to him.

Mr Batts said, "Good girl, Edith," and helped her over his lap. It was humiliating – there was no graceful way to do this. And also, up until this time, the wall of space that existed between student and teacher had been safely in place. This broke that safe wall, crashed it right down. Suddenly, her space was not her own anymore. And would not be until he was done with her.

He fished out a plimsoll from between sofa cushions, like it was a lost remote. Very handy, how he stored it in there, ready for the next unfortunate girl. Or ready for *her*, again. She remembered all too well how this felt on her bottom, and shuddered.

"Now we'll just be 'aving this up," and she felt Mr Batt's rough hands tugging her skirt over her hips, tucking her shirt-tails up underneath the folds of grey fabric.

"You've heard me talk of discipline and such before, young Edith, so I won't draw this out. You just consider what I've said previously, while I give you a firm reminder...."

And the plimsoll slapped down, sharp and painful even through her knickers. Indeed, her knickers were no protection at all, only a veneer of safety, a façade of privacy and some small amount of control.

And down the plimsoll rained, with only a brief pause when her flailing right arm was caught and pulled up behind her back, and then again when her flailing legs were trapped snugly under one of his own. She squealed and gasped and cried out in little wordless noises, but Mr Batts' room was down a long and mostly empty corridor, with the music practice rooms at one end, so her being overheard was most unlikely. And, she did have some pride. Or at least, she tried to have.

The deluge of sharp smacks turned her whole bottom and upper thighs into a burning, swollen-feeling area. She was panting, out of breath, when he finally stopped. She collapsed, pride forgotten in a moment of relief, but she knew with dread that it was not really, *really* over.

"Now, m'girl, I do have some worries from last time you were 'ere. I think I should just check on that situation, and see if there's any improvement—" She started to gasp, "No!" and try to squirm out of his grasp, but he was too quick, and his fingers had slid down her bottom, and were rubbing the fabric in-between her legs, the fabric that, inevitably, was embarrassingly damp.

"Oh dear, oh dear. You still having *that* problem, are we, m'girl? We've 'ad to 'ave a talk about this each time you've been in 'ere. That's very *tarty* that is, not lady-like at all. Still, I 'ope it's not as bad as it's been—" and with that, the questing fingers slid in the side of her gusset, and one insinuated itself inside her – and it didn't find much resistance; even though Edith had never had more than fingers in there, she was well slicked-up.

She moaned in shame, and buried her face in the cushion. This next part was even *worse* than the slippering, in some ways.

"Well, well, this is not a good sign, m'girl, not a good sign at all." His finger slid in and out of her, and at first it was easy to make the noises ones of protest and dismay, but all too soon they started sounded rather confused with noises of pleasure and gratification. "See, girl, this is not how a young lady like you should be reacting. It's this sort of thing that will give men the wrong impression, like with that lad I had to help *discourage*. This sort of thing is what you'd expect from a scrubber, and that won't help you at all, m'girl, will it? You need to learn to control yourself, you do, or men'll take advantage of you."

His finger slid in and out, and curved upwards, the tip moving right over the part of her core which made her eyes roll back in her head. There was no way he could miss the spasms in the muscles which surrounded his finger, grabbing onto it eagerly, wanting more, more, more, not wanting to let that deeply pleasuring digit – which was at the same time that horribly invasive, unwelcome thing – and yet somehow the contradiction just made the pleasure al the stronger.

She knew from various classes over the years that she was having a normal physical response, at least to that specific stimulation. Everything else was just Mr Batts' funny old-fashioned ideas. But still, she *was* very embarrassed by it all, and his talk of shame and disgrace just made the fireworks go off more explosively. In the moment, she *did* feel all that shame. And indeed, she felt a different sort of shame for returning to Mr Batts' room even once more than she'd absolutely had to. But they both sort of, well, made things more intense.

Those things Mr Batts were saying had melted into a background sound of, "Hmph- hmph- hmph- shame- hpmh- disgrace- hpmh- you- should- be- ashamed- you- lady- hmph- not- the- sort- of- thing- hmph" etc. While she was cresting those waves, thinking straight wasn't an option. There was just a rush of embarrassment and a sense of feeling out-of-control, and then there was just *sensation*.

Of course, there was *one* sensation that she couldn't avoid. It had started during the slippering. It involve the increase of pressure under her stomach, something getting bigger and harder every minute. She knew what it was. And it was gross ... yet, well, it also added to everything else, making things that much more intense.

Again, she flopped in exhaustion when he stopped, pride evaporated for a moment while she got her breath back. But Mr Batts didn't give her long to recover.

"Well, Edith m'girl, I must say I'm quite disappointed, I am. You don't seem to have learned any self-control from our previous sessions. It's on to stronger disciplinary medicine for you, girl."

And there it was. She knew he'd never let her off without this. Still, she didn't have to do much. She was so flustered by both the slippering and the invasive, so very *intense* bit, that he had her up off his lap, and she was teetering unsteadily while he got up, gruffly instructing her, "Over the arm of me settee, m'girl."

She froze, again. Each stage just got *worse*, in its own way. She knew what was coming – she'd been here before – why, she asked herself, was she *back*?

Mr Batts moved her into place, admonishing her about discipline the whole while. "Bend on over, young Edith," he instructed, waited a few seconds, and then, "Bend over, young lady! Now!"

Finally she forced herself to move without thought, most decidedly *not* thinking about how she looked with her bottom jutting out as the bent down at a sharp angle over the high arm of the sofa, her face between her hands on the cushion. She continued not thinking about the sight she made as Mr Batts replaced her skirt up around her waist and then, with rough fingers tugged her knickers down to her thighs. She tried not to listen to him, either, but already knew what he would say, "This is just the sort of thing a scrubber can expect, Edith. You don't want to end up like this, do you? 'Course not! That's why your Mr Batts is here to help. Shows you the shame of it now, gives you a whiff of the humiliation. But you're safe of course, safe with 'Old Batty'. "

"But now's the time for the real discipline, girl. I'd hoped a taste of the plimsoll would be enough for you, but there's nought for it but the belt." Indeed, she could hear – *trying not to* – the sound of the leather sliding through the fabric loops at his waist. It flexed silently in his hands, but the last time, she'd opened her eyes – which were well closed now – and burned into her memory was the sight of the well-worn leather being bent in half.

Mr Batts continued discussing her disappointing tendency to slutty ways, and how he hoped this taste of discipline would wake her up, give her something to think about. Actually, she was hoping it would put to bed her incomprehensible urges to end up in the position, would keep her from thinking about it again. He started talking about the shame she should be feeling, bent over, with her naked bottom all exposed like that.

She found it doubly mortifying because she knew he was holding forth on the topic while he got in a good eyeful of her – and she knew how much she showed in this position, now, because she'd tried it in front of a mirror. She'd nearly *died* when she realized he could see *everything* when she was bent over that like. Yet, still, here she was again.

And then, with an always startling *crack*, the belt landed, burning its impact across both cheeks. She buried her face in the cushion. She never made a peep at the first one – she was always a bit too much in shock. For the later whacks, she shoved her face as hard as it could go into the cushion, and it helped muffle the sounds she couldn't help but make.

Crack, again, and unlike the slippering, this pain went straight *through* her whole body. Somehow, she flailed less during the strapping – she held on with a death grip, instead, because it was that or fall over.

Again and again, the pain shot through her whole self, as the belt painted red stripes which would be slowly fading off her for at least a week. She'd have to be careful when changing her clothes, and take showers when no one else was around.

That thought had distracted her from her grim focus in holding on to herself, and a very low crack of the belt caught her off guard. She could not handle the pain of that stroke, and well before she had herself under control, the next *thwack* had tears starting to make lines down her face, echoing the lines being etched on her bottom. They started slow, and then, as the pain continued uncontrollable, inexorable, she began sobbing. Not crying, but sobbing, from a place deep, so deep inside her.

Mr Batts got in another nine good whacks before he stopped. The first time, he stopped when she started sobbing. But since she'd started returning to his room, each time he'd kept going just a bit longer while she sobbed. In the moment, she just wanted it to end, and knowing it would be a bit longer this time, an unknown amount longer, was terrifying. But, later, when she was *not* thinking about it, not thinking about it at all, she'd remember the strokes given as she sobbed more than anything that came before. It was like those were the ones that really counted.

Of course, she'd also remember what came after. It was hard to forget that, as much as she'd try.

He hadn't just taken the belt off, earlier. The first time she'd peeked back at him, maybe when her eyes had burst open in shock at a particularly painful stroke, and seen the shocking sight of his … *thing* … sticking straight out from the fly of his trousers, obscenely prominent against the battered dark grey work trousers.

Now she knew not to look, to keep facing forward no matter what, or to hide her face in the cushion of the sofa, pretending that she didn't know what was about to happen. Her bottom was still well up in the air, just like Mr Batts preferred. She might have rocked a little forwards and backwards with the thrust of the belt-whacks, but she'd mostly stayed in position. Sometimes her foot

143

would have kicked up – as much a reaction as when the doctor thumps your knee with that funny triangular rubber hammer – but she always put it right back down. And once she started sobbing, she really had just gone still, limp in some ways, but still holding in position like it was her life-line.

He'd stopped. But she kept sobbing. It was safest that way. If she was crying, he wouldn't expect her to talk, to give consent to What Came Next. That she returned to knock on his door, that she acquiesced each time to all of it, that she stayed in position at this very moment was a consent of sorts (consent enough for him, and almost too much consent for her) and it was another thing to spend time and effort seriously *not* considering.

"Right, m'girl. Now you know what's next. The final bit of discipline. This is for your own good, inn' it? This is the sort of thing what happens to little slags, takin' it like this, and you'd best get used to it if you're going to keep up this sort of wanton behaviour."

As he spoke, his hands grabbed for her hips. He'd a bottle of some sort of lotion somewhere, and his right hand was greasy with the stuff. More importantly, so was his ... his thing. Which was now pressing up against a most embarrassing spot, a spot she now knew was really shown off by the way she was bent over.

From that initial shock of contact from the hard smooth thing pressing resting against her, it built fast into pressure, pressure and a sensation almost like burning, as he thrust his way inside her. She felt the pressure, pressure and then the sudden "pop" of penetration. Then more pressure, pressure ... each millimetre experienced intensely.

"See, m'girl, this is the kind of rough business what happens to girls when men find out she's no better than she ought to be. Take – *this* – as a lesson. Remember how you're feeling *now* next time you feel a bit of tingle 'tween your legs. Old Batts is givin' you your lesson now, he is!"

The words helped. She could loose herself in the humiliation of them, the story he built – his excuse and hers. He couldn't say he liked spanking and buggering the student body (or at least some

144

of the bodies) of Chasforth College. And she couldn't say she thought about, dreamed about it, *needed* it, and had come back for more. So she held onto Old Batty's myth of the over-sexed young lady needing her discipline to set her on the straight and narrow.

After the initial sensations of his imposing himself inside her, things settled down to a combination of exquisite discomfort, with occasional shocks of intensity, almost like the strapping, yet even more *within* her.

Mr Batts had stopped talking, and was now panting. She was panting, too. He was almost done, although that itself entailed the final humiliation of knowing he was pouring himself out inside her. It was in the condom, yes, but he had *done it* inside her, anyway.

She took the final humiliation with a gasp.

The first time had set the pattern – she stayed bent over (the first time, too stunned to move) while he cleaned himself up and tucked himself away. When he told her – with gruff tenderness – to "get up and fix yourself up," she'd see him standing there, as if nothing had happened.

Once she had her knickers up over her smarting, aching bottom, skirt smoothed, he clap a hand down on her shoulder, as if no more intimate touching had ever occurred. "I hope that settles things for you, young Edith. Everything's put straight, eh? You come back and see me if you need m'help again. I'm here to help you girls."

"Oh, I don't think I'll need it, again, Mr Batts." What she always said. And then, sotto voce, "Thank you, sir." And she fled that room.

She absolutely wasn't going to think about what had happened. Again. And she was never going back there. This time she really meant it. Really. No, really! But she was already thinking, "What if, next time…."

♦♦♦♦

This story © Zille Defeu 2011

About the author:

Zille Defeu is a kinky American Anglophile who was brought over from the BDSM world to the spanko world thanks to the wonderful Janus and Blushes magazines, given to her by the man she later married. She documents her spanking adventures with both words and pictures at her blog: <u>zilledefeu.com</u>

That Charming, Disarming Man
William & Catherine

Richard's Diary
14th June

First day back in London! Staying in David's flat with his daughter Catherine. Haven't seen her since she was 14 and she seems to have grown up into a really good looking girl and quite fun company too, I think, based on less than half a day spent with her! Saw her briefly en route from bedroom to bathroom for a shower and she certainly has a nice looking body – she might have sensed I was looking too as she sort of hitched her towel further round her in case I saw any of her bottom (I didn't...more's the pity!).

I'll certainly be keeping a close eye on C while I'm here. I always did think she was a girl that looked like she needed a bit of discipline, the few times I met her – maybe a chance will present itself while I am here? She said she has a boyfriend (Jake? I think) – maybe I'll try the angle of asking her one or two innocent yet personal questions and see if I get a blush from her! She was still tidying up the flat when I arrived today from some drinking session she'd had with him and his friends last night – maybe I'll teasingly ask her if she always lives such a dissolute life or something.

I'll go to the British Library tomorrow and start to plan out my research for the book. Can't wait to get going finally on it after so many delays. (I wonder what C will say when she finds out that I'm writing a book on underground Victorian erotica..no doubt she will want to know what I am working on at some point!).

Time now to finish unpacking. Perhaps I'll leave my two hairbrushes and the tawse accidentally on purpose on top of the chest of drawers and see if they get moved at all while I am out tomorrow!

Catherine's Diary
17ᵗʰ June

I've not written in this diary for ages but I need somewhere to put down these thoughts! Dad's friend Richard, the one he went to University with, but who moved to the States, is staying here for 6 weeks. When Dad said he had offered him the room here I didn't want to make a fuss, as it is Dad's flat after all and I'm very lucky (as all my friends keep telling me!) to have the use of such a lovely central flat in London, so near to Uni too. Also, I have met Richard a few times, maybe not since my early teens, but I'd always remembered him as being fun and charming, a bit like Dad really.

But, there is something about him! I don't know what it is yet but it is really unnerving. There is a way he looks at me, the way he just glanced a little too long as I crossed the landing the other morning wrapped in my towel. I felt so self-conscious all of sudden, which is so unlike me. The look in his eyes made me feel like my towel was invisible so I tightened my grip around it and scurried in to the bedroom. The oh-so-cool-and-collected Catherine that saunters confidently past the rowdy college boys when I am in the student bar seems to have disappeared around him.

Then this afternoon I came home early from college and tidied up a bit before planning to get down to some study. Richard had left out some of his washing on the balcony to dry so I thought I'd be helpful and tidy it away, folding it up and taking it in to his room. And that was 3 hours ago, I still haven't got any studying done, because I've been sat here turning over in my mind what I saw. It would be normal for someone to have a hairbrush amidst their belongings, but not a women's hairbrush and not two. And there was something else beside them. A leather thing, which I thought was maybe a belt curled up but it wasn't, it was like a strap. All 3 things were layed out on the chest of drawers, almost on display. Maybe he collects women's hairbrushes? Maybe he just prefers them to use ? But the strap in particular, I had to Google it. I literally typed in to Google "hairbrushes & straps" and the first thing that came up was "The Urban Dictionary of Spanking"… spanking??!

So, 3 hours later I am still sat here, wondering why I have been thinking about that word, those objects, Richard, the way he looked at me, and now I am late for meeting Jake and totally behind on my study.

Richard's Diary
19th June

A VERY interesting day...! At the British Library, I found some unexpected and very useful correspondence about Mayfair brothels in the papers of Lord Wilmingshurst – a gentleman with a taste for exchanging details of his visits to such establishments with a small circle of other members of the nobility including (amazingly) the wife of the then Foreign Secretary!

Matters concerning my "hostess" in the flat, Catherine, have also taken a very pleasing turn! Yesterday evening, I arrived back after a full day at the BL to find her looking rather glamorous in a vintage frock and about to go out for dinner and then onto a party. I took the opportunity to ask her, in a deliberately semi-serious, semi-teasing manner whether she shouldn't be spending the evening at home catching up on her studies instead and she blushed quite distinctly and shot me quite a fierce glance for a split second but then laughed it off by saying "Yeah..you're probably right but Jake says there's going to be at least two Oscar nominees at the party so I'm NOT going to miss that!".

After she'd gone out I made myself a light supper in the kitchen and I saw that she'd left a load of her laundry in the washing machine. Not wanting it to be left all damp in the machine overnight, I took it out and hung the clothes on the airer. This gave me an excellent opportunity to examine Catherine's taste in underwear as there were three or four bras and several pairs of pants in the washing. I was pleasantly surprised to find that she is certainly not a thongs girl: there were three pairs of boy shorts and the same again in full-cut cotton briefs (two pairs white and one duck egg blue, for the record!). I decided to advance my little game with her a stage further by leaving a note for her on the kitchen table. This read:

> "Naughty girl!! Not only do you go out to a party when you should be studying but you leave your washing in the machine! Smacked bottom for you I think! Pleased to see that you like to wear proper pants though...Richard x"

One other straw in the wind is that I am pretty sure Catherine DID see the hairbrushes and the tawse where I left them out in my room as the brushes were swapped over on the chest of drawers from where I had left them...all very intriguing!

Catherine's Diary
20ᵗʰ June

It's 1am and truth be told I'm a little be tipsy, but dear diary, I really don't think I have had that many glasses of wine to be hallucinating, as much as I wish I were. There is a note here from Richard that I've re-read about 1200 times just to check it does actually say what it does. For a start he called me a naughty girl... GIRL?!... nobody calls me a girl, I'm a 22 year old woman.

He had also taken my washing out of the machine and hung my underwear out neatly in a line on the airer. Not only did he see my underwear (this wouldn't actually have particularly phased me in the past) but he commented on it like he'd been inspecting it with a certain consideration. Just the thought of him caring that much about my underwear makes me feel a bit flustered and there's something wholly disarming about him now knowing what underwear I may have on.

But worst of all he actually wrote the words... "smacked bottom"... which means he must have imagined smacking my bottom....almost too embarrassing a thought to have written here. And who thinks a 22 year old woman deserves a smacked bottom? I am FAR too old for that.

It should be that simple really. Of course he knows I am too old to have my bottom smacked. Of course he is not planning on actually doing that. My intermittent feelings of outrage can be surpassed knowing he is probably just teasing and it's all in a harmless light way. Maybe it's even some kind of American humour he has picked up after all these years in the States.

So why is it not that simple. My head is telling me to be outraged or to take it lightly but my tummy is turning and I've been blushing constantly since I came home from the party (and I really know that neither of these things are cider-induced)....

I'm in utter conflict. Why am I blowing this up out of all proportion? Why is there something about his taking an interest in my studying versus partying that I kind of like (I hope he never reads that!). I've mostly got by in life so far getting away with the odd thing, on the whole Dad's always trusted me to be responsible and I've honoured that. But right now I am liking Richard pulling me up on something, nobody has ever done that before. I think most of all though it is just the very matter-of-fact way he seems to have asserted himself in that role, and that tone of voice I can just imagine it as I reread the words on his note.....

Okay, I have to go to bed and try and sleep. Right now though I'd say my only plan is to never ever leave my bedroom or certainly make sure that if I do so in the morning it will be when I'm absolutely sure he has left the building! I don't think I'll ever be able to face him again....

Richard's Diary
21st June

Writing this at 5.30pm waiting for Catherine to come home from her afternoon at university (she had a supervision with her tutor this afternoon). What a day so far...

Of course I couldn't wait to find out her reaction this morning to the note I left for her last night. She didn't get home before I retired to bed so I mentally made a note of that as a further reason to embarrass her and (who knows!) to punish her when I next saw her. I didn't have to go into the BL until later on this morning so I was able to wait until Catherine was up (no doubt she was hoping I had already gone out!) to make my appearance. I was rewarded with the delightful sight of her blushing pink before I even said a word to her...and her blushes doubled when I innocently enquired whether she had seen my note?

She looked a mixture of furious and mortified and muttered something about "Yes, thank you very much" and sat down to eat her toast. She was looking especially attractive this morning, wearing just a simple white cotton dress with bare legs. I did notice that I could see the outline of her underwear beneath it nice and clearly, something which gave me a little frisson of enjoyment. I decided to make the most of her confusion and to see where it might lead.

I sat down opposite her at the kitchen table and looked at her with a smile. "And what did you think of the note might I ask..young lady?"

The "young lady" was deliberate... to see if my instincts about Catherine were on the right track. Her renewed blush at those words told me that they were.

"I think you had a cheek writing it really!" she muttered, unable to look at me directly.

"Because I mentioned about your choice of underwear and that I approved o of it...?"

"YES!!! Because of that and...."

She faltered, obviously wishing that she hadn't alluded to the other part of my message.

"And.. what young lady...?"

She looked at me with that same mixture of crossness and embarrassment that I was starting to find quite charming.

"Don't call me that! Please...."

"Why ever not Catherine? You ARE a young lady...but if you prefer I can always address you as I did in the note..as the naughty girl you really are!!"

I said this last with a new tone of authority and standing-for-no-nonsense in my voice. She noticed it straight away and looked up, rather startled. I met her gaze and eventually she lowered her eyes. I decided to press home my advantage and added an extra dash of stern-ness to my voice.

"It's true isn't it Catherine? You can be a very naughty girl at times..not just in doing things like leaving the washing in the machine when you went out...but in your rather lax attitude to your studies...the amount of time your spend indulging yourself in all sorts of ways with Jake, especially sexually I am sure, when you should be doing other things..it really isn't good enough is it?"

I waited with baited breath to see how she would respond to this rather dramatic upping of the stakes. To my delight and relief she kept her eyes lowered and simply said: "No..I suppose it is not really..."

I saw that this was the time for action. I moved my chair back a little way from the table. She looked up at me.

"Catherine..stand up please...and come here..."

She looked at me uncomprehendingly for a moment and then slowly stood up, her face flushed pink. She knew what was coming as well as I did and had obviously decided not to fight it any longer.

I wagged my finger at her. "YOU need a good smacked bottom, as I said in that note..and I was right, wasn't I, young lady mmm?"

She swallowed and did not speak..but then just nodded her assent quickly.

"Then come and place yourself across my lap, Catherine..."

She did so, her sweet smell of soap and a dash of perfume wafting past me. I settled her into place and rested my hand on the seat of her dress, noticing with pleasure that her bottom felt just as springy and rounded and firm in the flesh as I had imagined it would.

I decided that I'd spread this particular pleasure out as much as I could.

"Catherine... I'm going to give you a taster now of a more extended and thorough spanking I intend to give you this evening. If you had plans to see Jake tonight you will cancel them...is that clear?"

I'd expected her to argue and make a fuss when I said that...but all I got was a quiet "Yes Richard" and a slight stirring of her body as it lay over my lap. I could feel my cock getting hard already and decided to just let her feel that against her tummy.

I sent her off to university around 20 minutes later with her bottom smarting and glowing from the application of my palm over her dress and then over her pants. I decided to keep the pleasure of spanking her bare bottom for this evening. I could see anyway that her cheeks were a very nice shade of crimson round the legs of her knickers (the white full cut briefs I'd put out for her on the airer last night). I could also tell from her wriggling, the little noises she made and the definite dampening of her pants between her thighs that she found the experience far from unpleasant.

She'll be home shortly, I think. She's going to feel my hand again and also the brushes and the tawse across her beautiful backside before I am done with her. And I fully intend to teach her the meaning of sexual submission too before the evening is done. We shall see...

Catherine's Diary
21ˢᵗ June

I can't keep my eye from the clock. He will be expecting me any time now but the butterflies in my tummy are keeping me firmly stuck to this seat. I wish I could stay here in the University library all night, hiding behind this gigantic copy of Anna Karenina and writing down all the things that I do & don't want to happen. Although if I organised that in to two lists they'd be interchanging all the time.

It's only in the last few hours I've been able to sit down without wincing a little. It's hard trying to hide you have a sore bottom and mortifying too, imagining if anyone might guess. And this isn't anywhere near as sore as it is going to be tonight, this morning was just a warm up apparently (?!). Plus he has assured me that tonight he will be removing my knickers and spanking me on my bare bottom. And not just with his hand either. That hairbrush and tawse are coming out to play. Diary, if you could see the colour of my face now as I write that you'd also encourage me to stay firmly put where I am, and not even contemplate going back home, where he is waiting for me. Where later on he will see my bare bottom and no doubt my face is going to be a million times more pink and flustered than it is just now.

As much as I am resisting it, I know I will go back though. That command in his voice is so utterly compelling. It even made me cancel my night out with Jake, his demand that I do so was something I readily accepted. What is that about huh!? Since when did independent, self-assured Catherine take orders? When did anyone actually even bother to tell her what to do? And since when did being told what to do offer such a thrill?

Let alone when did a woman of 22 so readily agree to being put across an older man's knee to be spanked.....

It's not even the pain that I am nervy about, it is the undertones (quite literally under my tummy) that I'm trying to get my head around. I felt his erection there as he held me over his lap, and he knew I felt it too...I couldn't help my body squirming a little. I'd hoped I'd disguised it as wriggling from the pain, but it was like he recognised it as a tremble of arousal and pushed his hardness up in to my tummy just that bit harder.

If a pencil could whisper..... now would be the time. Worst of all..... I actually think I was aroused too. If he removes my knickers tonight, what if he sees that?! What will that invite him to do? It really is like he's found a secret window in to my deepest and darkest imaginings and is slowly bringing them to life. His hand on my bottom, then wandering somewhere in between. His eyes holding their gaze on me, stripped naked facing him, with the deep crimson glow of my bottom in a mirror reflection behind me. Instructing me to stretch my body out across the arm of a chair and the sharp, stinging whacks of that leather strap falling hard against my bottom. Being beckoned back over to him and ... and... how far might he go.? I'd want to please him, I know I would. Knelt down between his legs after he is thoroughly satisfied with my chastisement, I'd do everything that he asked.

That was my phone...he just called.

"Catherine, where are you? You do realise that every minute that you are not home from here on, will have earned you an extra slap of the hairbrush?

And…young lady…something for you to think about on your journey back here……the very first thing I shall do as you step inside the door, will be to inspect your knickers to see just how much the thought of what lies ahead with me this evening has had an effect on you…"

****

This story © William & Catherine 2011

About the authors:

Catherine & William are based in London. Neither of them have a public blog or website they can direct you to but rest assured if they did have, you would not be disappointed. You'd likely find a whole variety of vignettes, images and tales touching on topics as far ranging as traditional discipline and on to the delights of embarrassment and sexual obedience.

They both share a fascination with derrieres, knickers and the blushing of both pairs of cheeks. Catherine is quite possibly the more filthy minded of the two but then again William did introduce her to everything she knows. They hope that those reading their story derive as much pleasure from reading it as they did from writing it together.

The Royal Wedding

Pandora Blake

The road to Zadir was dry and dusty. Sometimes they would stop at one of the walled caravanserais lining the spice road, and Tabina would rinse the sand from her hair and enjoy a day or two of feeling relatively fresh. But no sooner were they on the road again than the wind would start to slap against the canvas coverings, and they would snap and flap until a corner was tugged away, and then the dust and sand would swirl in and they would both be covered all over again.

It was only the two of them sharing the carriage, Tabina and her old nursemaid Anar, who had scolded her and told her stories since before she was weaned. For once, on this journey Tabina was glad of her company. Apart from the honour guard riding alongside, the old nurse would be the only person she knew in her new married life. Tabina only sometimes wished for a companion better informed about the Zadine people, with whom she could have talked about their politics and mythology. But even the stories Anar had told twenty times before were welcome on those long, hot, tedious days.

Tabina had ample time to review what she knew about their destination. It was less than she would have liked, but more than people might expect. Her father had an extensive library, and he had always insisted that a princess should know how to read and write, study history and economics, and be able to tell when her advisers were lying or misinformed. Tabina had never been as accomplished as the other court ladies at singing or embroidery, but she could sit a horse better than any of them, and she was certainly educated enough to sit on her prince's council – if he would have her.

"Are you sure they don't say anything else about Mihran?" she asked.

Anar looked up from her sewing. "*Khanzada* Mihran - and I daresay they do, rani, but not where I've heard it. I've told you what I know. He's the youngest son of the noble Khafalid dynasty, and he became heir when his brother was killed on the banks of the river Jarun. He's a skilled swordsman. They say that since the death of the *khanzada* no-one has been able to defeat him."

Or no-one wanted to, Tabina thought. People behaved strangely around you after you'd lost a brother. She hoped that fighting wasn't all Mihran could do. Of course a king needed to command the respect of his lords, but he also needed to be able to negotiate. Still, if a king was not so skilled at diplomacy - well, that was why he had a queen.

Tabina picked dirt out of her fingernails. "I just hope we get a chance to bathe before we're presented at court." She would need to before being introduced to her husband-to-be in state. She'd seen her father receive ambassadors from other kingdoms to his durbar, watched them arrange their retinues so as to have the best possible impact. One old nursemaid and an armed escort wasn't much of an entourage. If Tabina had her way, she'd have been accompanied by zamindars and jagirdars, nobles of high birth and great renown. But all the Karathi lords were needed back home, to help Raja Selim rebuild the kingdom after the war.

Her parents had worked almost as hard during the treaty negotiations as they had during the war, she knew. It had taken all their bargaining power to arrange this marriage, and with it the hope of a peace between Karatha and Zadir. Everything depended on it now; everything depended on *her*. People said she should have married sooner, but her parents hadn't want to rush into a match. After Damush died she became their heir, and her little sister was still only ten, too young to marry. They had held her in reserve as their most powerful bargaining chip. Now, she was tasked with her first serious diplomatic mission: to be her country's ambassador at the Zadine court; her prince's advisor. It was of utmost importance that she make a good impression.

She hoped that the gifts would suffice. Her guards surrounded an entire carriage full of riches to be presented on their arrival. A polished spear of teak and steel for the crown prince, and an embroidered robe of the type that only married Zadine men could wear. For his mother the Khatan Jalapuya, an emerald necklace that had belonged to her grandmother, and a gold-embroidered veil beaded with carnelian and jasper. Khan Emed would receive a handsome turban and an ornate curved sword, the blade engraved with animals and flowers, with a sheath of black velvet, tipped in bronze. The carriage was also packed with bolts of silk and casks of wine, spices and saffron. Her father may have haggled long and hard over the treaty, but no-one could describe the dowry as ungenerous. Of course, Tabina herself was the most valuable gift of them all.

It seemed as if they'd been on the road for weeks when the domes and minarets of the great city of Shiradan appeared on the horizon. For a few days it felt like they weren't getting any closer, and then suddenly they were almost at the gates.

The bearded lord dressed in flowing silks who met them on the road introduced himself as Akartha, vizier to Khan Emed. He was accompanied by an armed guard wearing the distinctive spiked Zadine helmets, and he was unfailingly courteous.

"Most gracious Rani Tabinayanti, I am your humble servant. It is my greatest pleasure to welcome you to our city. Many sacrifices have been made in hopes of your safe arrival."

"My lord Vizier Akartha." Watching the way he looked at her, Tabina was grateful for the small privacy afforded by her veil. "It is delightful to be here at last. We met little danger on the road, although little variation in the view, either. Sand and more sand."

He didn't smile. She hoped he wasn't insulted.

"The preparations have all been made for your glorious presentation at our humble court," Akartha announced. "You will shine like the full moon, and hold eternal sway over the domains of beauty." At least, she thought that was what he said; she'd spent many months studying the Zadine language, but would not be fluent until she'd lived among native speakers.

"I thank you for your kindness, my lord. This moon will shine all the brighter once she has washed off the dust from the road." If

159

she was mispronouncing anything, he was being very polite about it.

They rode into the city together: her personal guard, the Zadine escort, both carriages and the vizier. She lost count of the number of gates they passed through. Somewhere within the palace, she realised her guards were no longer with them. Even Anar had been whisked away, presumably to her own accommodations.

The vizier personally escorted her to a suite furnished with carved rosewood and intricately patterned carpets. Tabina wondered if these were to be her rooms, but she did not see her baggage anywhere. Still, there was a bathtub with jasmine scented steam rising from it, and that was good enough for now.

She was so tired she had to remember to smile at the two young palace servants who were provided to help her bathe. She wished she could linger in the fragrant water forever. They washed her hair and brushed it until it was as glossy as a blackbird's wing, and dabbed perfume at her throat and wrists. After weeks under canvas her copper brown skin had faded to olive; she wasn't sure whether to wear the jade green dhoti for her presentation at court, as planned, or whether the peacock blue would suit her better now. Both had matching veils, and her green and silver silk wrap would go as well with either.

Her baggage still hadn't arrived. Presumably it was in her rooms, wherever they were. She would need to send a servant to fetch some clothing for her. She wondered if these girls were to be her handmaidens, but it seemed impolite to ask.

"Which colour will the esteemed Khanzada Mihran prefer, do you think - jade or peacock?"

The maids seemed perplexed. "Most gracious lady," one of them said, "robes have been provided for the ceremony."

"Oh, you mean the exchange of gifts?"

They exchanged glances. "Were you not informed, *khatani*?"

Tabina rose from the bath. "What ceremony is this? Tell me." Whichever of the local marriage rituals it was, she needed to prepare. She hoped it wasn't the one where the bride gives her swaddling cloth to the wedding fire, because she hadn't brought hers with her.

"Gracious *khatani*, this is not a common wedding." She learned more as the handmaids dried her limbs with polished curves of wood. The ceremony had not taken place for more than two hundred years. A political marriage alliance hadn't ended hostilities since the civil war, when Musavi, sole daughter and heir of the victorious House of Khafalid, wed Ayed, son of the House of Sammir. Ayed married the Khafalid claim, but before putting a Sammir on the throne they decreed that Ayed must perform a ritual atonement for the atrocities committed by his deceased father and generals.

"There was no other way," the taller one explained. "The Khafalids needed the Sammiri to support Musavi's claim. But how else could the son of the traitor be accepted, unless he was ritually cleansed and forgiven?"

She had read something about that. The marriage had ended the civil war. Songs had been sung about the humility and dignity with which Ayed endured a whipping in front of the eyes of the court, and he went on to become a just and honourable Khan.

"But Khanzada Mihran has his own claim," said Tabina, "he doesn't need to marry mine. And I won't go on to rule. Our terms were more than fair, and my dowry represents atonement enough."

"Your gifts are gracious," the girl replied solemnly, "but your people have done us great wrong. You will bear the next heir of Zadir. How can our *khanzada* accept you into his bed, tainted as you are by blood? How can the Khan and Khatan welcome you into their household? Only blood can pay for blood. You must pay the same price as Ayed."

Tabina had time to think on this, as they braided her hair and painted her nails. Why hadn't she been told? They had planned this all along. *This* was what Akartha had meant by her "presentation at court". They had toyed with her, and now she was trapped.

Her parents would never have agreed to the marriage if they'd known. They would not have accepted this condition. Although perhaps they should have; *she* would have, if she'd only been forewarned.

Or maybe they *had* known. Maybe everyone had known all along, maybe it was only she who had been kept ignorant. She hadn't signed the treaty agreement. They had presumably wanted to spare her from needless worry, but she would have appreciated the chance to read up on what was expected of her.

If they didn't know, what would they think when they found out? It was a great insult, of course. Perhaps the gifts were too generous after all. She wished her father was here to advise her, her mother to help her think it through. What would a diplomat do?

Tabina knew the answer as soon as she asked herself the question. A diplomat would smile, and bow, and do what must be done. A diplomat would courteously endure any number of indignities in order to procure peace. What, did she think her father had had an easier time at war? Had Damush died so that she could flinch away from the one task assigned to her? Would a public whipping be as bad as childbirth, as hard as losing an eldest son and two babies before they were named? No. To endure this would demonstrate her honour and humility in the eyes of the court. It was expected of her; refusing would be arrogant and cowardly. She would return in disgrace, having failed at the greatest responsibility she had been given.

The robe that had been provided was plain cotton, dyed dark red (so the blood won't show, Tabina wondered). She was permitted some adornment: the handmaids tied a belt of gold links around her waist, hung gold hoops from her ears, slid bangles onto her arms and embroidered slippers onto her feet. A golden veil was draped lightly over her hair, and made the whole world shimmer. She was ready.

Guards stepped out behind her as she left the bathing room. They were not her men. She wondered what Ravi, the brave captain of her guard, thought about that. She imagined him arguing with court officials, insisting on being returned to his rani's side.

162

Vizier Akartha met her at the first courtyard with a sweeping bow. "Many a beautiful star have I seen, gracious glory of the heavens; but you are something unique."

Tabina tried not to glower at him. She arranged her face into a smile as he fell in step beside her. "My lord, I feel much refreshed by your generous hospitality. I'm greatly looking forward to presenting the gifts we have brought, as gestures of our esteem for your noble house. Will there be time after the ceremony?"

Did his moustache twitch as she mentioned it? Yes, he replied; after the ceremony she would be formally presented to the crown prince and to the Khan and Khatan, and gifts would be exchanged. Her attendants were making the requisite preparations. Once she was officially accepted she would sit beside Khanzada Mihran on the dais, and all the Zadine lords and ladies would pay court to her. The rest of the day would be spent in feasting and celebration.

She wanted to ask him about the ceremony itself, but didn't dare. They were acting as if she already knew about it, and she was minded to play along. She was determined not to let them believe they had the advantage.

They were joined by attendants, and a robed man who seemed to be a priest. At the entrance to the hall where the Khan received his audiences a crier announced her: "Presenting Rani Tabinayanti of Karatha, daughter of Raja Selim, heir of the House of Kuru." The hum of conversation quietened for a moment as she stepped inside, then started up again; waves of talk rising from a brightly-coloured sea of courtiers. From somewhere came the sound of a singer, accompanied by flute and tanbur. She glanced at faces as she passed, but it was difficult to identify members of the noble Zadine houses through the blur of gold gauze.

After a few paces she finally saw her honour guard, surrounded by a much greater number of palace soldiers. Her captain Ravi looked stricken and furious all at once. Tabina guessed that he found out at much the same time she did. She gave him a small nod, making a mental note to find him later and reassure him.

The dais was a long way away. She wanted to catch a glimpse of Mihran, but instead she concentrated on walking gracefully along the richly-patterned carpet, keeping pace behind the priest, eyes not roaming overmuch. She hoped the incense filling the air wouldn't make her too dizzy.

Between her and the dais was set a block of dark wood, smoothly polished and curved like half a barrel. The priests parted around it, and she stood before it for half a minute before she realised what she was looking at.

Once she was sure her face was under control, she checked to see if there were any leather straps or ropes attached to it. She would endure this with good grace; she couldn't bear to be restrained, as if she were unwilling. To her relief, there were none.

At least, Tabina told herself, there was no established precedent she must follow. No-one else would have witnessed anything like this in their lifetime. They wouldn't know what to expect any more than she did. Infinite god, but she hated having to do anything in public unprepared.

The priest was talking now, in an archaic form of the language that was hard for her to follow. Sitting on the dais, beyond the block, she could see Khan Emed in his high turban, and the glittering jewels at the Khatan's throat. That must be Mihran wearing white beside her, but it was hard to see clearly from this distance.

She had seen a public whipping once at the palace, ordered by the Rani her mother. The thief was tied upright to a wooden frame, and the blood ran along channels in the flagstones. He had screamed at first, but after a while he had just sort of hung there.

Tabina had of course been thrashed in the nursery (admittedly, not as much as some of her cousins), but not since her betrothal. And only ever in the privacy of the household, among family and servants. Back home, for an adult of high birth to be publically flogged was the height of disgrace, the end of their political existence. It was ironic that in Zadir, it would mark the beginning of hers.

By the block stood a man dressed like an executioner, looking somewhat incongruous holding a cane rather than a sword. She had seen children and servants punished with such rods, but this was longer and thicker, more akin to those used by officers of the law. Ah; so she was to be beaten as if she were a criminal. She couldn't fault the symbolism.

The priest's speech was clear enough for Tabina to understand when she was asked for her consent. She gave it, with as much courtesy as she could muster. She was a step away from the block when an attendant moved forward.

"Most gracious lady, it is customary that you remove your veil."

Tabina had half-expected this, but revealing herself was the worst thing so far. She handed it to the attendant, and the room seemed to buzz more loudly and brightly once her head was bared. *At least I don't have to worry about it falling off during the whipping.* She could see more clearly now – except she couldn't see at all, everything was a blur.

Heart pounding in her throat, the toes of her gold slippers found the solid curve of wood. As she leaned over, the smoothness of it against her belly and thighs was cool through the cotton robe. She saw handles discreetly set into the wood below her, and reached forward. Her heels lifted off the floor as she grasped them, leaving her poised on tiptoe.

Someone behind her lifted her robe. Tabina was not sure which awareness struck her first - relief that her betrothed and his family could not see her nakedness, or shame that the whole court could. First her veil, and now this! They might as well take the robe off and be done with it. She wanted to tell them that she was willing to be humble; they didn't need to force additional humilities on her.

Being bent over was hard. She would have liked to lift her head proudly, to look out over the crowd and not be seen to flinch. But a small, shameful part of her was glad to be able to hide her eyes. And ... what if she *did* flinch? She realised that it was very possible that she might flinch.

Everyone watching was someone she would need to work with; the same nobles who would shortly be paying her their respects. She was going to have to learn their every strength and weakness.

165

Right now, however, they were anonymous, and she was exposed before them.

She was trembling; she hoped not visibly. Her hands were slippery with sweat. *Oh, come on,* she thought, *let's get this over with.*

The first stroke was so hard it expelled the breath from her lungs. She grunted - and then she would have screamed if she hadn't clamped her mouth shut and groaned through her teeth instead. This was her battle, she reminded herself fiercely. Did warriors scream on the battlefield? Actually, she suspected they probably did.

The next one seemed to be even harder. Each cut felt like a brand had been put to her, a fierce high pitched slice of pain. By the sixth she was aware that her neck was damp with sweat, loose strands of hair clinging to her skin. She nursed a growing terror that the next one would wrench a scream from her. Tabina counted the strikes in her head, biting down on the numbers under her breath. When she realised that she was also shouting curse words silently to herself, she forced herself to think *thank you* after each stroke instead, *thank you, thank you,* in case she accidentally yelled the words out loud. It would not do to shout abuse at the whole court.

Between each stroke her whole backside seemed to pulse and throb, feeling twice its usual size. Her legs were shaking with the effort of holding herself on tiptoe, and the robe was drenched in sweat. Anger rose up in her alongside the bloody weals rising on her skin. She raged that *she* had been chosen for this, used like this, that she could not just have married some nice highborn Karathi boy. The welts were burning appallingly, so raw that the merest whisper of air seemed to inflame them. Then the next stroke would slam her hips against the hard wood, and she would sense deep slabs of bruise forming under the skin.

Those standing on either side of the block could almost certainly see the screams her mouth was forming, although so far she had restrained from crying out. Blood roared in her ears. When a low cut sliced into her upper thighs she genuinely believed, for a moment, that the cane had been swapped for a sword. Her breath

166

was coming in ragged gasps. It was too much, unbearable. She wasn't getting enough air - she was going to faint -

Fiercely, she clung to the spar of her rage. She forced herself to focus not on the pain, but on her anger at those who had brought her here; with everyone who had fought in the war; with the captains and the soldiers who had desecrated Zadine temples and burned their villages. It should be those captains here, stripped and made to suffer before the court. It should not be her. All she had ever done was what she was told.

The last number she had remembered to count was twenty eight, and that had been some time ago.

By the end she did scream, a little. It was ripped out of her despite her best efforts at self control, but once it was out she thought sod it, and gave it a good yell. Better a yell than a sob. And who knew, maybe if she hadn't made a murmur they wouldn't have considered the ceremony to have had the desired effect. Who could tell whether screams or silence would be more appropriate? There was no precedent for this. She was the precedent. She bet Khanzada Ayed yelled when they scourged him.

She was waiting for the next stroke to land, eyes screwed shut and breath coming very loud, when she realised it had stopped. She opened her eyes. She had to blink tears, or maybe sweat, out of her eyes. Wetness prickled on her cheeks, and she could feel a drop of sweat crawling down the back of one leg - except of course perhaps it was blood. She couldn't tell.

Suddenly, she realised it wasn't just blood thundering in her veins she was hearing, but shouting and cheering. The anger surged up again: how dare they cheer her disgrace! But … it wasn't disgrace, not any more. She'd made it through, she'd survived. *Would you have preferred it if they'd booed?* They were cheering her success. It meant they had accepted her.

Experimentally, she tried to unclench her hands, and slowly unpeeled her stiff fingers from the wooden handles. They looked pinched and bloodless, and tingled sharply as the blood returned. Her backside was one great throb of hurt. The saddle had never made her feel this sore. She squeezed her hands open and shut a few times and then rested her palms on the block, pressing against the smooth wood to push herself upright. The wood was warm where her body had rested against it. Suddenly she was grateful for the simple comfort of the cotton robe, without any sequins or stiff thread to dig into her skin. Hands at her elbows guided her upright, and the robe slipped back down her legs to the floor. She glanced at her feet quickly, but couldn't see any drops of blood, so perhaps it had just been sweat after all.

Someone lightly pressed a hand on her shoulder, which she guessed meant she should kneel, so she did. It wasn't easy - all the muscles in her backside felt knotted and stiff, and twinged horribly as she tried to use them. She felt very exposed with her head uncovered. Her hair was damp, and the braids fell across her face as she bowed her head.

The priest scattered petals and perfumed water over her hair and said, "Your suffering has cleansed you of the blood spilled by your people." He touched water to her forehead, her lips. "Be relieved of your burden of guilt. No vengeance shall be sought for past wrongs. You have atoned." He met her eyes then and almost smiled, and she guessed that meant she could stand up.

She was a bit unsteady on her feet, and pain was swelling up from her bottom through her entire body. An attendant stepped forward with a bowl of water, and she splashed her face and took a swallow or two. Another held out the gold veil. Once the shimmering fabric was arranged over her hair she felt better. This was her armour.

Tabina stood a little taller and wiped her hands on the robe. She supposed she should say something, and she struggled to remember the words she'd come up with earlier in the bathing room.

"I thank you for the blessing of forgiveness," she said loudly, and encouraged by the pause that followed, continued: "It is most gracious of you to grant me this opportunity to demonstrate my goodwill towards your people, and my commitment to this marriage. I look forward with great eagerness to be presented to your most royal Khan and to set eyes on the noble prince who is to be my husband. I hope this heralds the beginning of a new age of peace, and a lasting friendship between our houses." They were cheering again - that was good, she supposed. She was swaying a bit.

The priest said something else and then the vizier, Akartha, was by her side, a cool hand on her elbow. "Very pretty, princess," he said.

"The whipping?"

"The words. And your glorious self, of course."

"The court seems happy."

"They do. It seems to have gone rather well, don't you think?"

I was about to ask you that, she thought, but she was reassured nonetheless. He led her around the block, which she hoped wasn't a permanent feature as she would prefer never to look at it again, and towards the dais. The Khan and Khatan had stood up, the queen very elegant in her long gown, and was that a welcoming smile on her face? Mihran was standing too, his body language uncomfortable. I bet he's more comfortable than me, she thought fiercely, but she lifted her chin and carried herself proudly as she walked that final stretch of carpet towards her new family.

****

This story © Pandora Blake 2011

About the author:

Pandora is a kinky blogger, activist, performer and producer. This is her first spanking short story, and she enjoyed the opportunity to bring to life one of her more unrealistically high budget film ideas.

You can find more of her writing at her blog, PandoraBlake.com, and films exploring her corporal punishment fantasies on her new site:

DreamsOfSpanking.com.

Trouble in Telesales

Domino

Mrs Doris Crammond was very happy in her job. The company she worked for was not a huge one, but to her that only meant that her position was the more respected. At 61, she was the manager of the telesales department, and answered to no-one other than the Board of Directors, of whom she was one.

The telesales department comprised fully half of the employees, and 50 girls together with 4 supervisors were under her command. There were five large offices on Mrs Crammond's floor, with ten girls and a supervisor in each one. Mrs Crammond had a small office of her own, but she chose rather to keep her finger on the pulse of her little empire and preferred to fill the position of the 5th supervisor herself and sit in one of the rooms with the girls.

Unlike most telesales departments, the staff consisted mostly of ladies of a certain age, who had been with the company for ten, twenty or more years! Mrs Crammond herself was proud to boast that she had joined the company at age 15, and had worked there for 46 years! She prided herself on running an orderly and ladylike operation. Not for her the hard selling techniques that the word telesales conjured up in this modern world. Mrs Crammond and her 'girls' conducted their business in a pleasantly refined manner.

Naturally, Mrs Crammond decided who would join which office. Younger staff who were allocated to Mrs Crammond's room were generally troublemakers and not destined for a long career at Grimsteads. However, for the most part Mrs C preferred to have the older ladies in *her* room. They were old friends, and socialised on a regular once-a-month basis. Mrs Crammond knew she could rely on them to maintain her high standards, in the tradition in which she had been trained as a fifteen-year-old all those years ago, when sales were made by writing polite, neatly-typed, individual letters to all the clients.

There had only been ten girls then in the typing pool, governed by Mrs Taylor, who had inspired a sense of awe in her girls. Being cheeky to Mrs Taylor, or disobedient, was considered to be far more dreadful a sin than being disobedient to God, because whilst with the latter you only had to worry about the hereafter, with Mrs Taylor, retribution occurred in the here and now!

When called to the time of reckoning with Mrs Taylor the sinner knew there was no hope of divine forgiveness. There was only the certainty of being ordered to reach under her skirt, lower her knickers, clear her desk, then lay across it. Mrs Taylor, possessed of a solid wooden ruler fully a quarter of an inch thick would then move behind the typist, raise her skirt and proceed to deliver a stern lesson in no uncertain terms.

Mrs Taylor's ruler was brought into action for the slightest infraction. Careless typing mistakes, clumsiness, tardiness, indeed, anything which did not conform to Mrs Taylor's strict standards would end up with a very sorry little typist, red-eyed and red-bottomed, tenderly perched on her chair at her work, not daring even to sniffle lest that brought on further recrimination for unladylike behaviour and lack of a clean pocket handkerchief! (Was it only in the imagination of the girls or was the punishment really more severe, did it last longer, if the typist was a dolly bird sporting one of the latest-fashion mini skirts?)

Doris herself had been subjected to humiliating punishments on more than one occasion, it was impossible to avoid them. Every girl who worked under the aegis of Mrs Taylor's weather eye, be she ever so ladylike and conscientious, had, sooner or later, earned herself a salutary spanking.

Doris had always comported herself in a ladylike fashion, not for her the short skirts and outrageous styles that had blossomed during the 60s, yet she had earned her fair share of Mrs Taylor's efficacious lessons. A lack of decorum, unpunctuality, too many typing mistakes - there were always numerous infractions which Mrs Taylor, at any given moment, could choose to correct.

With a mental shake, Mrs Crammond pulled herself out of her nostalgic reverie, thinking with a smile that Mrs Taylor would certainly have scolded her for day-dreaming, and given her something to buck up her ideas! Looking away from her computer screen Mrs Crammond cast a glance in the direction of a somewhat stout matronly lady, who occupied the desk just across from her own. Marlene was the proud grandmother of 4 gorgeous babies whose photos were pinned up on the wall behind her desk.

With an inward smile, Doris wondered what Marlene's children and grandchildren would have said, had they seen their mother and grandmother, on the fateful day she had arrived at the office fifteen minutes late, wearing a Mary Quant mini dress which, standing straight, only barely covered her knickers.

Or rather, as they all shortly discovered, when Mrs Taylor ordered Marlene over her desk, the dress only just covered the area where knickers were supposed to be! Doris remembered Mrs Taylor's gasp of astonishment that any girl should be so deliberately wanton as to parade around with no knickers on. Grasping the ruler from her desk, Mrs Taylor advised Marlene to grip the end of her desk and remain bent over until she was given leave to rise.

Doris had never witnessed a thrashing like it before or since. Even having been raised in a culture when cane, tawse and slipper were all freely administered at home and school, this was truly a punishment to outdo all others. Mrs Taylor had wielded her ruler with all the strength of a long-time golfer, painting bands of fire across Marlene's white cheeks. Taking a step to the rear, Mrs Taylor raised her arm, then stepped swiftly forward whilst swinging the ruler down on Marlene's pale nether cheeks, using the added momentum to increase the severity of the strokes.

Again and again the dreaded ruler rose at Mrs Taylor's direction, and over and over it painted a blazing red stripe on poor Marlene's bottom. In vain did Marlene try to defend herself with stories of a bus delayed, of laundry undone and an ailing parent. To no avail did she plead for mercy. Mrs Taylor's ruler struck relentlessly, covering the whole of Marlene's bottom to half-way down her thighs, overlapping each stroke. Marlene's backside seemed to expand as it grew hotter. It blushed pink as if embarrassed, then began turning even deeper shades of red.

All the watching girls knew Marlene would be wearing bruises for some time to come. Doris herself recalled feeling that Marlene deserved what she was getting – she had never heard of any girl forgetting to wear her knickers – and with a dress that short – why if you sat on the bus like that, or in the park – then any man could look up your skirt and see... Doris blushed to think of it! She had no sympathy then for Marlene, who shrieked loudly, ignoring Mrs Taylor's admonitions for her to comport herself silently. To add to Marlene's humiliation, old Mr Grimstead came through from his office to discover what all the palaver was about. Folding his arms, he stood impassively observing the scene, much to Marlene's chagrin.

Mrs Taylor was determined to drive her lesson home; the entrance of Mr Grimstead, the Company owner, did not deflect her from her self-appointed task, nor did it cause her a moment's pause. Unflinchingly Mrs Taylor persisted in her exertions, beating Marlene through the cries, through the shrieks and wailing, through the sobbing, until the girl was capable of nothing more than loud blubbering.

With a smile and a nod at Marlene-the-grandma, Doris remembered, when at last allowed to rise from the desk, how Marlene had been chastened, how she had hung her head in shame when Mrs Taylor had given her some money and ordered her to immediately proceed to Marks and buy a decent pair of underwear, and informing her that the money would be deducted from her weekly wages. Doris could still see the anguished look of shame on Marlene's face as she realised that she would perforce have to display her punished thighs through the streets to the shop and back.

Poor Marlene's humiliation had been complete when, on her return Mrs Taylor commanded her to raise her dress so that she might ascertain that the knickers were indeed decent. Mrs Taylor had been truly an expert in ensuring that offenders lived to regret their misdeeds. For weeks after Mrs Taylor had greeted Marlene every morning with a steely enquiry as to whether she had suffered any lapses of memory that morning. The other girls too had not lost an opportunity to tease, and when Mrs Taylor was out of earshot they too would make remarks such as offering to lend Marlene a pair of their granny's bloomers. For years, the word knickers had made Marlene flinch.

Times had changed indeed! Nowadays it was all panties and tiny briefs and scraps of floss that covered nothing at all! The girls got away with so much more. Tardiness, carelessness – indeed nothing short of gross misconduct in the way of stealing was a punishable offence. The world had indeed changed, and not, reflected Mrs Crammond, for the better. Crime rates were up, and in their quest for equality it seemed that young women sought to descend to the depths of the worst male behaviour – public drunkenness and lewdity – yes, Mrs Crammond had observed all these things as documented on her television screen.

Mrs Crammond remembered how unfair she had thought it when new rules introduced in the mid-seventies meant that the newest employees were now exempt from corporal punishment. She had been of the school of thought that believed that a girl who earned her whacks should be given them, just as she and her other colleagues had received theirs. Still, reflected Mrs Crammond with a gratified smile, time heals all wounds and the clock had now turned full circle. The change of government had brought in interesting changes in the law.

A conservative government, brought to power on a ticket of traditional family values, decency and public order had vowed to put right the increasing lawlessness which abounded. New legislation was proposed, debated and passed at record speed into law.

Less than a month ago, in response to this new legislation the Company Directors had laid their proposals before the Board. These proposals were in turn raised at an Extraordinary General Meeting of the shareholders. Being a small private company, there were few shareholders, young Mr Grimstead, who had followed in his father's footsteps as General Manager was also the largest shareholder. His two brothers, Head of Finance and Head of Production respectively each had their portion, as did their sister Agnes and their late father's sister Aunt Ursula who was in her late 70s.

The EGM was largely called, as any of their shareholder meetings were, more as a nod to propriety than anything else. The brothers were confident in the compliance of Aunt and sister. Mrs Crammond was also present, the only female in the company of status high enough to be entrusted with the sacred taking of minutes.

In the event, as always, more time was taken up in consuming elegant cups of tea accompanied by delicate biscuits than in business. Eventually after a round of small talk, Mr Grimstead, chairing the meeting announced that what with the economic crisis and the ensuing new government and new legislation, measures would have to be taken.

Sad as it was, it would no longer be possible to carry any of the older staff who were no longer capable of carrying out their jobs. Aunt and sister nodded... they knew that this was targeted at Jones, the faithful handyman who was well past retiring age. He refused to leave but sadly had long since been unable to perform most of the tasks required and it was only the fact that his junior took up the slack that he had been able to stay.

Aunt Ursula suggested that he be offered a grace and favour cottage on a corner of her small estate. She would ask him to take it as a favour so that she, as a weak and feeble female, would always have a man to hand, should one be required. A polite ripple of laughter was raised at the thought of Aunt Ursula being considered in any way as weak and feeble, however the brothers felt that this was a plausible excuse to use with Jones, who, being a gentleman of the old school would not suspect the deception.

Young Mr Grimstead, nodding in satisfaction at this resolution, expressed his regret that they must now move on to weightier issues – namely terms and conditions to be offered to staff following the recent changes in the law. The government had, in its wisdom, recognised that discipline in schools, on the streets and within some organisations was non-existent to all intents and purposes. This, claimed the government was the root cause of laddish behaviour, teenage gangs and other societal ills. In a rousing speech the new prime minister had instigated a variety of solutions, amongst them repealing the laws which had banned corporal punishment.

Indeed, not only were the laws repealed, but everyone in any position of authority was enjoined to be pro-active in installing new disciplinary proceedings within their organisations and institutions. The Home Office had acquired a new Advisory board and no time had been lost in issuing pamphlets and instructions to all and sundry. The civil rights groups had objected and protested of course, but in the end had failed to rise to the challenge to find any workable alternative.

With this in mind, the Board was proposing that all employees under the age of 30 were forthwith to be advised of a change in their terms and conditions of employment. Namely, that in addition to current disciplinary procedures, staff were also to be subject to corporal punishment at the discretion of their manager.

The resulting discussion was the liveliest one ever seen around the Board table, as the various schemes and proposals were discussed, until the new rules were decided upon. It was agreed that anyone over the age of 30 would of course still be answerable to their manager and the board as previously, but that otherwise all younger employees would be subject to discipline of a corporal nature by their line manager. Any employee who refused to accept these new conditions was welcome to seek other employment. As these laws were being implemented throughout the nation, the Board was confident that there would be few, if any, resignations. Indeed jobs were at a premium and with strict disciplinary rules being introduced at the job office, it was expected that not many would be stupid enough to choose to leave.

To ensure matters were dealt with fairly, the employee would be given the choice of accepting corporal punishment there and then from their manager or being referred to the Head of Human Resources for an adjudication. Mr Henshaw could, if he deemed it necessary consult with a quorom of three board members, and their decision was final. If corporal punishment was deemed appropriate then the only options open to the employee were to accept it or immediately tender their resignation.

Once an employee accepted the punishment from their manager, they could only appeal to Mr Henshaw after the punishment had been completed and only on grounds of undue severity. Determined to leave nothing to chance, employees were advised in their new terms and conditions that bruising and marking would *not* be considered unduly harsh, as per stipulations in the governmental guidelines. Punishment was to be applied to the posterior only, however, it would be on the bare and it would take place in front of whoever chanced to be present at the time, thus evading the whole question of improper behaviour.

There had, naturally of course, been considerable mutterings from the ranks when these new terms and conditions were announced, one or two disgruntled employees had departed, only to return some weeks later humbly begging for their jobs back, having realised that with added CP, the dole was no longer the gravy train it once had been.

As agreed, there had been a period of easing in, a breathing space as it were, with plenty of reminders and verbal warnings, but that initial period had expired last Friday, and here it was Monday morning and the first day of the new regime in all its glory.

Mrs Crammond had done her quick round of the office, touched base with all her supervisors and ensured that everyone knew what tasks they were performing that day. Annie, the most junior of the girls had brought in her first cup of tea of the morning, and Doris sipped it while scanning her emails. Spam and junk were assigned to the trash, then came the internal email and finally customer queries.

One of the internal emails caught Mrs Crammond's eye. It was from Mrs Wilson, one of her supervisors, expressing her concerns over one of her younger members of staff. Try as she might to instil the company values in the girl, nothing seemed to work. Vikki was brash, curt with clients, hectoring even. Her work was slap-dash. She spent far too long chatting to other girls and took several cigarette breaks every day! She frequently arrived late for work, clearly the worse for wear from the previous night. Lately she had taken to using foul language to impress the younger girls, and in an attempt to appear hard was telling all and sundry, clients included, that Victoria being an old woman's name and Vikki being a baby name, she was now to be known as Vyxen!

Any of this would have been bad enough, but Vikki's latest debacle involved the Company's most important client. At a time when cashflow was tight the silly girl had allowed an invoice to be sent from Finance without a corresponding purchase order number. The fiasco only came to light when, instead of receiving the expected fat cheque from the client, Mr Justin Grimstead (middle brother) had received a polite letter from the client, requesting an amended invoice.

Mrs Wilson was perplexed by the request – the purchase order number had certainly been received. Yes, there was the email from the client with the PO number, there was her email to Vikki emphasising the importance of this invoice and exhorting her to ensure it was included. Did Mrs Crammond want Mrs Wilson to take it up with the girl, or....

Quite appalled at the possible consequences to the company due to unwarranted delay of the single largest payment of the year, Mrs Crammond reached for her phone and buzzed Mrs Wilson. "Rachel," said Doris, "Leave it with me. I'll come through as soon as I've calmed down!"

Always a lady, Mrs Crammond suppressed the fury coursing through her. The only signs of it would be evident in her steely look and scathing tongue. She shook her head. Did the stupid girl not *realise* that it cost good money to keep all the staff employed, and that it was imperative for all their good for the company to keep solvent! A shortfall of this magnitude in the quietest month of the year could be disastrous for them all, and even if it were not, Doris was sure that this would cause problems in paying invoices on time thereby hurting their good reputation.

An example would have to be made! Vyxen indeed! Who did that silly child think she was! What on earth possessed her to believe that any of this silly posturing impressed anyone at all who was worth impressing. Ah yes... Miss Victoria was desperately in need of a good dose of reality!

Calling up the appropriate document, Mrs Crammond re-read the official guidelines and the new Company regulations. She nodded, accepting that this unpleasant duty could not and should not be shirked. She buzzed Mr Henshaw to advise him of events, then rising from her seat, Mrs Crammond, with a measured, regal gait, made her way through to the central sales office. She smiled a greeting at Mrs Wilson but did not pause until she stood in front of Vikki's desk.

"Victoria," began Mrs Crammond, only to be interrupted by the girl who instantly piped up saying that she would prefer to be called Vyxen.

"Nonsense" replied Mrs Crammond. "Your name as shown in your record of employment is Victoria, and while I am willing to use the more modern Vikki, I think on this occasion Victoria is more appropriate and there is to be no further discussion of the matter."

Something in Mrs Crammond's stern delivery must have penetrated Vikki's self-absorbed ego, as this time she forbore to answer back. "Victoria," continued Mrs Crammond, "Would you kindly show me the account details for customer number 24191."

Vyxen looked at Mrs Crammond, as if wondering why the old bat didn't do it herself - it was surely easy enough to call up an account on the system, but again she said nothing, just called up the details and turned her monitor so that Mrs Crammond could see it. "Thank you Victoria," persisted Mrs Crammond. "Now, would you kindly point out to me where you have entered the purchase order number?"

"Sure, it's," began Vikki. "Well – it's.. ummm it's not there," she tried to bluster, her face reddening. She recalled being told how vital it was for a PO number to accompany invoices, and she also knew that 24191 was their biggest customer. The lie that she had never received the number died on her lips as she recognised that Mrs C would not have commenced this line of questioning unless she knew full well the number had been sent to her. Furious at having been caught out Vyxen whined "but I put it in, I know I did. Someone must have..." Even Vikki herself could not continue that train of thought and she faltered

Mrs Crammond folded her arms, and with ice-cold eyes waited for Victoria to finish spluttering her excuses. The atmosphere in the room could have been cut with a knife – everyone had ceased their work to follow the saga unfolding before them.

As Vikki's voice trailed off, Mrs Crammond spoke again. "Victoria, the management team has been seriously concerned for several weeks now over your behaviour and performance. We have overlooked your penchant for grotesque makeup – if you choose to come into the office with so much black around your eyes that you look like a panda, then that is your choice." Mrs Crammond hid a smile at the effect of her words on the girl – Victoria had an expression of dumb insolence on her face, but her eyes sparked with anger at the remark.

"Unfortunately," Mrs Crammond resumed, "your work is lackadaisical. You are frequently late, you badger our customers. It seems to me that you are not really cut out for a job in telephone marketing. No!" Mrs Crammond raised a hand to prevent Vikki who had been about to speak. "Say nothing until you are allowed to. Your attitude is disgraceful, your work is sloppy and the repercussions of this invoice fiasco could well be drastic."

A moment's pause, the Mrs Crammond carried on, "Do you have so little idea of how a business works, girl? In plain, simple english, if we do not make enough sales, if customers don't pay on time, then how is the company to pay your salary? I don't think you would like it very much if Mr Harry said he was very sorry but he couldn't pay you this month!"

Still struggling to appear tough, Vyxen gave a little shrug, which prompted Doris to acknowledge that in this particular case she would positively enjoy doing her duty! Outwardly ignoring that defiant gesture, Mrs Crammond said, "I know you have read the new regulations, or at least I know that you duly signed the form saying that you had read them. So, first things first - you will kindly remove all your possessions from this desk and place them on the vacant desk in my section. From now on I shall keep you under my personal supervision, to see if you can improve, given one last chance. Come on girl – hurry up."

Vikki appeared somewhat taken aback by this but she slowly rose and began collecting her things. Mrs Crammond beckoned two of the younger girls to give her a hand, and the desk was soon emptied. Vikki, in the meantime was simultaneously trying to take in this turn of events and desperately trying to remember quite what was in the new regs. Something about discipline and a whole new strict outlook – and corporal punishment, although what on earth the death penalty had to do with anything, she didn't know. Had Mrs Crammond been privy to the girl's thoughts she may not have been able to suppress a smile. It was quite obvious that Vikki's education and upbringing had been sadly lacking if she could confuse corporal with capital punishment, but she was due a rude awakening!

With all her belongings all in place at her new workstation, Vikki returned to Mrs Crammond, who was waiting for her with a sheet of paper in her hand. Passing it to Vikki, Mrs Crammond asked her to read and sign it.

Grasping the sheet, Vikki read :

> This is to certify that I have read and understood the regulations pertaining to discipline in the workplace. I hereby acknowledge that my recent behaviour warrants punishment as decided by my Manager Mrs Crammond, to be meted out by her in the main Sales office. I further confirm that I accept this punishment freely and that I do not wish to seek adjudication from the Human Resources Director or the Board of Directors. I understand that this agreement does not invalidate my legal rights as established in the British Bill of Rights and Duties 2010.

"Punishment?" squeaked Vikki, "What's all that about then?"

"Enough of your nonsense my girl," responded Mrs Crammond, "If you have managed to avoid all the political brouhaha of the past months over the introduction of discipline in the workplace amongst others then you are deaf and blind and as stupid as you look! You signed the forms accepting the new regulations – you had ample time to reflect on the laws and ask questions. All you need to know right now, my lady, is that I have the legal power to order you to bend over that desk, raise what there is of your skirt, lower whatever underwear you are wearing and prepare yourself for a good sound spanking!"

As Vikki stared at her, slack-jawed and wide-eyed, Mrs Crammond, in a slightly sharper tone of voice barked, "Enough shilly-shallying. Sign the paper and bend over the desk or else it's off to Mr Harry and from there to the dole queue."

As realisation dawned on Vikki of what was about to happen she glanced around her in consternation. She did not like the idea of that ruler one little bit. Sadly for Vikki, a youthful indiscretion meant that she was the mother of a young child whom she had to support. Her own mother, with whom Vikki and baby lived had warned her often enough that if Vikki lost her job she would also be thrown out of the house. All these thoughts darted through Vikki's mind in the couple of seconds it took for Mrs Crammond to make her way across to the stationery cupboard, in order to withdrew a stout 18 inch wooden ruler.

With a stifled howl of rage and frustration, and something that was almost a stamping of her foot, Vyxen made a last determined attempt to retain a semblance of control over her destiny. Turning to her desk, doggedly making an effort not to let old Mrs C win, with an infernally cheeky swing of her hips, she slid her hands under her short skirt and lowered her panties for all the world as though she were performing a strip tease, then stepping out of them, she draped them artistically over a monitor.

Mrs Crammond raised an eyebrow, but said nothing, merely hefted the ruler in her hands. The younger girls in the office were wide-eyed in astonishment that someone could be so cheeky in the face of such a punishment. The older ladies exchanged knowing smiles – they had been there and done that, and knew just how deflated Vikki would shortly be.

"When you are *quite* finished with your inappropriate little display," said Mrs Crammond, addressing Vikki, "kindly bend over the desk and raise your skirt. No-one here is interested in anything other than seeing you get the comeuppance you deserve my girl."

If looks could kill, Mrs Crammond would have been seriously injured by the vicious darts emanating from Vikki's eyes, but since, happily, Vikki was not endowed with superhuman powers, the only consequence of the nasty looks an exhortation for Vikki to get on with it.

Still bent on being as unmanageable as she could, Vikki gyrated against the edge of the desk, thrusting her hips backwards and forwards as she gradually lowered her torso to the desk and ever so slowly reached behind her to raise her skirt.

"You will keep your hands out of the way," said Mrs Crammond, unimpressed. "You will hold on to the opposite end of the desk and if you reach back there is a chance that your hands will receive a blow intended for your behind. So don't do it."

Pressing her left hand into the small of Vikki's back, Mrs Crammond raised the ruler and swung it down smartly onto the creamy white flesh before her. A band of red flared up, although the stroke had not been terribly hard.

It was hard enough for Vikki! Having it in mind to deprive Mrs C of her satisfaction by not uttering a sound, Vikki's resolution went out the window as she felt what was probably the worst pain of her life. Her head shot up and she bellowed in pain. She would have leapt off the desk if Mrs Crammond had not been pressing down on her back.

With a short pause for the stroke to take its full effect, Mrs Crammond again raised the ruler, swinging it down to overlap the red band already there. Another roar from Vikki, who jerked and bucked.

"Good heavens girl," said Mrs Crammond, "I really did expect you to have more gumption than that. I thought you were supposed to be a hard case, and here you already in a state are after only two strokes."

She delivered another one, not quite as neatly this time, but obviously as effective, because Vikki responded to it with yet another loud shriek. "I hope you take this time, Vikki," advised Mrs Crammond, "To reflect on the behaviour that has reduced you to this condition."

Raising her arm once more, Mrs Crammond deftly flicked her ruler down onto Vikki's backside, just at the crease where thigh meets buttock. It was quite evidently effective as the result was a high kick from Vyxen and an accompanying oath. Quite undaunted Mrs Crammond laid on 4 swift strokes to mid thigh and mid-calf. "You will not curse and use bad language my girl," she said, "Nor will you kick out like that, or you *will* regret it."

As Vikki wailed, again Mrs Crammond drew back her arm to place another cracking blow on Vikki's backside. Vikki howled, and jiggled her buttocks from side to side in a vain attempt to shake the pain away. Not likely, thought Mrs Crammond. She knew just what needed to be done to break the arrogant wilfulness of the girl. She continued scolding, crashing the ruler down as emphasis for each word.

By this time Vikki's bottom was mottled, with patches of red on deeper red which surely preceded various shades of purple bruising, but this did not deter Mrs Crammond, who was determined not only to set an example to all the younger girls under her aegis, but also to break Vikki so that Vyxen would nevermore rear her arrogant head.

"Punctuality," said Mrs C, ignoring the yells, which were becoming ever more desperate.

"A painstaking, conscientious approach to your work" – the ruler by now was positively bouncing off Vikki's backside, searing, burning, roasting her bum. Vikki had never experienced anything like it before. Childbirth had been a doddle compared to this. The entire universe shrank and the only thing that existed was hanging on as wave after wave of indescribable smarting, stinging agony washed over her. Her pleas became ever more incoherent.

She did not realise, nor would she have cared, that tears were flowing unbidden out of her eyes, smudging her make-up so that her appearance was quite grotesque. Her sobbing was ragged and Mrs Crammond sensed that the crisis was approaching. Wielding the ruler ever faster and harder Mrs Crammond played her opus to a crescendo. The ever-decreasing kernel that was at the core of Vyxen finally disappeared. Vikki wept, her breathing was laboured and came in snatched gasps between her howls. All thought of resistance was long gone – all of Vikki's focus was on the searing white flash of pain which exploded in her head each time a fresh stripe landed on top of the background omnipresent smouldering.

Satisfied that her job was done, Mrs Crammond stepped back, folded her arms and waited. It was some seconds before the realisation seeped through to Vikki that her punishment was over. "You may rise," said Mrs Crammond, somewhat unnecessarily. When she sensed that the restraining hand had left her back, Vikki leapt from the desk, and to the sniggers of a few of the less sympathetic girls, performed a little comic act as, desperate to assuage the pain in her bun, Vikki first tried to massage her nether cheeks, but when that proved too painful, resorted to patting them, then massaging again.

Mindful of her position, Mrs Crammond let this go on for a minute or two before announcing sternly that it was time for Vikki to pull herself together.

"Kindly go and re-arrange yourself in the ladies Vikki," said Mrs C, "I shall expect to see you in my office in ten minutes. Do you understand?"

"Yes Mrs Crammond," whispered Vikki, recognising with a sinking heart that a new era had begun, that Vyxen was gone forever and that in future she would have to become a responsible, model employee.

****

This story © Domino 2011

About the author:

Domino is a 50-something Smart Ass Masochist. She lives in the north of the UK, where she is very happily spanked (some would say not frequently enough!) by the love of her life.

Domino says :

Spanking has been a part of my life since I taught myself to read, aged 4, so I could indulge in the story of Fairy Tina spanking the naughty elf.

The stories which I enjoy the most are non-sexual ones, set in a Victorian or historical period where the person being spanked is a pre-adolescent child, particularly when it is a good child who is being unfairly punished by an over-zealous parent/ guardian/ authority figure. Anyone who wants to debate this theme with me is invited to email me at domino@domin-o.org.uk

I discovered around the age of 11 or 12 that the spanking stories which I enjoyed the best were the ones produced by my own fevered imagination, and I have been writing for my own amusement ever since then. If others find pleasure in my stories too, then that gives me pleasure too, and I invite you to my website:

domin-o.org.uk

Heatstroke

Penny Docherty

No matter how many times I've heard its little daily-check whine, my pager always startles me when it goes off in earnest. Startling isn't good. Startling keeps you from concentrating, right away, on the cool voice crackling out from it – and you need to concentrate, believe me, you need to know where you're going and why. Even in a small place like this, heading down the wrong driveway into the woods can be a disaster for the guys waiting for your backup.

It almost made me jump this time too, when it erupted into a sudden fizz of static and then voices reciting the regional code for the call, directing it to first responders, fire and emergency medical technicians. That's me – fire. Trying to stop 'em anyway, or at least stop 'em really getting going. So my head was up the minute she called it out. It was a hay bale fire, down on Andrews Farm, a little ways out of town off the main road. At least it was by the road – or at least I hoped it was, in the main field out where I'd seen old man Andrews hay-baling yesterday. By now he could have worked his way further in and be out of reach of the engines, hell of a big field to haul the hoses across. I hoped he was okay, anyhow, they hadn't put a call out for an ambulance, so I reckoned he was out of danger. I stopped my truck, jumped out of the cab and pulled my bunker gear out of the back. Easier said than done: that son-of-a-bitch weighs a freakin' ton, all the fireproof gear, boots and respirators and all. I'm used to it, though, and I'm no wallflower. I dropped the pants on the ground and stepped into them, grappled with my boots, threw the jacket over my back and hauled ass on out of there up out towards Andrews Farm.

I was hardly even close before I saw the smoke column rising up on the other side of the trees. Andrews' field was smoking up but good. I pulled in by the fence, to one side of where the first engine had gone through. There was a few guys already out there, scattered out in a fan across the field stomping at hay stubble –

Kay, Pete, Jim Thornton and Trisha, who waved. I gave her a nod back; I know some of the guys get weird about women being in the team, but Trisha's tougher than near on any of them. Got a way of fixing you with her blue eyes like there's something real funny about you, but she's not going to tell you what it is, just laugh until you figure it out for yourself. Pete says she's stuck up but I reckon he's just sore about the time she knocked him back for a dance when we were all down at the Pinedale Inn that time. There's a difference between being stuck up and just having someone's number, and she had his that night, for sure: that Dutch courage, sweaty hands stuck in his jeans and his hair all slicked back, and her just sitting there cool as you like with those blue eyes on him. She had on this old brown suede jacket, real soft, with fringes, but something about that jacket made her look like a hunter, like she was about to head on out of that bar with her dog and go shoot deer. Had a look in her eye, like she was sighting down a rifle through the brush and Pete was the deer about to get it in the head, only he didn't see that 'til she leaned forward and said something real soft in his ear, which made him go red as a sunset, and then he backed off in a hurry. He muttered afterwards that she made him look like a fool, but he didn't need help. He did a fine job of looking like a fool all by himself. I don't know her so well to talk to, but I bet she knows me better than my own brothers do, she just don't let on. I'm kind of scared to talk to her, is the truth, but she's always been pretty nice to me.

I looked for the Chief and he motioned me over. 'Hey Preston. Andrews is OK, we got no casualties here' he reassured me, lifting his respirator. 'Just a hell of a lot of burning grass and I don't know what kind of damage to his baler. Damn thing got some kind of kink in the machinery, set up a spark and lit the place up. The northwesternmost corner was the first to go and the fire's been spreading in a southern direction evenly since then, not much windspeed to push it, though'. I nodded. 'So we don't need the hose, but we're figuring on dampening this place down, get some bucket chains set up and make sure it don't spread over to the house or the perimeter of the property. There's a livestock trough over there, about enough to keep us supplied. You want to get to carrying buckets, be my guest'.

'Sure thing, Chief'. I had that kind of a thrill in my chest like when you're going to be useful, really helpful. Maybe not a hero now, although I was glad that Andrews was out of danger, but I was going to get that burn under control. I ran, didn't walk, over to where an old livestock tank was and grabbed a pail from the heap someone had rustled up and put there. Not much of a chain, yet. I filled it up from the trough, ran up to where the edge of the fire was smutting up the grass. Man, hot in this suit on this hot day. Soaked it where I could, ran back. No joke, this gear was heavy. Filled the bucket up again, ran on back, soaked the ground, jogged back to the tank. Another gloop as the bucket filled up, another run back to the edge. Splash. Run. Splash. I wish I could empty some of this cool water over myself. Run…

I came to face up to the sky. My hands tickled against the cropped grasses. Wait, where was my respirator? My face was damp, and stinging. Someone was kneeling next to me. Someone else standing over me. Chief! What happened, Chief? The person by my side spoke.

'Preston? Hey there buddy, you doin' OK? Yeah, he's gonna be fine. Plenty of fluids and not so much excitement.'

Kathy? Kathy the EMT? What had happened? The fire hadn't been that bad. 'Chief?'

He looked down at me, relief tinged with scorn around his eyes. 'Preston, you got so het up running back and forth in your bunker gear you about gave yourself heatstroke. You collapsed right on the ground over there. Hot day ain't no time for a man to go about exerting himself'.

Flushed and grimy as I was with heat, I swear my face burned even more red. I had…fainted? Given myself heat exhaustion, outdoors, manning a bucket chain? I'll tell you, I never felt so mortified. How many good people had been diverted to get me out of my gear and make sure I was OK? How much more of the field had been burning while they saw to my sorry ass? Dumbshit didn't begin to cover it. I closed my eyes and willed it all to go away. It didn't. I sat up instead and put my face in my hands.

The guys were good about it, really – almost too good, if you know what I mean, I know I'd been a bonehead, so when we were all back at the station getting showered down and talking over the day, I kept my mouth shut and changed in the corner. I didn't go out to the bar with them later, either, just went home with a six-pack of beers and shot up some pixellated aliens to make myself feel better. At least I could run after them without making myself pass out.

The worst part was how, the next day, the Chief didn't say anything to me about that foolishness. He'd go past us in the kitchen down at the station, get himself some coffee, look at me and then look away again. Tell you the truth, it made me jumpy. It wasn't that I was trying to get out of discipline, more like I wanted to get it over with. The other folks picked up on it too and pretty soon they were ignoring the fact that I'd made such an idiot of myself and kept us all back on that day. But what if there had been casualties? What if it had been a house and not some stupid stubble fire? Those thoughts kept pinging round my head, and I couldn't ignore them. The fire service can't carry liabilities. Break your leg, fail to engage your respirator, just act like a damn fool and it might be two bodies your buddy has to carry out of that burning house instead of one. You can bet your ass I learned my lesson about running in bunker gear under hot sunshine, but I was worried about future foul-ups. Could everyone else depend on me not to do some other butt-stupid thing in a future emergency situation?

I could feel it at drill, too, not just the first one we had after Andrews' fire but the one after that, too. Their doubt crept around me like mist or smoke. I tried to keep my head down, go through the exercises as quick and good as always. Some of them were fun ones, like cutting open a car someone had donated as though we were getting an old lady out. It should have been good for all of us, running round hollering for the bolt cutters and with all the sparks flying. It wasn't, though, not for me. Something in me locked up, down in my belly, and I just did what I had to do and kept in my position 'til it was over, sweat running down my back. I had lost my nerve.

I don't think it was anything the guys did or said. They weren't mean guys, they were solid. Good pals. I think it was the stuff they didn't say, the way they avoided horsing around with me like we'd always done. Hell, I'd known some of them my whole life, pretty much. Of course I was going to notice when they quit taking a rise out of me. The sight of one of them, just one, running round at a practise like a chicken in a coop going, 'I'm Preston, ain't it hot, watch me faint like a little girl!' would have picked me right up. At least then we could have all laughed. Laughing wasn't what bothered me – it was letting them down. That fear in Kathy's voice when she had been stood over me in a field, thinking I might have just fallen down in a swoon and wasn't going to get up, like happened with old Casey Davis when he just keeled over. He had cancer all up inside him, though, which was why he collapsed, and no-one knew, not till he just fell down like that right in the middle of the store parking lot. Amount of pain he must've been in. Nobody had a clue.

Well, I didn't have any cancer, I was pretty sure, but this shame was starting to feel like a big red weight in the middle of my head, blocking out my usual self. I'd shot about enough aliens to defend the world from ten invasions, so I started hitting the weight room down at the station instead. Exercise always made me feel better, and I didn't have to talk to anyone. I was hitting my sixth rep on the weights for your deltoids when guess who comes in. Walks right in like she owns the place, never seen anyone look so dignified in jogging sweats. No prizes, it was Trisha.

'Hey there, bud,' she called out, and sat right down on the machine opposite me. I grunted back at her and avoided her eyes. That isn't easy, you should know, avoiding Trisha's eyes. She's got that kind of gaze you can feel on you even when you're looking at the ground, that kinda draws your eyes back up onto hers. And then she went ahead and ignored the whole rest of the room and just started doing tricep curls on the machine right across from me like she was there on her own. I watched her. I couldn't help it. She does landscape gardening and it shows: she's got those worn, calloused hands that gardeners get and when she's got a sleeveless top on you can see those muscles in her arm ripple right up to her neat shoulders, defined like neat little machines working under silky fabric. It makes me think of horses, the way you can see their big muscles work under the gleam of their hides. Pretty soon I realised I'd stopped doing deltoid exercises and was just staring at her profile. I hurriedly started doing stretches, so it would seem like I'd taken a break to do that. It didn't work.

'Got something on your mind, Preston?' she asked, straight out. It shocked me a little bit when she talked, and even more when she fixed those blue headlamps on me. It was the most natural, friendly thing in the world and at the same time it was like one of the posters off the wall had turned round and said 'hey, how you doing?'.

'Uh. How many reps you going to do there, Trisha?'

'I generally do about six, but I'm feeling kinda lazy today.' She reached into her bag and pulled out a bottle of Coke, unscrewed the top and took a pull. 'This heat just takes away my willpower, you know?'

I nodded. I didn't know what she meant – I liked hot workouts, I liked sweating through them – but I just nodded.

'Guess you know about heat affecting performance there, though, huh Preston'

I blushed – I am a twenty seven year old man! I weigh two hundred and twenty five pounds and I can bench press two hundred thirty, and I blushed. The blushing made me blush even harder, so I turned away and pretended to mess with the weights. I slotted in another ten pounds and was about to fix them there with the pin when she spoke again.

'It's really not a big deal, you know. I saw a guy one time down the Swinomish Valley, who got thrown off by the water coming through the hose. Didn't ground himself properly, got all off balance and was dancing around like Jiminy Cricket before he went over and knocked his head on a rock. He was out cold for hours and we got all tangled up trying to get the hose back. Passing out from heatstroke, I seen that a few times now. No big deal, Preston. Honest to God, no biggie',

I was still flushing, I knew she could tell. I couldn't turn round and look at her yet. I couldn't bear her talking like this, trying to make it better. But I couldn't bear it when she stopped, either.

'That kinda shit happens to everyone once. Maybe more than once. The trick is to come back from it, not have it happen again. Hell, a month's time and it'll be forgotten. But you can't go creeping round here like a kicked dog. That's the kind of thing that gets in the way of a good team. And we need a good team, here'.

I finally found it in me to look up at her. There was something about her face, right then, that made me think hard about what kindness was. There was kindness there, sure, but it was edged round with something harder. I liked the toughness in her jaw right then more than the gentleness in her tone. It was like an old sideboard with a crackle glaze on it, the hard will daubed over with soft words. That soft spoken woman stuff, I'll admit, it gets me going in a certain way, like that good hero feeling coming up through my chest. But it wasn't what I needed right then.

I sighed like a teenager in a sulk. 'I guess I just feel like everyone's not talking about it. It just keeps going in this spiral in my head. The Chief won't barely look at me and the guys are being too damn nice. I feel like if I'm going to act like a jackass, they should treat me like one'.

She smiled, and I could see that hard glint again. 'So what you're saying is you feel like you should be disciplined? Preston, if you'd put other people in danger they'd be talking about disciplining you. Not for something like this'.

'But I did put people in danger! They were taking care of me when they should have been stopping that fire! I held them up, I wasted time. You can't waste time'. I realised I was breathing heavily. 'I just want something to happen, to stop it going round my head. Let the Chief tear me a new one, or the guys play some

193

stupid joke, just not this...this tiptoeing round it! Dammit, I feel like I'm waiting outside the principal's office for him to paddle me'.

She did a double take at that. 'They still paddled you kids when you were at school? I thought that went out years ago. I guess your mom is pretty strict...'

I shook my head. 'No, no they didn't do it. I guess I just thought about it sometimes. You know, how it must've felt. My mom never did anything like that to us'. I almost laughed. 'Reckon she was pretty tempted sometimes, though'.

Trisha looked at me pretty closely, then, like I was a hedge she was about to trim. 'You think about this kind of stuff a lot?'

I shifted a bit, on the narrow seat of the weights machine. 'I guess. Hah, maybe that's what I need. A good paddling from the principal. Don't reckon I can ask the Chief for that, though, do you?' I couldn't look at her. I couldn't not look at her. I felt like her eyes were boring right inside me. Still gentle, and still with that resolve behind them. She stood up over me and said, 'I think you're onto something there. Stand up now, Preston. Turn around'.

I moved slowly, deliberately. I could feel her behind me, even though she was standing a foot away. Even without her telling me, I knew to kneel over the bench of the weights machine. The leather slid under my sweaty cheek.

'Take down your pants. I'm going to give you what you deserve'.

It was like her words moved my hands without my arms even intervening. I pulled the elastic of my jogging pants down to my knee, where they lay bundled on the carpet.

'Your boxers, too.'

There was a clamour in my head at that, even through how strongly I knew I wanted it. For the first time I thought about how public the weights room was. 'What if someone comes in?'

'What are you afraid of? They might enjoy seeing you like this? Stay there.'

She got up and walked out of the room briskly, and came back in a minute or two later. I couldn't see her, but I heard the door snick shut, and the lock click home. Then she was behind me again. 'I told you to get those underpants down. That was not a request'.

The kindness was gone now, and all I could hear was firmness in her voice. I wriggled around and pulled down my underwear. I could only imagine what my ass looked like, stuck up in the air. Thank Christ this room didn't have any windows.

There was a swoosh of air and then I felt her garden-calloused hand whack up against my buttocks. I let out a yelp, and this only got me another smack. I kept quite this time, even though it was harder than the last, but it didn't help: she pinned me down with her free arm, elbow crooked into my back, and brought her hand down on my bare ass til the ringing slaps filled the close air of the weights room. I tried not to cry out – two hundred and twenty pounds, remember? – and I did okay until she landed me one good blow in that crease between my ass and my thighs. Goddamn, that hurt. And then another and another til it felt like the underside of my ass was on fire. I wriggled underneath her like a kid, but she just kept whaling on me. Eventually, I relaxed into the pain, like when you get into your groove on a run: the smacks started feeling almost soothing, coming in a regular rhythm one after the other, building up and cooling down. I could feel the tension leaving me one jolt at a time. But then she did something far nastier.

She got three or four good swipes in before I realised what she was hitting me with. She'd taken the ping pong racket off the rec room table next door and she was spanking my ass with it. The flat rubber surface seemed to spread the blow out into a little mat of pain each time. I was yelping again, I was crying out but she wouldn't stop and I didn't want her to. She counted out twelve blows, each heavier than the last, and the three she finished with made a thwack that echoed round the room and left my ears ringing, never mind the sting on my behind.

She patted my ass when she was done, almost proud, like I was a dog she was pleased with. I was gasping and gulping into the bench where I'd been sitting so tense twenty minutes ago. It was like after a squash game, or a run through the woods. No, it was better. It was all that and that heaviness lifted off me too. It was like coming out from a fire and taking off my helmet and respirator, knowing I'd done my job. It felt that good.

When I made it up off that bench, pulling my pants up around me and turning around, I saw Trisha sitting just where she'd been doing tricep curls, with a smile playing round her mouth. She still had that damn ping pong bat in her hand, and she was toying with it like I've seen cops toy with their handcuffs. The thought of handcuffs made me shiver a little, all over again. She looked at me, and that hardness was back under control in her face, buried deep under a look of affection. She reached out and patted me on the shoulder.

'You're alright, Preston. You're a good kid.'

'Ma'am, yes ma'am. Thank you ma'am,' I said, and she smiled. Right then we heard the door open, the one that comes through from the truck shed. We both looked at the locked door. I leapt up, checking my pants were on right, and opened it up to see Pete King walking on in with the Chief. 'Hey Preston' he said, 'How's it going, guy?'

'Just been doing some time in the gym' I said, 'and I guess I ran round that treadmill so much I about passed out from heatstroke again!'

We all laughed, deep ho-ho belly laughs, and I knew it was going to be OK. As I walked with them into the kitchen, I heard the soft clunk of Trisha sneaking back into the rec room and putting the ping-pong bat back down on the table, and I smiled all over again.

****

This story © Penny Docherty 2011

About the author:

Penny Docherty grew up in Scotland and the USA, and now lives in London. She has previously had erotic fiction published in Filament magazine, and intersperses writing dirty stories with academic work. Her father is a firefighter, and told her the true story on which her piece in this volume is based.

Arlington Girls' Reformatory

Rayne

The night is young—the lights bright and brief, deep reds and blues, flashing strobe-like, enticing, electrifying.

The music is pounding, louder than words… the bass-beat reverberating through muscle and bone, loosening, freeing, pumping inward and forward… Forward through the crowd, bodies colliding in the hot air, hair flying, beer spilling—"Heyyy, dumbass, what the hell?" Shouting, through 120 decibels of blissful hearing damage.

Blank eyes, stupid grin. "You just sloshed me, jerk!" Shoving him away, his grin untouched, his brain beer-fogged and soggy. "Dipshit." A growled mutter under liquored breath—at least *she* can still stand up straight…

A girl, blonde, slight—slighter than she should have been, shoulders tense. Spotted, sitting, alone, at the bar, cradling her drink in both hands, as if tethered to a lifeline. "Her glass is still full…" Annoyed.

"Come on Cheryl, I brought you here to have fun, remember? Relax!" She is joining Cheryl now, her arm around those slim shoulders, warm skin, reassuring. "Why don't you just have a sip?" Helping her now, two guiding fingers on her hand, lifting her drink up. Cheryl can only manage a weak smile, an infinitesimal swallow of her iced Rum and Coke. *Pathetic.*

As if on cue, the beat changes—syncopated, a little faster, a little grittier. Cheryl's intake of breath and elevated heartbeat would have been imperceptible to any but the most watchful of souls nearby. Mira catches it—and leaps at the brief moment of opportunity.

"Let's *dance*." Grabbing her wrist, yanking her free from the drink, free from the bar, free from the awkward solitude of insecurity, unhelpful memories, irresistible longing.

Cheryl has neither the strength nor the time to resist—the sea of bodies swallows her up, Mira's bright face inviting, encouraging. *There she goes,* Mira finds herself thinking. *Just needed a little push. Let her lose herself, let her forget... Him, their mother, the baby, everything... Let her smile, for once in her life, really smile...*

"Mira, are you sure you can drive?"

Stupid question—of course she can drive —but she is trying to empower her sister, not shut her down. "Yes, Cheryl, you know how many times I've done this?"

"Yeah, but, remember, last time you got—"

The wheel slips a little, but Mira grabs it in time. These stupid little yellow lines don't really mean much this late anyway—it's 3am—who cares?

But Cheryl is tense again.

She'd been doing so well, at the club—feeling the music flow through her body, letting the corners of her lips curl upward ever so slightly, in the anonymous darkness. The music pulsing, the lights flashing—blues and reds, leading them both deeper into themselves, safe, oblivious to the tribulations of life. Blues and reds, strobe-like... Cheryl's voice, a wailing siren, "Mira! Mira pull over!" A hand on her arm, guiding, grounding.

"What?—Shit!"

A *cop.* Shit. Fucking *shit.* Just what they need now. Why *this* time after countless times when Mira had done this on her own? After finally getting Cheryl to open up—after finally seeing her smile for the first time in *months.*

A tap on the window. Too soon. Time is compressing...

Where is that button? No, not the locks, the window—the window, damnit—there.

"Miss? Are you alright?" Bright light. Flashlight—in her face? Really? Obnoxious?

"Yes Ma'am. We're fine." Blinking painfully—speaking to a watery uniformed silhouette behind the spotlight. "Just heading home."

"Where's home?"

Nowhere I want to be right now, Officer. "Not far…"

Cheryl is concave in her seat next to Mira. Her arms wrapped tightly around her thin frame, every nerve in her body on edge, hiding her face, beginning to rock, slowly, forward and back, forward and back.

Would you turn that friggin' light off and leave us alone, already?

"I'll need to see your license and registration, Miss."

License? …License? Mira can't pry her eyes away from her sister, so young, fifteen, so fragile…

"Miss? Have you been drinking?"

"I—" a defeated, rattling sigh. A sigh for her plight, a sigh for her sister. A sigh for the world gone wrong. *Why must things always end like this?*

"Miss, I'm going to have to ask you to step out of the car, please…"

The two girls are as unlike each other as any sisters Judge Ainsworth has ever encountered.

Miranda Wates: 18, dark and moody, loud, rude, piercings up and down her ears, donning ripped jeans and unlaced combat boots, in and out of this county court so many times that even her voice had become recognizable to the regular staff, clearly audible through the courtroom doors.

Cheryl Wates: 15, blonde and timid, painfully quiet, eyes downcast, wispy, frail, as if at any moment she could just fade away into thin air.

Odd, though—different as they are, Miranda seems to be harboring some kind of deep-seated need to protect her younger sister. She uses her volume and color to strike up a barrier around Cheryl, rather than to overshadow her...

"It wasn't her fault! She shouldn't have to be here—"

"Miss Wates, as you have already been informed, this is your sister's first offense, and the penalty for the purchase of alcohol as a minor is far less than—"

"But you can't—"

"Enough! Miss Wates, if you do not remain silent for the remainder of this hearing I will have you held in contempt of court!" The fire in her eyes does nothing to quell his ire. In fact, quite the opposite.

"Now. Miss Cheryl Wates, as you are a minor, we will need to wait for your parents' arrival later this morning before any sentence can be appropriated. But don't worry—" her terrified glance upwards only serves to remind him how distinct she is from her sister "—I'm sure we won't be giving you much more than some hours of community service."

Miranda's barely perceptible sigh of relief is not lost on Judge Ainsworth.

"Your sister, on the other hand..." He allows his eyes to lower for a moment, consulting the generous stack of paperwork laid out before him. Three accounts of disturbance of the peace, once caught in possession of a fake ID while attempting to purchase alcohol, and this would be her second time earning a DUI, driving drunk, let alone while her driver's license was still suspended from her last DUI, which he himself had adjudicated only just two months previous. Even overlooking the fact that a minor was present in the car with her at the time that she was driving with a blood-alcohol level above the legal limit, even for someone over 21 years of age and legally allowed to drink.

But when his be-spectacled eyes rise again to find Miranda, she is no longer glaring defiantly back at him. Her dark eyes are fixed at a spot on the floor some inches from the front of his pulpit, her lower lip uncharacteristically bitten back, her brow slightly furrowed. Concern? Guilt? ...Fear?

Well. In unaccustomed shock, Judge Ainsworth can hardly keep his eyebrows from traveling upward. He has never seen Miranda look anything other than downright belligerent.

"Hmmm." At his thoughtful hum, Miranda looks up, as if she can't help herself. He is lucky enough to catch her eyes, and hold them, over the top rim of his glasses. "When I saw your name again on this little piece of paper, Miranda Wates," lifting the sheet and waving it for emphasis, maintaining eye contact, "I had every intention, this time, of sending you on to the State Court, where you could be sentenced to up to two years in prison, for your latest offense." She wants to look down, desperately, he can tell. But he imbues just enough warmth through his gaze to keep her with him, even though his words are shaped to sting. "Your record is deplorable, and you are no longer a minor in the eyes of this court—therefore you must be held fully accountable for your actions. Your second DUI, on a suspended license, is considered a felony."

She betrays herself now more than ever before, with an involuntary glance toward her sister—concerned what would happen to her, no doubt, should Miranda go to prison.

"However, I fear that the state penitentiary may not be the most effective treatment for your string of obscene behavior, Miss Wates." Now Cheryl is even showing her face, stirring with some form of life other than abject terror.

"Instead, I am offering you an alternative: Plead guilty to the charges of underage drinking and driving under the influence, on a suspended driver's license, and accept the lesser sentence of six to eight months in the Arlington Girls' Reformatory."

There is her surprised comprehension, her mind working furiously, weighing the options, calculating the time... "Six to eight months, Miss Wates, in lieu of up to two years in state prison, should you force me to send you forward through the court system."

Her narrowed pupils give her away—she is looking for a catch, expecting some terrible twist.

"Do consider, Miss Wates, that the Reformatory is not very much unlike prison in terms of confinement, regimen, and expectation of compliance. The difference is, you will be only with convicted girls near your own age, you will be given much more opportunity for growth and development as a contributing member of society, and you will be subject to certain humane forms of corporal punishment."

If this had been Miranda's first felony before him on her own, she most certainly would have found herself in jail. But somehow, Cheryl's presence had brought out another side of Miranda that Judge Ainsworth had not yet seen in his courtroom. A glimmer of compassion—a shimmer of hope. How it would loathe him to have to see that brief sparkle eradicated, by a hardening two years in the state womens' prison.

"You need not decide this moment, Miss Wates." He is rising, signaling the coming end to the hearing. "Your parents should be here within the hour to collect your sister—both of you will remain here until then, in the holding cell where you were detained last night." Leaning toward them now with both his palms flat on the raised wooden block that serves as both his courtroom desk and his barrier of status. "You will have until the arrival of your parents, Miranda, at which point Cheryl will be returned to court, sentenced, and sent home." The court guards are moving now, closing in on the two sisters, sensing the arrival of their official moment to step in. "From that point, you will be sent on your way to one institution or the other—I do hope you choose wisely."

And with that, Ainsworth provides the guards with the obligatory nod of approval before an expedited retreat from the room, leaving the sisters to commiserate and reflect upon their respective fates.

The grass is green and neatly cut. The wrought-iron gates are tall, intricate—imposing. Inside the stone-cut walls tracing the perimeter of the property, a long, narrow path winds its way up through the front lawn to the carved mouth of a grand, fortress-like, graying old building.

The crunching of gravel under halting rubber car wheels lets her know, beyond a shadow of a doubt: this is it.

This place?

It's made of stone!

The only windows she can see are miniscule, in regimented little rows on either side of the second and third story. The roof is turreted, like a castle's would be—and is that a tower on the rear corner? Really? A tower? Who do these people think they are?

"Your subjects await, m'Lady…"

The snickering young police officer opening her car door apparently feels out of place here, too, the little shit.

"Let 'er alone, Harris. C'mere an' help me with this stupid thing—I never know how to—"

But apparently he did know how, because a terrible crackle of speaker waves suddenly issue forth from the keypad he had been attempting to operate, and a nasally woman's voice springs out from the metal box. "Arlington Girls' Reformatory. What is your business?"

Having leapt back at the noise, the older of the two officers leans forward to answer, as if unwilling to get too close again. "Er, …we have Miranda Wates."

"Ah yes, the new intake. One moment please." All three of them jump this time at the jarring BUZZ that clatters through the heavy iron of the gate—and something jolts in Mira's brain.

This is it, isn't it? Once she's beyond that horrible iron web, there's no getting back out—not until her sentence is complete. Why is she giving her life over to these people? What would happen if she just took off, right now? Who would care? There are plenty of trees on the other side of this gravel road—they probably get thicker. No police car would be able to follow her in there. They'd look for days—she could be out and off on her way to another state, another life… Why not? What does she have to lose?

Images of Cheryl, all alone in that god-forsaken house, shriveled and forgotten, surrounded by anger and alcohol and tears. Mira could never just leave her like that.

Their hands are on her now, gripping her upper arms, dragging her forward. The chance to escape gone—the trees moving away, the gates creaking to an irreversible close behind her.

Before they can traverse the complete path and mount the front steps to reach the door, it is swinging inward, much to the visible relief of the officer to Mira's right, who seems wary of having to deal with another confounded speaker system.

"Right this way, Miss Wates. Thank you, gentlemen."

Mira is swept into the foyer and cut off from the bright green lawn in a matter of moments—the heavy front door moving with more agility than something of its size and weight should be able to achieve. The sudden change in spectrum leaves her eyes useless and blinking inside the dimly lit stone corridor. She hadn't even had the chance to take one last look at her two escorts—leaving her bereft, cold, more alone than she can remember feeling in a long, long time.

"Where is everyone?" For her eyes are adjusting, and all she can see are thick walls, pristine floors. Closed doors, a grand, empty staircase. All she can hear is silence—emphatic. Uncanny.

"They are in classes." Blinking. *Classes?* "And Miss Wates, it would be advisable, while you are here, to speak only when you are spoken—"

"Shut the fuck up with this damn 'Miss Wates' crap—I don't want to hear it any more—My name is *Mira*—" she wants to continue, to explain how uncomfortable the decorum makes her, how unsettled she is with the frigid stone and the lack of life around her, how much she just wants to be able to connect with someone, to know their first name, to make them know her. She's not a convict! She doesn't deserve this!

But her expectation had been to be interrupted. When no interruption comes, her conviction fizzles—she is confused, lacking substance against which to push, standing over a precipice of territory entirely unknown.

205

"Are you finished? Good. I will not do you the discourtesy of interrupting you when I expect you not to interrupt me. We hold you to no higher standard than we hold ourselves. I expect you to call me Ms. Ruiz, therefore I will address you properly as well. It is a matter of respect, Miss Wates, not the opposite."

Her pause is not an invitation for Mira to interject.

Ms. Ruiz is holding her gaze, steady, clear and piercing, right through Mira's eyes to something deeper there. Awakening sensibilities Mira has long since distrusted—proven wrong again and again. But this woman, she seems genuine—truly. She seems real.

"You will find that your choices matter here, Miss Wates." She is pulling out paperwork now, retaining Mira's fixed attention with compelling words rather than purposeful eye contact. "Certain choices will be met with certain consequences, just like the choices you have made up to now that led you to this institution."

Holding out a sheaf of neatly organized papers for Mira to take. "Your daily schedule. The Handbook, which includes all Reformatory regulations, as well as the procedures followed upon non-compliance with those rules."

Her eyes again, sharp, hawk-like. "The consequences of any willful non-compliance, Miss Wates, I can assure you, will be quite severe."

The chill in Mira's spine has nothing to do with the lack of warm surroundings. What consequences? That Judge had mentioned "humane corporal punishment." Is that what she means? What exactly does that entail? What had come over her to accept this damn alternative? At least in prison she could have a better idea of what to expect...

"Your uniform." Mira accepts the bundle of cloth, curious, skeptical of the cottony navy-blue material which seems to constitute one single piece—a dress? Seriously?

"Come with me."

Lost in her thoughts, doubting whether she made the right choice in entering the Reformatory, clinging to what would soon become her only possessions in this place, Mira follows after an unsettlingly brisk Ms. Ruiz. At the top of the stairs, Mira peers to her left, down the open hall, where she can see the door to another room, marked 212, and an unmarked door designating the very end of the second floor. Ms. Ruiz has produced a key-card and is swiping it through the giant metal handle of room 213—rooms 214 and 215 reside further down the hall to the right, both locked shut from the outside as well. Swiftly, the door is open, and Mira finds herself gestured forcefully inside.

Nothing—nothing in this room but beds. Bunks, to be exact—stark white, pristinely made, four on each side of the room, lining the walls like some kind of infirmary. And three tiny, barred windows set precisely at face-level on the other side of the room. Flashes of her first glimpses of the building's front, as they drove up what seems like must have been hours and hours ago, play through Mira's immediate memory. Here she is now. Locked inside.

"Second bed to your left, bottom bunk. You have ten minutes, Miss Wates. I expect you changed into your uniform, all of your piercings removed, and your old clothes folded neatly at the foot of your bed by the time I return. The Deputy Head will then be conducting your official intake."

Yeah right. She's about to leave Mira alone in here? How big are those windows?

"And Miss Wates," half out the door, looking back over her shoulder, raising her eyebrows with practiced experience, "don't be fooled. Every inch of your life here will be under video surveillance, until you can prove that such a security measure is no longer necessary."

With the thud of the shutting door and the clank of a mechanical lock, Mira can feel the latent indignation rising in her chest. Surveillance? A rule handbook? Childish uniforms? Sixteen people to a room, no bathroom that she can yet see, barred windows, cold hard unforgiving stone everywhere—what makes them think they can treat anybody this way?

She wants to throw something. Anything. Anything hard, solid, with weight—something to heft and enact change upon her surroundings, exert some corporeal form of control—

Before she can think, her right shoe is off her foot and sailing across the room, the muscles in her right arm burning with the force of her explosion. There is nothing else heavy enough to throw—the other boot follows suit almost immediately.

She is screaming. Her hands are on the solid metal of the bunk frame now, pounding, pushing, trying to upend the whole structure.

How could she be here? How could she leave Cheryl? How could they do this to her?

Her shoulders are straining, her bare feet digging into the stone beneath her—battling for traction, for roots, for grounding. Her strength is waning—nothing is moving, the bed frame is anchored to the floor. The heat flushing her cheeks and searing her throat is incessant and suffocating. It is not until her body has pushed itself to the ground, thrown in futile desperation at the immobile steel, exhausted beyond logical physical measure, that she realizes: her face is wet.

She is being irrational.

She chose to be here—she didn't have to drive drunk. She didn't have to put her sister in danger like that. There are so many other ways she can try to engage Cheryl—to save her from the choices Mira has made.

The clinking of the door lock alerts her to the passage of time—has it been ten minutes already? Just one or two more—*I promise, I'll be ready, I want to be ready...*

Diving for her new uniform as the door swings open unceremoniously, fumbling for words, "I'm sorry—I'm almost ready..."

"Almost counts for nothing here, Miss Wates. You either are or you aren't. You are either a competent adult or you are not. Get up. Get dressed. You are now wasting not only your time, but ours as well."

The door is wide open, Ms. Ruiz is standing there matter-of-factly, showing no sign of turning or leaving. Mira understands that she has lost even the privilege of dressing in semi-privacy, and hurries to obey, struggling to wipe the tears from her face as she removes her own clothes. The plain, navy-blue jumper dress fits neatly over her head and around the light blue collared shirt provided to her—matching the light blue socks which cover most of her calves. Black, matted, boring flat shoes. The waist of the dress conforms to her own with a pull-string bow knotted in the back, and embroidered into the right upper corner of the chest, in red silk thread, are the initials of the Reformatory: AGR.

"Piercings in here, and we will be on our way." Ms. Ruiz is holding out a small plastic bag. Mira's identity, no longer external—forced inside, detached from what was once her own unique appearance.

As they return to the second floor hallway, a resounding bell sounds through the whole first and second floor. Instantly, the building springs to life: Classroom doors on the first floor bang open and girls pour out—all of them dressed identically. Hurrying out with heads bowed, not a word exchanged between them as they converge toward the back of the building, followed and interspersed by several commanding adults who seem to be surveying their progress.

Mira is watching, overwhelmed by curiosity, knowing that tomorrow, she will be one of them. One or two dare to look up as they pass, catching her eyes, some of them curious, some of them cold and challenging.

A click and a creak draw Mira's attention back to Ms. Ruiz. She is standing in an open door frame at the end of the hall, revealing a grand, circular, antiquely decorated office, complete with a vast, ornately carved desk, and high, orange-tinted windows.

"If you will wait here, Miss Wates." She is gesturing to a small bench just inside the door. "The Deputy Head will be with you shortly. He's just finished evening classes."

"Miranda Wates." He is regarding her from behind his desk with strangely amber-golden eyes. "You may call me Mr. Avery." He is younger than she had expected—most likely somewhere in the vicinity of his early thirties—but nowhere near short of the stuffy authority she is becoming to associate with this place. "I trust Ms. Ruiz has explained to you why you are here?"

Mira wants to scoff, standing there on the hardwood floor in the middle of the room. 'Official intake' is not much of an explanation...

"Yes."

"Yes, *Sir*, Miss Wates."

Oh *fantastic*. "Yes, Sir." More of these interminable *titles*...

"It is my duty as Deputy Headmaster to officially welcome you to Arlington Girls' Reformatory, and to begin your disciplinary process." He is pulling something out of the top drawer of his desk that suddenly turns her stomach to lead. Something she has only seen rarely in movies, read about in books.

"We use the cane here at Arlington, Miss Wates. I will be administering your weekly appointments as well as supplementary discipline for as long as you are living on this floor."

Cane? Weekly?

It doesn't look so bad—small, thin. Long. He had set it reverently on the cleared surface of his gleaming desk while he spoke. Now Mira can hardly keep her eyes from it.

"You have come to us because this is your *second* offense—a second DUI, among other offenses. Second offenders receive twelve strokes upon intake—double the usual sentence."

How bad could twelve be? A specific number at least... Not the unpredictable, flailing chaos of a drunken outrage...

"Your deplorable behavior thus far, however—your language toward Ms. Ruiz upon entrance, and your refusal to adhere to clear instructions—has earned you an extra four strokes: two for each behavioral disturbance." He is rising now, his black suit rustling with the motion, his cherry-red tie swinging from his neck.

"You will learn very quickly, Miss Wates, that certain behavior is not tolerated here at AGR. Our office is to do what we can to help you make better choices, but the decision is always yours." Removing his jacket, folding it over the back of the chair he has just vacated. "What you can expect from us is nothing short of absolute consistency." Now rolling up the sleeves of his crisp white shirt. "The choices you make will constitute clear rewards and consequences, the latter of which you are about to experience first-hand." Coming around the desk, picking up the cane.

"Any attempt you make to move out of position once I place you there will be met with an extra stroke, Miss Wates. Is that clear?"

Mira can only nod her comprehension, her throat dry, her heart gaining speed.

"Good. Come forward, position your hips near the front edge of the desk, then bend straight down, all the way, and place your forearms on the desk surface."

This is ridiculous! She is not a child!

"All the way down, Miss Wates. Elbows on the desk. Good."

Suddenly every inch of indignation inside her roars to burning, urgent life—he has just flipped up the back of her dress. "No way—" *Goddamn pervert!*

But he is ready for her. His trained palm is already firmly in place on the small of her back, pressing her down where she wanted to spring up and run, holding her fast, blocking her escape. "You consented to this when you signed the papers confirming your acceptance of Arlington Reformatory as an alternative to incarceration by the state government, Miss Wates. A wise decision—and hopefully the first of many more to come."

"You can't!"

"I can, and I will, and I *will* restrain you if need be, Miss Wates, is that really what you want?"

No. Forced restraint would leave her helpless. She doesn't know this man. How could she give up that control? *Just let him do what he wants. Let it be over with.* At least that way she knows she can still get away or fight back if she really needs to...

Sensing her compliance, he removes the weight of his hand from her back, and replaces the sensation with a cold, thin line across her backside, flush with bare skin where her panties don't cover. Mira's eyes are shut tight—she can't *believe* this is happening! Why isn't she locked in a tiny two-person cell right now, safe in a dignified orange prison uniform, with nothing to do but sit alone and contemplate...

"No need to count." The words come as he taps against her skin, marking his trajectory.

The first strike hits her with such force she is sure it must have cut right through her. *It's like a knife!* "Jesus fucking *Christ!*" How could something so thin and light hurt so much? Her fingers have balled into fists, her knees buckling ever so slightly.

"Language, Miss Wates. That will cost you another additional stroke."

Lining up for the second strike. This can't be happening—this can't be happening—thiscan'tbehappening...

Swish—CRACK!

Holy fucking—

The third stroke comes before she can breathe, and the fourth very soon after that. Her skin is on fire. Gritting her teeth does nothing—her voice still betrays her. "Shit-shit-shit, no stop, *shit*, no—" it all comes out in a terrible, urgent whisper. Mira has never heard herself sound like this. Almost like begging—begging for the pain to stop. *Pathetic.*

"Four down, and you're up to eighteen now, Miss Wates. I suggest you keep a better handle on your outbursts."

"No, please—" the fifth cuts her off mid-plea, a white line of pain erupting in her brain as she bites back a cry. She can't imagine *thirteen* more of these... Not possible!

After the sixth, he pauses—enough even to take a few paces away from her. Leaving her there, strung tight, waiting, wanting nothing more than to be finished and done, but at the same time never to feel that cane again.

"Had your behavior not dictated so, Miss Wates, you would be half-way done now. As it is, we are only a third of the way through."

God no please—nothing can hurt this much—nothing in existence...

Swish—CRACK! Pleeeeeeaase!

Swish—CRACK! No more no more nomore-nomore...

She is losing track, losing track of the count, of her body, of whether she is thinking or screaming, moaning or crying.

Swish—*CRACK!* Pushing, straining, *willing* against the dark wood, willing herself to sink straight through it, plunge into its cool, silent depths, let the silky polished mahogany embrace her. Yes, there are things in life that could hurt more than this. There are things that have hurt more. She just needed to remember—gain perspective.

The next three are quick—one right after the other, in successive percussive *whips* across her skin, strips of white and then brilliant red, settling into deep, biting ridges that will remind her of this encounter for days to come. The building speed elicits from the base of her throat a long, mounting, piercing squeal, higher and heavier with each stroke, until her arms have stretched to grasp the other side of the desk, and her toes are knocking alternately on the hardwood floor as she holds onto reality for dear life.

"That is twelve. The punishment sentence you will receive from me each week, a frequency which will decrease with good behavior, and increase otherwise."

He can't possibly mean each week. *This? Every* week? How long had her sentence been? Eight *months??*

"This time, as per the choices you have made since your arrival here, you have six more."

If only she could turn back time—do things differently. Learn how to cope in better ways, how to help Cheryl, how to move forward in life, together.

"Two, for disrespect. Ms. Ruiz deserves better, and you know it." The cane on her again, tapping out its target. "I expect you will show her thus from now on." *CRACK!* A pause and a whimper. *CRACK!*

Cheryl respects her—looks up to her—and she is the only person Mira has ever truly let down. Their mother couldn't care less—but Cheryl cares. She deserves better.

"For your childish outburst and unwillingness to comply with stated instructions, another two." Tap tap tap—*CRACK!* The tears are flowing freely down her cheeks now—she can't hide it, she can't hold it in any longer, she can't stand the burning pressure in her chest and throat, the fire alight on her sit-spot, scalding her flesh, wounding her pride.

Swish—*CRACK!*

Never again! Never again will she hurt Cheryl, she swears, never again will she cause herself pain like this. Please just let it be over—let her go back home, let her find her sister's arms, make her smile, scoop her up, carry her away, give her wings.

"And twice more, so you remember that profanity is unacceptable within these walls, and does not become you without them, either, Miss Wates." Swish—*CRACK!*

With the final stroke, Miranda lets out an expansive breath—her lungs releasing, her body quieting, her nerves screaming in pain, and yet somehow calm. She can do this. She can be better. For Cheryl. For herself.

"Stand up, Miss Wates, and straighten yourself out. I will be returning you to your room. Your only duty for the rest of this evening is to read your AGR Handbook—diligently. You will be expected to know it well by morning."

Stirring, rising, calling on age-old muscles to reawaken and give her strength. Finding her feet, painfully, readjusting her new dress.

"Oh, and Miranda," halting before her, his hand on the door, about to push through, looking back at her. "Welcome to Arlington Girls' Reformatory."

****

214

This story © Rayne Bailey 2011

About the author:

Rayne Bailey, born and raised in the United States, is currently working on completing her graduate education. She and her partner reside on the East Coast, and enjoy a continuously evolving spanking relationship together. Both love to write, whether the genre smacks of vanilla or slides to a silky darker shade— other than her blog, this story constitutes Rayne's first published work in the latter. You can find more of both writers on Rayne's spanking blog, Mischief Managed, at:

solemnlyswear-uptonogood.blogspot.com

Rayne would like to thank Abel and Haron, for making this book and its higher purpose possible, as well as all of the fantastic authors who color theses pages, and, not to forget, the readers— who bring our words to life. Without you, we would all be living in a very different world! Thank you, and happy spanking!

<u>Watching</u>

Discerning Dom

'Maybe,' said Sophie slowly, 'you'd like to watch.'

'Watch?'

'Yes.'

'Watch what exactly?' he said.

'You know, us.'

Jonathan swallowed hard. 'Doing what?'

Sophie giggled. 'What do you think?'

'I see,' he said. Not that he did, exactly.

'Maybe I can persuade him,' she said. 'I'd like to do something for you.'

'Thank you,' he said. 'You mean, on the webcam, like now?'

'No, for real,' she said. 'But it can't be the full monty.'

'No, of course not.'

'Watching, from a distance, no touching. He might buy that.'

'I see,' said Jonathan again. He was beginning to, now. 'You'd be OK with that?'

'Yes, I think so,' she said.

'Have you done that sort of thing before?'

'No. Have you?'

'No. Well, not exactly.'

'What do you mean, not exactly?'

He didn't want to raise complications right now. 'I'll tell you another time.'

She smiled. 'Such a man of mystery.'

He was silent.

'I expect there would be conditions imposed,' she said.

'Yes, I expect so. Whatever you say.'

'Good. I'll get back to you, then, shall I?

'Yes, do.'

He signed off with blown kisses, just enough to indicate some feeling, not too many to be pushily emotional. He sat for a while, thinking about what she'd said, how she'd like to do something for him. He knew there was affection there, even desire, but she had always kept it under firm control, because Roger wasn't inclined to do favours; he liked to keep close what was his. But lately, she'd been more forthcoming, more open. Were there difficulties with Roger? He was aware of some tensions. Things never stayed on an even keel for long. And when they weren't going quite right, she seemed to need him more, looked for him online more often, stayed longer. And lately, there had been some teasing revelations, the veil had been lifted a fraction. She'd given him some details, about the things she did with Roger.

And then there was the photo. He wasn't expecting that. He'd always supposed that was a no-go area, and so he'd never asked for a picture; not that kind, anyway. And one day it had just popped up in his email inbox, out of the blue. Unsolicited. Except that he'd solicited long and hard in his prayers, silently hoping that if only he was patient enough, one day it might come. And there it was. A bottom. A bare bottom, bent over the back of an armchair. A marked, bare bottom; six well-defined welts, red against the white skin, in parallel lines. And underneath, a message: 'What happens to naughty girls.'

He'd always behaved himself, tried never to put pressure on her, always understanding of her situation. I'm not going to cheat on him, she said, and he admired her for that. This didn't stop her flirting. I'm that sort of girl, she said disarmingly; just born flirtatious; do you mind? Of course he didn't mind.

So now she was contemplating an escalation, just for him. Although it wouldn't be just for him. He knew her well enough to be sure she would enjoy it. If it happened.

It was almost a week before she got back to him. He'd nearly given up hope.

'He says it might be allowed,' she emailed. 'Under strict conditions.'

'Any terms are acceptable,' he replied. 'Roger is the one in charge.'

217

Precise instructions followed. 'Come to our house tomorrow evening at seven pm on the dot. The front door will be open. Enter and come up the stairs. Just outside the first door on the right you will see a chair. Take a seat and wait. You mustn't move from that spot, nor speak, and you must go when told to do so.'

They lived only half an hour away. He'd been to the house before, once to dinner with a group of other people, once on his own when Roger was away. She'd been careful to keep him at arm's length, just a peck on the cheek when it was time for him to leave. He wondered if it had been difficult to persuade Roger to agree. Had she used her wiles? Roger was the sort of guy who, if she showed she wanted it too much, was likely to say no. She must have somehow piqued his curiosity, that there was something in it for him too. Jonathan always had the impression that Roger liked to show her off, that in a way she was a trophy to him. He might like the idea of another man seeing just what he had, and demonstrating just what he could do to her.

Five minutes to seven the next evening saw him standing outside their front door. Was this for real? Did she mean it? He didn't think she'd set him up. She wasn't like that, she was genuine.

His heart was pounding as he climbed the stairs. There was the chair, on the landing, outside the bedroom door. He sat down. The door was closed. He couldn't hear anything. After five minutes, it opened. He could see one end of the bed. Then she appeared, wearing a red dress he hadn't seen before. Roger appeared next to her. He said something to her which Jonathan couldn't quite hear. She started to take her clothes off, first the dress, then a black bra and knickers, finally kicking off her shoes. He'd never seen her naked before; only that one shot of her bottom. He admired her body, well-built but graceful. Roger stood her in front of him, put an arm round the back of her neck, took hold of her hair. He was saying something to her, something insistent. It sounded like it might be a lecture, a recital of her misdeeds, perhaps. Whether they were real or imaginary he had no idea, but she looked down at the floor, as if contrite.

Then, apparently following instructions, she knelt on the bed. She was sideways on to him, her bottom projecting out over the edge. Roger pushed her head down into the bed covers so Jonathan couldn't see her face. Roger disappeared, came back with a leather tawse. He said something and there was a muffled reply. Roger touched her bottom, adjusting her position, then stood back. His arm rose and fell quickly. Jonathan held his breath as the tawse slapped against Sophie's bare behind.

There was a pause. Then Roger's arm rose again. Jonathan winced as the tawse struck a second time. It was harder than he expected; the sound seemed to echo round the house. Not that he knew quite what he expected. Perhaps he had imagined it might be something more symbolic, not real like this. Though why? Had she not told him often enough how much she needed a thrashing?

That, it appeared, was what she was about to get. The tawse rose and fell with a steady rhythm, just enough of a lapse between strokes to let it sink in. He saw her buttocks ripple each time the tawse made contact, became aware of the noises she was starting to make as the tawse smacked hard against the bare skin. At first half-suppressed little squeals, grunts and groans muffled by the bedclothes, but the spanking went on and on, and the noises grew more insistent, true registers of pain. She kept shifting from one knee onto the other, anything to mitigate the stinging blows, though she managed to stay in position. Her bottom was bright red now.

Roger paused. He put his hand on her bottom, seemingly to feel its heat. Then he disappeared from the frame. Watching, Jonathan felt as if he was in a theatre, with a seat in the stalls, the frame of the door a proscenium arch, the actors appearing from and disappearing into the wings. Except that what was happening was real. It wasn't a play.

Roger reappeared. This time he held a cane, a long, thin bamboo cane. Jonathan felt a knot in his stomach. She was going to be really punished now. Could she take it? Could he? His cock twitched; there was his answer.

219

Roger spoke to her again. Jonathan heard her murmur something in reply. Roger touched the cane to her bottom, tapping, getting the range. He lifted his arm. Jonathan felt as if his head was reeling. He felt the rush of adrenalin, as if he himself were wielding the cane. He wanted it to be hard, he wanted to hear her cry out; and he wanted the poor girl to be shown mercy, to be comforted. But, he thought, not yet.

The cane struck her right across the centre of her behind. A welt showed, the skin raised, a darker red. The cane rose again. This time, when it landed, she gave a little cry of pain and shifted position. Roger put his hand on the small of her back to steady her. But the caning continued, implacable. Jonathan was gripped; he knew the fierce, wild excitement that comes from the infliction of sexual pain. There were welts all across her behind now, a neat series of parallel lines, purple against the red of her cheeks. She was shaking. Jonathan became aware of her sobbing, and now he wanted it to end, both the caning and the sobbing, but it didn't. It was vicious; Roger wanted to really hurt her.

At last it stopped. There was silence except for the sound of her whimpering. Roger walked towards the door, without looking at him, and closed it. Jonathan took that as his cue to leave.

He drove home and sat with a drink on the sofa, trying to absorb what he'd seen. It was quite a different experience from doing it himself. When he spanked, he was the one in control. But this time, he had no power. He was as much under Roger's control as she herself had been, for it was Roger who decided how much pain she should receive, and who decided what Jonathan might and might not watch. He felt, in a strange way, almost as if he had been cuckolded, as if he had offered her up to Roger, had allowed his own power to be usurped. Except of course that in reality he had no power over her. If anything, she had power over him, setting it up for him to observe, gaining the privilege for him from Roger, her gift to him. Purchased at what price? He didn't care to think about what she might have bargained with.

Later the next day she came online, smiling. 'Did you enjoy it?' she asked.

'Yes,' he said. 'Very much.' And it was true; whatever the complexities of his response, he wouldn't have missed it. 'But,' he added, 'I feel a little guilty too. He hit you really hard. Perhaps he wouldn't have been so cruel to you if I hadn't been watching.'

'Maybe that's true. I think he wanted to show you that he could do it as hard as he liked. But it was my gift to you. Don't be guilty, just be pleased.'

'I am. How was it, being watched?'

'Strange,' she said. 'Contradictory, in a way. On the one hand, it brought out the exhibitionist in me. But at the same time it was embarrassing, humiliating, even. I knew you could see me struggling to keep still, and I knew you could hear me crying out, though I tried not to.'

'What were you being punished for, exactly?'

'Best not to know,' she said. 'Something improper. Not concerning you.'

He felt a pang of jealousy; there was so much in her life that was closed off to him.

'Am I allowed to ask what happened when the door was closed?'

'Oh,' she said, 'you can guess.'

'He fucked you?'

She nodded. It didn't seem like it was important to her.

'How?'

'In the ass, eventually. And no, I didn't come.'

He was glad. Glad that she hadn't managed to find relief, and glad that she saw fit to tell him so. A crumb of comfort.

'So, tell me now, you've done something like that but not the same?'

'Not the same,' he said. 'One girl watched while I spanked another.'

'I wonder if I'd like that, watching,' she said.

'I wonder.'

'I'd be scared, in case I was next.'

'And you'd be wet,' he said.

'Yes,' she said, and fell silent. He watched her musing on that. He wouldn't force the issue. But he knew she would think about it. Perhaps her thoughts would bear fruit. He had the feeling this wouldn't be the end of it.

****

About the author:

Discerning Dom lives in London and has several years' experience as a practising dominant. As well as writing fiction, he has a blog, 'Sexual Dynamics: Memoirs of a Discerning Dom', to be found at:
discerningdom.blogspot.com

Wifehouse

Serenity Everton

Charlotte nearly looked up but then quickly averted her eyes as the footman appeared behind her to remove the charger plate and utensils. She dared not blink, though her body shuddered slightly as she sat primly on the edge of her chair. Dressed elegantly in stockings, petticoats, dancing slippers and an evening gown so low that her nipples would pop out if she dared to bend forward more than a few inches, she knew the footman had looked impertinently down the front of her gown.

Still, she sipped at the watered-down champagne and smiled in response to the commentary of the gentleman beside her. He, of course, was merely the dancing instructor, but he would report any hint of misbehavior. Charlotte dared not say a disapproving word, even as he openly kept a lewd eye on the skin her gown so shockingly displayed.

Further up the long table filled with colorful gowns and dark formal evening wear, Mistress Sherring was engaged in extolling Charlotte's virtues to the gentleman on her right. Charlotte knew not to listen openly, but it was difficult. She had excellent hearing, Mistress Sherring's voice carried easily and the dancing master seemed disinclined to discuss anything more interesting than the desultory habits of Handel.

"Of course, she is well-trained for both roles, sir," Mistress Sherring was now saying. "You've been seeing for yourself how composed and presentable she is even among this company, so she'll have no trouble with the daily round, even should the rector's wife come calling. Naturally, she is also prepared for the more private pastimes you'll want to enjoy."

The gentleman replied in a low voice that Charlotte could not discern amid the clinking of the silver and crystal. The footmen had begun serving the dessert course, though Charlotte had little interest in chocolate and cream.

Whatever had been said, Mistress Sherring replied confidently. "Absolutely. None of the girls are permitted to engage in such behavior while they are with us, sir. We use other methods to ensure they have the required skills."

The gentleman – Charlotte could not help but wonder if he would be the one – chuckled. From the corner of her eye, she heard him ask, "Would it be permitted, Mistress, to have a demonstration? I do require some proof that she is as accommodating as you say, even for the most deviant imagination."

Charlotte caught her breath. Mistress Sherring courted such men intentionally, offering up the girls in her care without compunction. These gentlemen looked to Mistress Sherring for presentable spouses in public, but ones who had no private defenses – without family or standing of their own. Young ladies who could be kept confined without comment, and subject absolutely to the will and hands of their husbands.

Still, this man looked frighteningly *normal. Staid.* Indeed, he was an upstanding – *respected* – member of Richmond society, a large plantation owner with a mother in town and a fine house in New York as well. She'd already heard Mistress Sherring's gleeful exposition on the subject during afternoon tea.

"Naturally! Would you prefer a public viewing in the drawing room, or something more intimate?" Mistress Sherring inquired. Charlotte kept her eyes on the dancing master and her back perfectly straight. Charlotte knew she had no physical defenses against the woman at the head of the table, but she had no wish for the mistress to gloat over Charlotte's inward reaction – no matter if waves of anxiety, skittering excitement and trepidation flooded her all at once.

One man – a 'customer' as Mistress Sherring termed them when with the residents of the House – had already walked away a few days earlier with a red-headed girl on his arm. Mistress Sherring had introduced him to Charlotte first. Inwardly shuddering, she'd hidden for longer than necessary in the withdrawing room until the man was distracted by the other girls in Mistress Sherring's salon. Charlotte had been relieved that the sixty-year-old portly banker had focused on the young redhead. The banker's first two wives had mysteriously fallen down the stairs soon after their 30th birthdays, and Charlotte had no desire to be the third.

Still, Charlotte knew Mistress Sherring was intent on dispensing with her. Doxies were expensive to house, feed and train, Mistress Sherring had said bluntly, and it was about time Charlotte turned a profit for the woman.

Though Mistress Sherring preferred to marry her 'students' off, the woman had made it clear prior to the dinner party that if Charlotte refused to cooperate with the process, she would be inclined to sell the young woman to a different sort of customer – one with a highly select clientele of its own, and one Charlotte would be equally unable to flee. It seemed, either way, she was trapped. She'd hoped this man would be reasonable, and indeed, until his exchange with Mistress Sherring, he had been eminently acceptable. How much worse could a whorehouse be than the wifehouse she lived in now?

Of course, Mistress Sherring herself had seemed a godsend, at first. With her mother dead and her step-father disinclined to provide her with any sort of home, Charlotte had found herself awkwardly and reluctantly serving drinks in her step-father's tavern. At fourteen, she'd worked in the kitchen, but at seventeen, he had forced her to start working in the keep. He'd pointed out she was too pretty to be kept in the scullery, and had followed that up by loosening the ties of her peasant's blouse and fondling her breasts himself.

Charlotte had been horrified but impotent to stop him. After that day, she spent most of her energy avoiding the small narrow rooms above the tavern when he was there. She did her best to find empty guest rooms and lock herself in when she slept, and made sure he was well off and away when she ventured there otherwise. But two years of sneaking around had taken its toll. Charlotte had been weary of the constant vigilance.

She'd been an easy mark for the serious gray-garbed middle-aged lady that had ventured in with two liveried servants. Charlotte had served them, and noticed the lady watching her. After a bit, she'd melted and answered the lady's questions. Yes, she was nineteen. Yes, she'd always lived there. No, she wasn't married and no, she'd not had a child. Yes, that was her step-father glowering at her from the tap.

He'd made Mistress Sherring pay him a small fortune to take her. Charlotte could have run away; but until she was twenty-one, he was her legal guardian. At least, he'd been her guardian until he'd signed over his supervision of her to the business-like lady in gray. Mistress Sherring had insisted, then, on doing everything properly; Charlotte now understood why.

Charlotte was now twenty and several months; she'd be her own woman on her twenty-first birthday, but she knew Mistress Sherring would have finished with her by then, whether it was to marriage or a brothel she went.

"I see we shall have some proper entertainment tonight," Monsieur said superciliously beside her. "I assure you, I shall look forward to it." Without disguising his lust, he let his gaze rest on Charlotte's cleavage.

Charlotte dared not respond to what would have been impertinent from a stranger, but was rather restrained from one of Mistress Sherring's employees. All the servants ogled her, and touched at will, even while the mistress herself watched. Indeed, she was not permitted to deny them, and only the nature of the meal and its company restrained the dancing master from baring Charlotte's breasts then and there.

The butler entered with the tray of ports, and Mistress Sherring rose. Rather relieved to escape from the dancing master, Charlotte stood as the footman pulled back her chair. Mistress Sherring's gaze rested on her, and knowing she was being summoned, Charlotte coolly circled the room and approached the head of the table. Naturally the men had risen as the women did, and Mistress Sherring's guest was standing, his eyes on her.

Charlotte did not look up at the man, but curtsied carefully to them both. "Mr. Briding, might I make you known to Miss

Charlotte Rothswell, of the Carolinas?" Mistress Sherring stepped back to make room for the introduction.

Only then did Charlotte dare to look up at the face before her. He was perhaps twice her age, though hardly in his dotage. His complexion was smooth and his dark eyes and hair were dramatic against his pale white skin. The square cut of his jaw gave him a stern demeanor, and he was undeniably taller and stronger than she would ever be.

She lifted her gloved hand, and bobbed as he bent over it, hardly concealing his review of both her attire and her décolletage. Charlotte smiled charmingly and in a flirtatious manner, as she'd been taught. "I suppose you know, Miss Charlotte," he said directly, "Just what I am looking for."

Charlotte raised her eyebrows. "Not precisely, sir," she answered. "Mistress Sherring believes I should fit your expectations and needs, however, and I am sure that with her experience in such matters she is correct."

"I prefer to judge for myself," he returned. "I suppose you have no objection?"

"I have no objection, sir," she confirmed, still smiling at him, deliberately projecting the prim innocence which came so naturally to her.

"Excellent." He had not released her hand, but continued to grasp it in his as he turned his head to Mrs. Sherring. "I'll want her in her shift and stockings, then, and I assume you have birches prepared?"

Mistress Sherring smiled, but Charlotte trembled, struggling to maintain her confident expression. She knew he felt her involuntary reaction, for his gaze smoothly returned to her face and he, too, smiled. Expectantly. Over the burning in her ears, she heard the woman respond, "Of course, as well as other items you might wish to employ."

"Are you nervous, my dear?" he asked, not releasing her hand.

To lie would be foolish. Charlotte attempted something close to the truth. "That which is difficult has the best reward, sir."

"Off with you, then," he said, and she sensed that she had somehow pleased him.

Mistress Sherring was less than gentle as soon as they had left the room. "You're doing well, whipping girl," she said, using the insult as she always did when not before strangers. "Don't louse it up, understand?"

"Yes, ma'am," Charlotte gasped as the mistress grasped her by the arm and fairly dragged her across the room. A maid was waiting, and she was quickly stripped down to the loose chemise and fine silk stockings with black garters. Without ceremony, the pair pushed her to her knees on the punishment bench kept in the room for just such events.

With little need or desire to offer comfort, Mistress Sherring had ensured the ledge for the girls' knees was as narrow as possible and nothing but hard wood. To keep Charlotte's thighs in place and apart, leather straps were buckled around them. The contrivance raised Charlotte's bottom to the height of Mistress Sherring's torso. With Charlotte bent over, the shift barely reached her mid-thigh and its hem brushed her garters.

For Charlotte, the difficult part was the width of the bench she was draped over. The shortest girls were able to maintain themselves in position by pushing their body down into the wooden bench, with their chins on the wood. Charlotte was too tall. If left to their own devices, her nipples would press down on the far edge, and be crushed and sore before the beating was over. In addition, her head was forced to remain up for the entire experience – if left to drop, her chin simply rested on her own cleavage.

"Now then," Mistress Sherring explained, coming around and grasping Charlotte's breasts decisively. She pulled them forward so that Charlotte's aureoles and a barely decent amount of the shift were just free of the wooden bench before continuing. "It must be clear to you now that Mr. Briding isn't interested just in a girl who likes fucking, although that's certainly part of it. He came to us because he wants a girl who won't be able to run away. He *likes* to beat his girls, and he's of the opinion that the safest woman to beat is one's wife. A slave is worth too much, and a prostitute is good for only one go-round. But, my dear, a wife can't say no, and isn't permitted to run away. So there you are."

She fondled the large bulbous tissue until Charlotte whimpered. "Of course, here we only beat you for punishment. Mr. Briding, however, would do it just because he wishes to. When he wishes to. As severely he wishes to. And I do think he'll enjoy you particularly," she smiled a bit contemptuously at Charlotte, "As it will soon be clear to him that however much you deny it, your cunt enjoys being whipped."

Charlotte whimpered, and grasped the edge of the bench tightly, but Mistress Sherring was having none of it. She dragged Charlotte's hands behind her, tying them easily with fancy black rope intended for curtain tie-backs. Charlotte groaned, but there was no help for it. Her upper body weight pushed the undersides of her breasts down onto the edge of the bench. Even through the fabric of her shift, the narrow ledge along the edge dug into Charlotte's tender skin.

She waited like that, helpless, as the maids scurried in and out, and then as the gentlemen flowed into the room. Charlotte tried not to listen, for she truly feared the humiliation of these public displays, but it was no use. The conversation was about her, after all, and the diners commented freely on her jutting breasts and her helpless bum high up in the air.

All too soon, she recognized Mr. Briding's waistcoat before her. "I was admiring your delightful bosom in the dining room, my dear," he said, his hands unabashedly reaching out to caress her globes through the shift. "And I do wish to see them." Without further discussion, he pushed down the finely woven cotton so that her nipples were bared, and then further, tucking the fabric down between her breasts and the bench so that it couldn't slip back into place on its own.

Charlotte couldn't help a small gasp of shame, as others crowded around "to have a look", as she heard them say. Mr. Briding squeezed and pinched and pulled while the men chuckled and some of the women even offered suggestions. "An excellent notion," Mr. Briding approved of one remark, smacking each one hard on the teat so that Charlotte whimpered. "But such amusements can be saved for later. Sadly, one cannot experience all delights in one evening."

Fear rose in Charlotte's chest. Mistress Sherring's threats, along with a sudden surge in her bladder, rattled her nerves. Anxiously, Charlotte took a deep breath. She'd been birched, paddled, fucked in her cunt and ass with vegetables of all sizes, and endured any number of other humiliating episodes in this drawing room over the last nine months, and had survived them all. She could survive this one, too.

Nevertheless, Charlotte knew this time was different. Those other numerous times had been for some perceived fault – a punishment for behavior gone wrong – in her carriage, demeanor, dancing, etiquette or dress. This time, though, there would be no experienced hand ensuring no scars remained.

Just as worrisome, there was little chance Mr. Briding would be concerned with satisfying her. Mistress Sherring always ensured she was brought to climax before the night's end. The mistress believed, and Charlotte agreed when she thought about it, that satisfying the girls increased their eagerness for sexual attention. Indeed, the five girls now confined upstairs were likely, as Charlotte had done on other nights like this, furiously touching their own and the others' cunts, wishing desperately for a live cock to ride.

Behind her now, Mr. Briding lifted the hem of the shift and slowly raised it. Pulling it past her bare rump, he rolled the bottom edge and then slipped it into Charlotte's nerveless fingers. Instinctively she grasped it, and he chuckled. "Don't let go of it, now, until I say so or I shall strap your hands, too," he whispered soft in her ear, so only she could hear.

Charlotte drew a quick, deep breath, but she couldn't prevent the instant sheen of wetness she knew was forming between her legs.

With a pleased chuckle, he returned to her rear. Charlotte could not see him, and ached to know what he was doing in silence. But it was soon clear what he wanted. His hands touched her and for some minutes her rear was pulled and poked and examined. Mistress Sherring bustled up, and Charlotte blushed red when Mr. Briding commented, "An excellent derriere. You've beaten her recently – I'm sure she deserved it – and I see it left a bruise."

It had left a number of bruises and welts, but for now, just that one patch along Charlotte's lower left cheek remained.

"I am afraid we are quite strict here. Even the slightest of offenses, you know, and we must respond. Otherwise these girls are likely to get out of hand." Mrs. Sherring's voice was apologetic, and Charlotte wondered if she was going to be blamed and punished if Mr. Briding passed her up for someone without marks.

"I completely understand," he said, his voice modulated perfectly so that Charlotte and Mistress Sherring could hear, though the other guests – currently engaged in retrieving their teacups from the teacart – could not. "While I naturally would not allow Miss Charlotte the opportunities to cause scandal, I can see that having a strict hand in the smaller freedoms surrounding etiquette and obedience is to be desired." He pressed a finger against Charlotte's anus, and she helplessly gasped. "Ah, and I see it is responsively sore. You keep it prepared?"

"She's cleaned daily. I find it helps her comportment," Mistress Sherring cleared her throat. "I realize it's not common but –"

"But I thoroughly approve," Mr. Briding returned. Against her bottom, Charlotte felt the cool familiar slide of wet ginger. She whimpered. "And the application of ginger root doubtless helps. I would certainly employ it regularly."

Swallowing heavily, Charlotte helplessly felt the root slide inside her. She could do no more than a little feminine wriggle of agony, which simply made Mr. Briding pinch her bruised cheek and cluck. "Now, now, I know this is neither the first nor the last time you'll be subject to such discipline. Indeed, if you're in my house, you'll have one inserted prior to dinner nearly every evening we're home, to remind you of your manners, young lady."

Though Charlotte couldn't see the lady, Charlotte heard Mistress Sherring make an approving noise. "An excellent notion, sir," the woman offered.

"Now then, the birches," Mr. Briding said. "You'll want to stand back of course, my lady," he prompted.

Charlotte listened as Mr. Briding drew the wet bunch of birch from the bucket that had been brought in. She heard him swing it through the air and instinctively stiffened ... but then Mr. Briding laughed. "Just a test swing," he commented, "Although that that was a lovely wriggle of fear, my dear."

A moment passed as Charlotte realized the burning in her bottom was spreading, thanks to her stiffening. She bit back a moan, hardly wanting her tormentors to know that the ginger brought her euphoria, rather than pain and dread.

In the next instant, he swung again. Charlotte gave a small helpless cry as pain burst through her bottom and across her hip. He'd delivered the stroke rapidly and forcefully, laying it expertly along the lower edge of her rear. Quite out of her senses for a moment, she rocked backward, but it only served to smash her breasts back down against the edge of the bench when she fell forward.

As soon as she was in position, Mr. Briding continued the assault. He walked in circles around her after each stroke, watching as she struggled to maintain her composure. The dancing master brought a chair around and sat in front of her, openly ogling her darkened nipples and her clear discomfort. Mistress Sherring took a position on the settee where she could observe both Charlotte's face and Mr. Briding's. The others – mostly men and women who made Mistress Sherring's girls their entertainment of choice – congregated in groups, openly watching.

Charlotte endured a dozen before Mr. Briding came closer. Drawing his fingers over the welts, he tapped her rectum, where a ribbon threaded through the ginger hung out. Charlotte couldn't help herself. This time, she moaned audibly, and Mr. Briding made an approving noise as his fingers drifted down and probed the juicy folds of her pussy.

"A fine, pretty cunny she has," he said to his hostess. "And it's best kept bare. I quite agree and would insist she be kept the same under my watch."

"I have her waxed as needed. It is not a thing she enjoys, but the results are satisfactory," Mistress Sherring murmured.

"Quite. In any event, it looks as if this one actually does enjoy being at my mercy." He slipped two fingers inside Charlotte's opening and pumped them in and out.

Charlotte rewarded him with another husky moan, this time openly encouraging. Her hips thrust involuntarily against his hand. She knew it was shameless, but couldn't control her body.

"Naturally," he went on, continuing to slowly stimulate her as he spoke to the lady on the settee, "Charlotte would be quite busy in my home. In the morning, of course, she would be exercised. I prefer riding as it helps keep the thighs and buttocks in fine condition, and is so pleasantly uncomfortable for girls who have been chastised. Do you know if she can keep her seat on a horse?"

Mistress Sherring pursed her lips. Riding was not a skill the girls acquired at this place. Indeed, they weren't permitted to leave the house or the narrow walled garden at all. "I'm certain she could learn, sir," she proffered after a moment.

Charlotte thrust her hips slightly again, this time in a silent plea that he fuck her faster. But he continued at the same slow, relentless pace. "'Tis a skill that can be taught, after all. In any event, afterward she would complete her *toilette* in the company of my very thorough staff. She'd be scrubbed, brushed, tweezed and outfitted as I directed, and of course she'd be cooperative throughout – even through the less pleasant aspects."

"Of course, all the girls from my house are well able to thrive under even the most invasive of regimens," Mistress Sherring murmured.

It seemed clear to Charlotte that though his words were addressed to Mistress Sherring, he intended for her to listen as well. Indeed, she was listening, but mostly she wished only for Mr. Briding's two fingers to get on with it. The small movements of her hips were now in rhythm to his thrusting fingers; she closed her eyes, shutting out the gloating stare of the dancing master before her.

"She'd share lunch with me, and I am afraid that due to my relatively unusual tastes, chances are she would find herself bare-breasted at the table regularly. Then there would be an afternoon devoted to whatever was pressing: errands, tea with my elderly female relatives, household matters or the dressmakers, or possibly something refining like practicing her musical skills. I assume she has some hobby?"

"As it happens," Mistress Sherring confirmed, "she's excellent at sewing and embroidery, and she has a lovely singing voice."

"Well, then, off she'd go to prepare for dinner. And it would be an invasive regime, let me assure you," Mr. Briding said, his fingers beginning to plunge more quickly into Charlotte's anxious depths. "Of course, after dinner, her primary duty would be to entertain me."

"Ah yes," the good lady answered. "The young ladies are excellent at providing us with evening distractions."

Mr. Briding added his thumb to the pulsing fingers. The pad slipped between Charlotte's labia and pushed firmly against her hidden pearly nubbin, even as his fingers dove rapidly inside her. Charlotte gasped, arching, feeling the sunburst break and wash over her.

The man chuckled and withdrew his hand, as Charlotte slumped forward, her breasts again crushed under her weight.

"This one truly is a naughty slut, isn't she?" he heard him inquire, disapproval and amusement threaded in his voice. "I can see I will have to be cautious about giving her any freedom at all. It simply wouldn't do to have her sharing such favors." Charlotte's eyes opened in alarm, but before she could order her wits into some sort of thinking, Mr. Briding had drawn out a new bunch of birches from the bucket and had slammed it without pity against her bottom.

This time, there was no pausing while she recovered. Relentlessly he delivered twelve hard strokes with the beribboned bunch of knobbed wood. By the end, Charlotte knew she had screamed – likely earning another punishment from Mistress Sherring before she would be allowed to sleep – and believed the welts on her backside might be bleeding.

Hopelessly she slumped on the punishment bench, the pain reverberating in her shoulders and head.

It was some minutes before, dimly, she could listen to the conversation around her.

"If that's all then?" she heard Mr. Briding say.

"I do believe," Mistress Sherring murmured. The lady was close to her ear. "As you insist, she'll go with you tonight. One of the maids will bring down a gown and slippers and we'll send her trunk along in a day or so. How foresighted of you to have arranged this evening in conjunction with your return from New York, sir."

"How like me to bring home a bride from the Carolinas while on a trip to New York. My elderly mother will be shocked, but hardly surprised," Mr. Briding deadpanned.

"I can hardly disagree," Mistress Sherring agreed, clearly amused. "Well then, young lady, stand up," she said sharply.

Charlotte blinked, but apparently Mistress Sherring was speaking to her. She moved her legs and found they had been unstrapped, so she stood, wobbling on her feet. Her chemise was still pulled down and her breasts stood out. Behind her, her hands were still bound, but at least her rump was covered.

With a growing sense of dismay, she realized the hem of the chemise Mr. Briding had ordered her to keep in hand had fallen, whether during her orgasm or the horrific birching that followed. Hardly able to conceal her concern, she looked up.

As she suspected, a small knowing smile was on his face. "Never mind, my dear, you'll learn soon enough to keep it in your hands," he said softly, raising a brow. "We'll take care of your punishment for that when we get home." He glanced at the group around him and took her by the arm, steering her toward the front door. "As your bottom is unexpectedly covered, I shall simply have to divert my attention to a part of your body that is on display."

Blinking, Charlotte tried to think, but they were in the front hall and a carriage had already drawn up in the drive. After installing a bag with a few of Charlotte's belongings in the equipage, the liveried black servant stared unabashedly until Charlotte physically had to resist the urge to squirm. Behind her, Mr. Briding signed a few papers and presented Mistress Sherring with a bank draft. Charlotte knew that among the papers would be a wedding certificate, duly signed by a local judge. No wedding was actually required, as long as the judge signed the certificate swearing it had taken place.

After a few moments, Mr. Briding took Charlotte gently by the arm and descended the front steps. Her cheeks flushed red as his man held open the carriage door. Noticing, Mr. Briding murmured in her ear, "That's Toby, my valet. You'll find yourself in all sorts of shameful situations in his presence, I assure you." He lifted her up into the coach and followed her in, settling beside her on the bench and flipping her face-down across his lap with hardly a word.

Charlotte gasped at the abrupt maneuver.

"Now, then, my dear," he asked, his fingers already playing with the ribbon that still dangled from her anus. "When was the last time you had your lovely breasts cropped?"

"Never!" Charlotte gasped.

"Ah, then, my dear, you have so much to learn…"

****

This story © Serenity Everton 2011

About the author:

Serenity Everton is a mostly rational kinky wife and part-time perverse writer who authors the blog *At A Kinky House* at:

serenity.kinkyfirehouse.com

She lives with her husband and daughter somewhere in the enormous state of California, travels too often for it to be enjoyable, drives as little as possible, and gets spanked several times a week.

Serenity's publicly available stories can be found online at the website *Out of My Mind*, located at:

fiction.kinkyfirehouse.com

The author dearly looks forward either to retirement or her daughter's teenage years, so that she has more time to write. Meanwhile, she dabbles in the art of capturing the attention of other kinky minds, both the romantic and the perverse.

Honour Among Fools

Haron

The hope, the fear, the jealous care,
The exalted portion of the pain
And power of love, I cannot share,
But wear the chain.

Lord Byron

From the hallways lit with neon - into the bright sunshine of the Quad; I didn't stumble or sway or anything, that stuff only happens in movies. Our hero, shocked to the core by cruel events, is unsteady on his feet as he walks away from the scene of his disgrace, the world spinning in front of him - yeah, rubbish. Nothing spun. There was no dramatic background music. I just walked, bag slung over my shoulder, putting as much distance as I could, without being too obvious, between me and Isabel bloody Walters.

"Do you realise that if you ask her out after prep, you can have banged her by dinner time?" my subtle friend Richard Delvig asked me the other day. We were sitting at the prefects' table, and although I was doing a reasonable job ignoring the looks Izzie was casting at me across the refectory, Richard wasn't according her the same courtesy.

"Yes," I said.

"And?"

"And what? I'm supposed to take advantage of the poor fool's crush on me? Come on, Rich, you know me better than that." I shovelled a large forkful of bread and butter pudding. Much as I'd

238

have liked to, I couldn't fail to notice Isabel follow the food's journey from the plate into my mouth with focus she rarely displayed in prep.

"Oh, for god's sake, Ben. You're being an idiot. You like her, don't you?"

"Yes. Exactly."

Izzie was a good kid, and popular. Not exactly the queen of the Fifth Form, but she was cute enough, and had a good head on her. She didn't run with the pack, nor squawk with the flock: she was sound. The only thing that was really bloody annoying about her was that she thought she was in love with me (she wasn't), and behaved as though I was about to change my mind any minute (I wasn't). I was hoping that with a good, hard ignoring she would get over it.

"I don't know, man," said Richard. "Maybe if you paid a bit more attention to the fine goods on offer around the school, you wouldn't need to spend this much time in the boat shed with your porn collection."

"Jeez, man! Keep your voice down!"

He smirked at me over the rim of his mug. That's the thing with friends: they know how to poke you right where it hurts.

I thought back to this conversation as I sat in assembly two days later, terror twisting my guts, as the Head peered at us from the stage. He tapped a cane against his trousers.

"I'm waiting," he said. "The person who left these disgusting materials in the boat shed has twenty seconds to come forward. If I don't hear from him, the spring ball is cancelled. Make your decision quickly."

I'm not a coward. If it had been about the cane - just the cane - I'd be raising my hand right away. Fuck the cane. I'm not going to lie: it was about my prefect's badge. The day I was made a prefect was the first time my father started actually looking at me instead of through me, talking to me instead of at me. This was going to take more then twenty seconds to untangle.

I felt Rich squirm in the seat next to me. The spring ball was going to be his chance to get off with Amanda Purnell; he had it all planned out. "Come on, man," he hissed.

"He's bluffing," I breathed.

"Yeah? You wanna believe that?"

"Ten seconds," said the Head, looking at his watch.

I wondered if Richard would shop me. He could be a selfish sod at times. But then, I was the one to bloody talk.

"Five. Four."

"Please, sir?" A lone hand raised two rows ahead. I saw Isabel Walters get to her feet, and remembered, with a sick feeling in my gut, that she had a habit of following me everywhere. I didn't think she'd seen me go into the boat shed. But maybe she had. Maybe it was revenge time; that would teach me to spurn the advances of lovesick fifth-formers. And here was me, thinking I was being all noble in not taking advantage of her.

"Yes, Miss Walters?" said the Head.

"I'm sorry, sir," a feeble, faltering voice. "They're my magazines."

"Jesus holy Christ," Rich whispered. There was nothing much to add.

The Head's face and bald patch grew so red, I could get worried about him going apoplectic on us. "Are you telling me that you, a young woman, have been keeping a collection of obscene material?"

I wish I could see Izzie's face, but she was two rows ahead of me. "I'm sorry, sir," she repeated. "Girls have needs too."

"Needs! What you need, young lady, is a serious lesson in appropriate behaviour. Come to the podium."

Isabel walked to the front, ascended the four steps that led to the stage. The world didn't spin, nor did a lightning bolt thwack down from the sky to turn me into a pile of ashes, but I tasted bile when I knew, without a doubt, that I would sit there in silence and accept her sacrifice.

"Miss Walters, lift up your skirt, bend forward and touch your toes," said the Head. "With your back to the school."

She complied. I imagined that she saw herself as Joan of Arc, stepping up to the pyre, but it was nothing like that. There's no such thing as dignity when you're displaying your underpants to the entire school.

The Head stood to the left of her and tapped the cane against the seat of Isabel's knickers. He was saying some bullshit about the evils of porn, about propriety and all that stuff. I wondered what porn he bought, and stifled a hysterical laugh.

He brought the cane down with a crack. No sound from Izzie; she must have been floating on a cloud of her own nobility. Stupid idiot.

"That's love, man," Richard whispered.

"Shut up."

Another stroke. No sound. My jaw ached from the effort of gritting my teeth. Another stroke.

There was a hush over the school. I wondered if it was obvious to every single person there that Izzie Walters was covering for someone. Covering for me. Seriously, they couldn't believe she was keeping porn in the boat shed, could they? I surreptitiously looked around, but nobody was staring at me: they were all gawking at the stage, where Izzie was burning up on her pyre.

Once I discovered the secret of looking away from the stage, you couldn't make me turn my eyes back to it. I looked at curlicues around the edge of the ceiling. Drawn blinds on the windows. Backs of heads of my schoolmates.

The cracks of the cane; the silence.

She never did cry out. He gave her twenty-four, and I could only imagine how much they hurt. When she was allowed to rise and turn around, her face was crimson, eyes wet. But she never cried out. Joan of bloody Arc. She didn't look at me as she descended from the stage and walked back to her place.

"I shall be writing to your parents, Miss Walters, to explain to them why you've been suspended for the rest of the term," said the Head. Izzie didn't even twitch.

The school was dismissed. I grabbed my bag and headed out, elbowing my way though the agitated masses: into the bright sunlight of the Quad.

I skipped breakfast. I walked to the rugby pitch and sat at the top of the stand until the Third turned up for games. Coach Davidson shouted up at me to hurry up if I didn't want to be late for my first lesson. I couldn't think of anything less relevant to my life right now than business studies, but I cleared off and pretended I was heading towards the school. Maybe I'd get the cane for skipping lessons. Maybe it would make me feel better. I was unlikely to be demoted for something like that.

Around the school, towards the bike shed. Quiet now that the lessons had started. Was she in her lesson? Was she happy with her idiot self? I leaned against the wall. If I'd been a smoker, now would have been the perfect time to light up, but I was a big proponent of indulging in one vice at a time. Mine was porn. I liked porn: girls together, kissing, groping each other, pussies and tongues, nothing so nasty as a knob in sight. Shit, oh shit, if she had followed me, if she knew the stash was mine, had she looked through it too? I felt breathless with shame. There was only so much shame one man could take.

"Ben?" a familiar, tentative voice nearly made me jump out of my skin. She was standing by the corner of the shed, looking up at me, eyes still red-rimmed.

"Christ, Isabel." I didn't know what to say. I wanted to called her a stupid idiot, but that was hardly appropriate, no matter how true it was. "You should be in your lesson."

"I've been suspended. I'm waiting for Mum to pick me up."

"I'm sorry," I said. I didn't know if I meant it.

"No, no. It's okay. I wanted to find you to say, it's okay. I'm not expecting anything in return. It's just, you're a prefect, and I thought…" a little shrug. Puppy-dog eyes.

Too right she was expecting something. She was expecting me to take her into my arms, and tell her how much her heroic act had meant for me. How my eyes were now open, and I didn't want anything as much as to be her boyfriend, forevermore.

It would have been a perfect solution: an easy way out. We would have snogged, and then she'd be gone till the end of the term. I would be her favourite person in the whole bloody world.

I had already taken one easy way out that morning, and it was still making me sick.

"Look," I said. "I really like you. Always have. But I don't like you like that, and frankly, you deserve someone better than me." Someone who wouldn't sit silently while you're being caned in front of the school assembly.

Tears in the red-rimmed eyes. "It's fine," she said.

"Bollocks it is!"

"I... what?"

"Christ, Isabel. You're being an idiot. Why would you even try to pretend it's fine? You should be furious with me right now; raving. You should be turning on your heel, marching into the Head's office and shopping me to him. It's not fine."

She shook her head, tears running down her face. "I knew you'd be angry," she said. "You're too good to accept stuff people do for you. It's okay, though. It wasn't just for you, it was for me, too. Anyway. I just wanted to say good-bye before Mum picks me up. I need to pack my stuff."

She turned and ran towards the dorms.

Love. I wasn't sure about love. It made idiots out of the most reasonable girls, and it messed you up in every possible way.

She didn't love me. I didn't love her. It was lunacy.

I yanked the prefect's badge off my lapel and started towards the admin building. I knew the Head was in.

****

243

About the author:

Haron writes spanking stories because she doesn't know how not to. When she isn't writing fiction, she blogs at <u>spankingwriters.com/blog</u> and <u>adelehaze.com</u>; you can also hear her chat about spanking at <u>spankingcast.com</u>. She is a co-editor of this anthology with her husband Abel.

"The Slipper": Cover Art

Catherine Thomas

Cover art © Catherine Thomas 2011

About the artist:

When a young Catherine Thomas disapproved of the way her parents were bringing her up, she turned to 1950s school stories for guidance. Having ticked off the stereotypical milestones (brown public school uniforms, bullseyes, ginger beer and lacrosse), she discovered an enthusiasm for another ritual of the era: corporal punishment. This eventually led her to the kinky school scene, where she attended Lowewood Academy and made lots of new friends - including Abel and Haron.

Catherine's previous forays into illustrating CP scenes have included an edition of the Lowewood Academy magazine "Glory in the Fight", and the front cover of Abel's previous book "The Punishment List".

Catherine and her (vanilla) dog Furball now share a house with Emma Jane. If you should ever visit, you'll find that the ginger beer is always flowing and lights-out is at 10pm.

Cover art models: Emma Jane Woodhouse & Abel Jenkins

Editors' Note

Abel & Haron

So many people are fascinated by spanking. Some embrace their kink, living lifestyles filled with roleplay, discipline and punishment. Others love reading about it. Yet relatively few of us find our tastes satisfied by the mainstream publishers of erotica.

Hence, an idea was born - to bring together a selection of our favourite authors from the spanking web, and to ask them each to write a story for an anthology.

We gave them relatively little by way of instruction - a rough idea of the length of story that would fit, and a requirement that their piece had never previously been published - and let them loose. We are delighted with the amazing quality and variety of the contributions that they have submitted.

Not, of course, that we paid them! A key principle from the outset was that all profits would be donated to cancer research charities. So, in buying your copy, you are helping an important cause.

We'd like to thank all of those involved for their support. And we hope that you, the readers, will enjoy devouring the volume as much as we've enjoyed pulling it together.

Abel & Haron
spankingwriters.com

www.ingramcontent.com/pod-product-compliance
Lightning Source LLC
Chambersburg PA
CBHW031831090426
42741CB00005B/206